KT-504-753

The Knitter's Bible

04113100

CLAIRE CROMPTON

The Knitter's Bible

David & Charles

About the author

Claire Crompton is a talented needlewoman with over 15 years experience. Her degree in Knitwear Design took her to the knitting industry and she has worked as a pattern designer for major wool manufacturers such as Sirdar, Courtaulds and Hayfield, as well as for the needlework company DMC. She is the author of *Cross Stitch Card Collection*, also published by David & Charles.

A DAVID & CHARLES BOOK
Copyright © David & Charles Limited 2004

David & Charles is an imprint of F&W Media International, Ltd
Brunel House, Forde Close, Newton
Abbot, TQ12 4PU, UK

F&W Media International, Ltd is a subsidiary of F+W Media, Inc
10151 Carver Road, Suite #200,
Blue Ash, OH 45242, USA

First published in the UK in 2004
Reprinted 2004, 2005 (three times), 2006 (twice), 2007, 2008, 2009 (twice), 2010, 2011,2012

Text and designs copyright © Claire Crompton 2004

Claire Crompton has asserted her right to be identified as author of this work in accordance with the Copyright, Designs and Patents Act, 1988.

All rights reserved. No part of this publication may be reproduced, stored in a retrieval system, or transmitted, in any form or by any means, electronic or mechanical, by photocopying, recording or otherwise, without prior permission in writing from the publisher.

The designs in this book are copyright and must not be made for resale.

The author and publisher have made every effort to ensure that all the instructions in the book are accurate and safe, and therefore cannot accept liability for any resulting injury, damage or loss to persons or property, however it may arise.

Names of manufacturers, paper ranges and other products are provided for the information of readers, with no intention to infringe copyright or trademarks.

A catalogue record for this book is available from the British Library.

ISBN-13: 978-0-7153-1799-0 paperback
ISBN-10: 0-7153-1799-7 paperback

Printed in Singapore by KHL Printing Co. Pte Ltd
for David & Charles
Brunel House, Newton Abbot, Devon

Executive Editor: Cheryl Brown
Editor: Jennifer Fox-Proverbs
Art Editor: Prudence Rogers
Production Controller: Ros Napper
Project Editor: Joan Gubbin
Photographer: Karl Adamson

David & Charles publish high quality books on a wide range of subjects.
For more great book ideas visit: **www.rucraft.co.uk**

CONTENTS

GETTING STARTED

Introduction 8
Introducing Yarns 8
Choosing Yarns 10
Needles and Equipment 14
Holding the Needles 16
Casting On 17
Introducing Knit Stitch 18
Binding (Casting) Off 20
Introducing Purl Stitch 21
Combining Knit and Purl 23
Advanced Casting On 24
Advanced Binding (Casting) Off . .25
Increasing Stitches 26
Decreasing Stitches 28
Ribs 30
Gauge (Tension) 31
Knit Perfect 32
Abbreviations 33

CREATIVE OPTIONS

Introduction 34
Lace Knitting 34
Fair Isle 37
Cables .40
Embossed Knitting 42
Short Rows 44
Twisted Stitches 46
Intarsia 47
Circular Knitting 50

EXPLORING CHOICES

Introduction 52
Medallion Knitting 52
Beaded Knitting 54
Looped Knitting 55
Entrelac 56
Mitred Squares 58
Fulling .60
Smocking 62
Reading Knitting Patterns 63
Knitting a Garment 64
Other Garment Details 68
Adapting a Pattern 72
Knitting a Patterned Garment . . .74
Tassels, Fringes and Cords 76
Edgings 78
Buttons 80
Flowers and Leaves 82
Embroidery 83
Correcting Mistakes 86

STITCH LIBRARY

Introduction 88
Knit and Purl Stitches 89
Gansey Patterns 97
Texture Stitches 101
Rib Stitches 106
Cable Stitches 108
Lace Stitches 117
Edgings 125

PROJECTS

Introduction 128
Garter Stitch Scarf 129
Flower Top 130
Striped Bag 131
Cable Throw 132
Place Mat and Coaster 133
Fun Children's Mittens 134
Rib Stitch Scarf 135
Short Row Cushion 136
Beret .137
Garden Plot Squares Throw 138
Beaded Bag 139
Sheep Toy 140
Fair Isle Baby Blanket 141
Scented Sachets and Cover 142
Lace Bags 143
Funnel Neck Sweater 144
Lace Cardigan 146
Baby Bootees 147
Dainty Knitted Trims 148
Drawstring Bags 149
Patchwork Cushion 150
Greetings Cards 151
Gift Bags 152
House Sampler 153
Intarsia Cushion 154
Motifs .155

Yarn Details 158
Suppliers 159
Index .160

top and above left: Christmas Tree and Valentine
Cards – see page 151 for pattern instructions.

Intro

This book will take you through the basic techniques that you need to begin knitting, such as casting on, and knit and purl stitches. It encourages you to try new techniques including cables and fair isle knitting. There is a wide range of projects for you and your home, ranging from simple ones to more challenging designs as your confidence and skills grow.

duction

How to use this book

The book has been divided into colour coded sections to help you find the information you need quickly and easily. Each new technique is explained with clear diagrams, photographs and step-by-step instructions.

Getting Started is colour coded purple and teaches you the basic techniques you need to begin knitting straight away. It offers invaluable information about yarns and choosing the correct needles for your work. At the end of this section is a page of useful hints and tips to improve your knitting and a list of the abbreviations that are used throughout this book, each clearly explained.

Creative Options pages are coded blue, and introduce more techniques to expand your range of knitted fabrics, such as lace knitting, cables and colour knitting. Circular knitting is also explained.

Exploring Choices is colour coded green and features many exciting techniques to encourage you to experiment and discover the wide variety of fabrics that can be knitted. Beads, embroidery and looped knitting decorate the surface whilst mitred squares and entrelac illustrate the creative use of shapes. This section also includes information on working from knitting patterns, how to alter patterns to fit and how to adapt patterns with new stitches.

Throughout these three sections, there are Knit Perfect boxes, which focus on the important points of each technique and give hints and tips to improve your knitting.

The Stitch Library pages are coded turquoise and include a wide range of over 100 stitches that you can use in the projects or for your own designs.

Throughout the book, the techniques are illustrated by projects, beginning with a simple garter stitch scarf that can be knitted with three basic techniques. Other projects include a cable throw, and bootees, sweater and blanket for baby.

The smaller items like gift bags and scented sachets are quick and easy to knit and will encourage you to try new techniques.

Measurements are given in imperial with metric conversions in brackets. Use either imperial or metric when working, do not combine them since in many cases they are not a direct conversion.

Two ways of holding the needles and knitting are explained: the English method and Continental method. To avoid confusion, throughout this book the diagrams show the English method of holding the needles. Knitters who prefer the Continental method can easily use the diagrams since the position of the needles and the working yarn around the needles are the same for both methods.

Whether you are a complete novice wanting to start knitting, or an experienced knitter searching for fresh ideas and inspirations, this is the essential handbook that will always be at your side.

Getting Started

This section contains all the techniques you need to start knitting, beginning with how to hold the needles and yarn, how to cast on and work the knit stitch, and how to bind (cast) off. These basic techniques will then allow you to complete your first project. Learn how to purl, the other basic stitch, and combine it with the knit stitch to produce stockinette (stocking) stitch and ribs. More projects follow, using the techniques just learnt. There is useful information on choosing and using different yarns, and an explanation of the different needles and equipment you will need to begin knitting confidently.

INTRODUCING YARNS

Fibres

Yarns are spun from natural or synthetic fibres. Natural fibres include wool, silk, linen, cotton, cashmere and alpaca. Synthetic fibres include polyester, acrylic, viscose, rayon and nylon. Yarn can also be a mixture of each, for example, wool and acrylic, or wool and cotton.

The following list describes the most common fibres used in knitting yarns:

NATURAL FIBRES

Alpaca hair from the alpaca (llama)
Angora hair from the angora rabbit
Cashmere hair from the cashmere goat
Cotton plant fibre, from the boll of the cotton plant
Lambswool sheep's first shearing, usually the softest
Linen plant fibre, from the stem of the flax plant
Merino wool from the fleece of the merino sheep
Mohair from the angora goat, the softer and finer kid mohair is from the kid goat
Shetland wool traditionally from Shetland sheep
Silk continuous filament secreted by the silkworm larva
Wool from the fleece of a sheep

SYNTHETIC FIBRES

Acetate, rayon and viscose chemical treatment of cellulose fibres from wood pulp
Acrylic, polyester and nylon made from petro-chemicals, nylon is the strongest textile fibre, elastane is an elastic fibre

PLY OR THICKNESS

A ply is a single twisted strand and, as a general rule, the more plies that are twisted together, the thicker the yarn but, confusingly, the plies from different manufacturers can be different thicknesses themselves.

A tightly spun ply will be thinner than a loosely spun one. In order of thickness they are:

I ply which is used for gossamer lace knitting like traditional Shetland shawls
Baby and fingering (UK 2ply or 3ply)
Sport (UK 4ply)
Worsted (UK DK – double knitting) the most widely used weight which is suitable for most garments without being too bulky for indoor wear.
Fisherman or medium weight (UK aran)
Bulky (UK chunky)
Super bulky (UK super chunky)
and **Big** yarns are even thicker

big

super bulky (UK super chunky)

bulky (UK chunky)

sport (UK 4ply) mohair

sport (UK 4ply) wool

2ply Shetland wool equivalent to sport (UK 4ply)

worsted (UK DK)

fisherman or medium weight (UK aran)

Texture

Most yarns are plain – simply plies twisted together but there are other yarns called novelty or specialist yarns.

Chenille has a core of strong plies spun together to trap the short velvet pile threads.

Boucle has two plies spun together at different speeds so one bunches up around the other creating a towelling look when knitted up.

Slub yarns alternate between thick and thin creating a very textured fabric.

Ribbon yarns are exactly what they sound like; knitted up they form a loose fabric with plenty of drape.

Mohair or angora yarns have been brushed to raise the hairs of the fibre and make a soft fluffy fabric.

Fun fur yarns with short or long piles knit up for an extra furry garment.

Fleece yarns knit up to make a soft all-over pile.

mohair

long-pile fur

fun fur

fleece

slub yarn

ribbon

chenille

boucle

Special features

Due their different characteristics, some yarns are more suitable for certain uses than others. A child's garment that needs frequent washing should be knitted in a hardwearing, machine-washable yarn rather than one that has to be hand washed. Fun fur yarns make cosier cushions than rough natural wool and linen yarns drape better than crisp cotton.

Wool is the best yarn to use. It is strong, durable, elastic, takes dye well and feels soft against the skin. A garment knitted in wool will hold its shape, have excellent insulation properties and the surface will not pill like some synthetics. As there are different breeds of sheep so there are different types of wool; lambswool is soft, merino and wensleydale have long fibres and a lustrous sheen when knitted, and shetland wool is available in a wide range of colours for traditional fair isle knitting. Natural, undyed yarn, usually straight from the wool producers, comes in range of colours from cream through to soft browns and charcoals, and has a real rustic look and feel. Wool

that has machine washable or tumble dry printed on the ball band has been treated to not shrink or full in the washing machine and drier.

Cotton is a heavy yarn, so the weight of a finished garment can cause it to drop and the garment will get longer. It also lacks elasticity and so ribs become baggy, though this is restored after washing. Cotton blended with a synthetic fibre will have more stability. However, cotton is a great yarn to use for crisp stitch textures and looks beautiful in lace knitting. Mercerized cotton has been treated to add lustre and take brighter dyes; it is stronger than untreated cotton and harder wearing.

Silk is a luxury fibre that is beautiful to knit with and creates soft, fluid garments to wear against the skin. If loosely spun, it will not be hard wearing, so use it for special garments only.

Cashmere is an expensive yarn but its soft, light and luxurious qualities make it a good investment. Knit it into classic garments that never go out of fashion.

Synthetic yarns are hard wearing, and can be pulled in and out of the washing machine without suffering shrinkage or fulling, making them ideal for children's clothes. But some knitters find them uncomfortable to knit with, as stitches tend to cling to the needles. The surface pills easily, and submit them to a steam iron and they lose all elasticity and life.

Blended yarns of natural and synthetic fibres combine the natural yarn's qualities with the hardwearing and stable features of the synthetic.

When you are learning to knit, start as you mean to go on – choose a 100 per cent wool yarn; it is easy to work with, can be unravelled and reused, and whatever you knit will look gorgeous.

CHOOSING YARNS

When selecting yarn for a particular garment or accessory, bear in mind the way in which it will be used once finished, and the overall effect you want to achieve through the colour and texture.

Yarns for baby

Yarns specifically for babies are treated to be softer, and made to withstand frequent machine washing and tumble drying. Suitable yarns are baby and fingering (2ply) in 100 per cent wool for white lacy heirloom shawls, sport (4ply) nylon/acrylic mix in traditional blue and pink, fashion worsted (DK) nylon/acrylic mix with a pearlized thread or 100 per cent wool in soft colours for cosy sweaters and bootees.

Crisp cool yarns

Pure 100 per cent cotton, cotton mixes and natural fibres such as linen and silk are perfect for summer but can look good all year round. Hardwearing, they also give a classic look to soft furnishings, knitted into throws and cushions. Worsted (DK) denim yarn fades and ages like jeans, tweed yarns with a touch of silk make relaxed holiday wear, and spaced-dyed yarns give a blended look. Worsted (DK) cotton comes in bright colours for crisp ribbed sweaters, worsted (DK) linen mixed with viscose has drape, sport (4ply) mercerized cottons have a sheen, and a cotton ribbon yarn is ideal for slinky summer evening wear.

nylon/acrylic mix with pearlized thread

nylon/acrylic mix in traditional pink

fingering (2ply) wool

worsted (DK) and sport (4ply) wools

cotton denim yarns

worsted (DK) cotton

cotton ribbon yarn

tweed and space dyed cotton mix yarns

sport (4ply) mercerized cotton

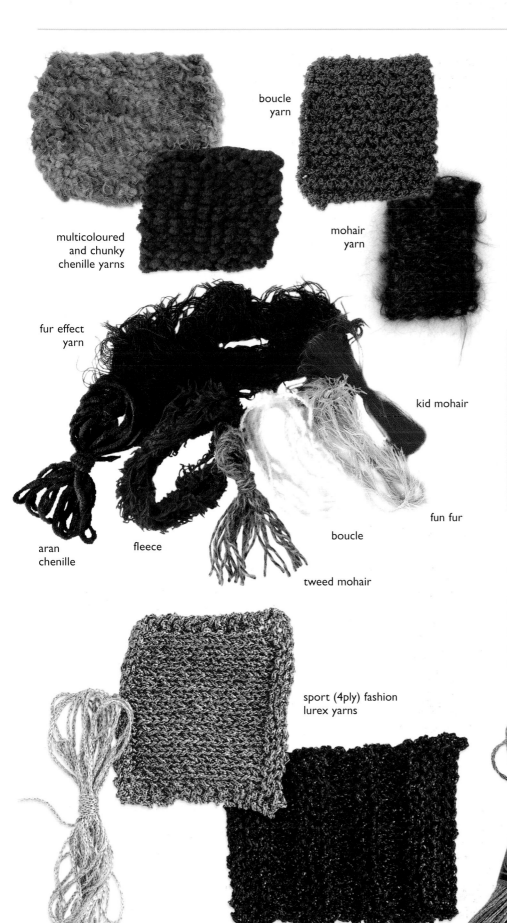

boucle yarn

multicoloured and chunky chenille yarns

mohair yarn

fur effect yarn

kid mohair

aran chenille

fleece

boucle

fun fur

tweed mohair

sport (4ply) fashion lurex yarns

metallic embroidery threads

Yarns with texture

Knit them in simple stockinette (stocking) stitch and let the yarn make the difference. Use soft, velvety chunky chenille for opulence and a multi-coloured version for fun. Mohair makes huggable sweaters in medium (aran) weight mohair/wool mix, sport (4ply) kid mohair creates a delicate fabric and a sophisticated tweed is ideal for city wear. Boucle yarns are great for summer tops. For a fun look, knit a top in funky fur yarns in variegated or bold colours while fleece yarns are great for outdoor wear.

✓ Knit Perfect

Dye lots of the same colour may differ slightly in shade, so always buy enough yarn of the same dye lot to complete your project. The dye lot number is printed on the ball band next to the shade number.

Yarns with sparkle

A lurex and viscose mix is perfect for evening wear and adds an unexpected accent to fair isle knits. Metallic embroidery threads add small glints of sparkle when combined with a plain yarn.

choosing yarns

Natural fibre yarns

The best knitting yarns are made from natural fibres. Tweeds for a cosy country look, thick yarns for warmth in the great outdoors and stylish yarns for urban wear. Try using small amounts of tapestry wools for their great range of colours in fair isle or for embroidery. Shown here are truly rustic fisherman (aran), bulky (chunky) and worsted (DK) weight yarns in tweeds and soft greens, a soft sport (4ply) 100 per cent alpaca yarn, traditional shetland wool sweater yarn and tapestry wools equivalent to worsted (DK) weight.

bulky (chunky) tweed wool

aran weight rustic natural wool

worsted (DK) tweed wool

two skeins tapestry wool

sport (4ply) tweed wool

2ply shetland wool

aran weight tweed wool

luxury alpaca

worsted (DK) soft merino wool

bulky (chunky) wool/ alpaca mix

bulky (chunky) tweed wool

worsted (DK) tweed yarn

Every one of these adorable bags was knitted in basic stockinette (stocking) stitch (see pages 18–23) and measures 4in (10cm) square, but the varying choices of yarn and needle size have resulted in very different effects. See page 152 for the full pattern and details of trimmings.

Gold ribbon star knitted in stockinette (stocking) stitch using a cotton ribbon yarn on size 8 (5mm/UK6) needles.

Heart and bird knitted in stockinette (stocking) stitch using a chunky fleece effect yarn on size 9 (5.5mm/UK5) needles.

Rosebud knitted in stockinette (stocking) stitch using a silk and kid mohair yarn used double on size 5 (3.75mm/ UK9) needles.

100% pure silk
hand dyed yarn

aran weight chenille

super bulky
slub yarn

sport
(4ply)
thread

skeins of
sport (4ply)
weight
hand-dyed
embroidery
threads

thick slub
wool yarn

aran weight cotton
ribbon yarn

Hand painted, hand made yarns

For a really exclusive garment, how about an individual yarn, hand painted in multi-colours or a big bold slub yarn for texture and colour? Add an extravagant touch by using small amounts of embroidery thread, the mixed colours guarantee no two are alike. Multi-coloured chenille and ribbon yarn come in sophisticated colours like these berry shades and for pure luxury try a sport (4ply) 100 per cent silk yarn in soft azure shades. Slub yarns make unusual fun sweaters and embroidery silks can be added for a little touch of magic.

Denim heart bag knitted in stockinette (stocking) stitch using a cotton yarn on size 7 (4.5mm/UK7) needles.

Hologram daisy bag knitted in stockinette (stocking) stitch using a lurex yarn on size 3 (3.25mm/UK10) needles.

Snowflake bag knitted in stockinette (stocking) stitch using a boucle yarn on size 6 (4mm/UK8) needles.

Fluffy pink ribbon bag knitted in stockinette (stocking) stitch using a funky fur yarn on size 6 (4mm/UK8) needles.

13

NEEDLES AND EQUIPMENT

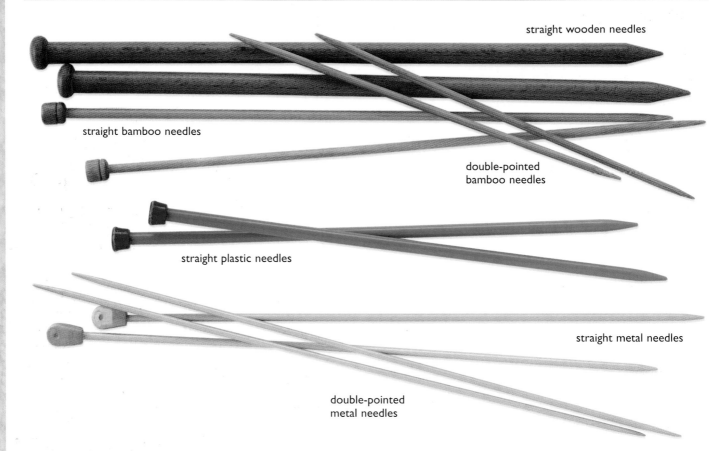

straight wooden needles

straight bamboo needles

double-pointed bamboo needles

straight plastic needles

straight metal needles

double-pointed metal needles

There are three types of needles, in a range of sizes, lengths and made from different materials.

Straight needles are used in pairs and have a point at one end with a fixed knob at the other. Stitches are worked using the pointed end; they cannot be removed from the other end. They are used for flat knitting, working across a row of stitches moving them from one needle to the other, turning the work and working back again, and continuing back and forth.

Double-pointed needles are used in sets of four or five and have a point at each end. Stitches can be worked with one end and can also be removed from the other end. This means you don't have to turn your work at the end of each row. In fact you can continue knitting in a spiral and produce a seamless continuous tube. This is called circular knitting.

Circular needles consist of a pair of needles joined by a flexible nylon wire.

They have a point at each end and, like double-pointed needles, you can work from both ends and so knit in rounds to produce a seamless tube.

Plastic, metal or wood, including bamboo are used to make needles. Each has its own characteristics and can help or hinder your knitting experience. Metal can be cold and inflexible to work with, but it is more slippery than other materials and can help you knit faster. Wood, bamboo or plastic on the other hand are warmer and more flexible, and are smooth rather than slippery. They grip the stitches a bit more which is quite useful when you're beginning to knit and don't want stitches sliding off your needles. Wood and bamboo warm up in the hands and are light to use. Try different materials and find the one you are most comfortable with.

The tip of the needle is also something to consider. Some needles have a blunt tip and some have a sharp tip. A blunt tip is harder to insert into stitches but is better to use with a loosely spun or

thick yarn. A sharp tip can split the stitches but is useful when working pattern stitches or knitting with a tight gauge (tension).

The size of a needle is determined by its diameter and there are three sizing systems. In the US, needles have the American size and metric equivalent. In Britain, they have the metric size with the old UK size. The table shows you how these sizes compare; however some needles have no exact equivalent.

Three standard lengths are available, 10in (25cm), 12in (30cm) and 14in (35cm). Use longer needles for projects with a large number of stitches and shorter needles for fewer stitches. The stitches should fit snugly along the length of the needle, not crammed together where they can easily fall off the end. Long needles can be awkward to knit with; you need a lot of elbowroom to work comfortably. Many knitters find it easier to use a circular needle instead, working as for flat knitting, and turning the work at the end of every row.

Needle sizes

US	METRIC	UK	US	METRIC	UK
0	2mm	14	10	6mm	4
1	2.25mm	13	10½	6.5mm	3
	2.5mm			7mm	2
2	2.75mm	12		7.5mm	1
	3mm	11	11	8mm	0
3	3.25mm	10	13	9mm	00
4	3.5mm		15	10mm	000
5	3.75mm	9	17	12.75mm	
6	4mm	8	19	15mm	
7	4.5mm	7	35	19mm	
8	5mm	6		20mm	
9	5.5mm	5			

Additional items beside needles and yarn will be needed as you progress with your knitting. These include:

• A needle gauge to check the size of a needle; circular needles and double-pointed needles tend not to be marked.

• A pair of small sharp scissors to cut the yarn; never be tempted to break the yarn, you will stretch the fibres.

• A non-stretch fibreglass tape measure for checking your garment measurements and a ruler for measuring your gauge (tension) square.

• Cable needles are used for manipulating stitches whilst working cables. They are short needles, pointed at both ends, and some have a kink in the middle.

• Stitch holders to hold stitches not being worked; you can use a safety pin for a small number of stitches.

• A tapestry needle with a large eye and a blunt end for sewing pieces together and sewing in ends.

• Bobbins for winding off lengths of coloured yarns for intarsia or fair isle knitting.

• A pad of graph paper is useful for charting garment shaping or stitches, giving a clearer picture than written instructions.

• A row counter that slides on to the needle to keep track of the row being knitted.

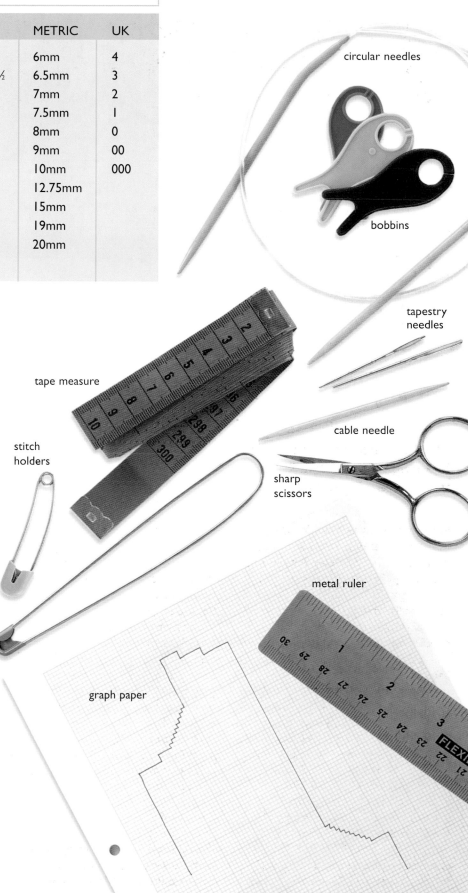

circular needles

bobbins

tapestry needles

tape measure

cable needle

stitch holders

sharp scissors

metal ruler

graph paper

HOLDING THE NEEDLES

Not every knitter holds their needles and yarn in the same way. The yarn can be held in either the right or left hand, the needles can be held from above or below. Try each of the methods described here and work in a way that is most comfortable for you. They are all bound to feel awkward and slow at first.

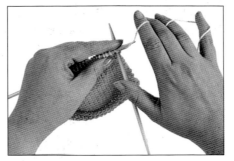

English method
(yarn in the right hand)

Left hand: hold the needle with the stitches in your left hand with your thumb lying along the needle, your index finger resting on top near the tip and the remaining fingers curled under the needle to support it. The thumb and the index finger control the stitches and the tip of the needle.

Right hand: pass the yarn over the index finger, under the middle and over the third finger. The yarn lies between the nail and the first joint and the index finger 'throws' the yarn around the right-hand needle when knitting. The yarn should be able to move freely and is tensioned between the middle and third finger. You can wrap the yarn around the little finger if you feel it is too loose and it keeps falling off your fingers. Hold the empty needle in your right hand with your thumb lying along the needle, your index finger near the tip and the remaining fingers curled under the needle to support it (see right hand in Continental method).

Some knitters prefer to hold the end of the right-hand needle under their right arm, anchoring it firmly. Whilst knitting this needle remains still and the right hand is above the needle and moves the yarn around it.

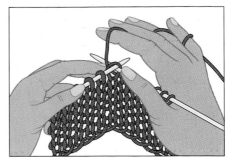

Alternative hold

Left hand: hold the needle in the same way as shown left.

Right hand: hold the yarn in the fingers the same way as shown left. Hold the needle like a pen, on top of the hand between thumb and index finger. The end of the needle will be above your right arm, in the crook of the elbow. As the fabric grows longer, the thumb will hold the needle behind the knitting.

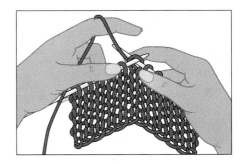

Continental method
(yarn in the left hand)

Left hand: wrap the yarn around your little finger, under the middle two fingers and then over the index finger between the nail and the first joint. The yarn is held taut between the index finger and the needle. Hold the needle with your thumb lying along the needle, your index finger near the tip and remaining fingers curled under the needle to support it. The thumb and index finger control the stitches, yarn and needle tip.

Right hand: hold the empty needle in your right hand with your thumb lying along the needle, index finger resting on top near the tip and remaining fingers curled under the needle to support it. The thumb and index finger control the stitches and the needle tip, which hooks the yarn and draws the loop through.

✔ Knit Perfect

If you learn both the English and Continental ways of knitting, you will be able to hold a different colour yarn in each hand which will make fair isle knitting (see page 37) easier and quicker. As you start to knit you will soon find a way of holding the yarn and needles that is right for you. Whether you hold the yarn differently, have it wrapped around more or less fingers to control the tension or hold the needles from above or below, as long as the yarn flows freely through your fingers and the tension on it is consistent, stick to the most comfortable method.

CASTING ON

To begin knitting, you need to work a foundation row of stitches called casting on. There are several ways to cast on depending on the type of edge that you want (see also page 24). The cast on edge should be firm; too loose and it will look untidy and flare out, too tight and it will break and the stitches unravel. If your casting on is always too tight, use a size larger needle. If it is always too loose, use a size smaller needle. Remember to change back to the correct size needle to begin knitting.

Thumb method

This is the simplest way of casting on and you will need only one needle.

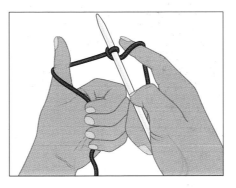

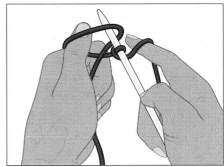

1 Make a slip knot some distance from the end of the yarn (see Knit Perfect) and place it on the needle. Hold the needle in your right hand. Pass the ball end of the yarn over the index finger, under the middle and then over the third finger. Holding the free end of yarn in your left hand, wrap it around your left thumb from front to back.

2 Insert the needle through the thumb loop from front to back.

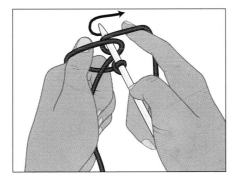

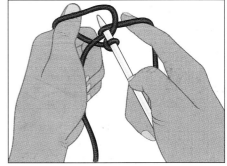

3 Wrap the ball end over the needle.

4 Pull a new loop through the thumb loop by passing the thumb loop over the end of the needle. Remove your thumb and tighten the new loop on the needle by pulling the free end. Continue in this way until you have cast on the required number of stitches.

✓ Knit Perfect

The slip knot counts as the first cast on stitch. It is made some distance from the end of the yarn and placed on the needle. Pull the ends of the yarn to tighten it. You now have two ends of yarn coming from the slip knot; the ball end attached to the ball and a shorter free end.

For the thumb method of casting on, you will need approximately 1in (2.5cm) for every stitch you want to cast on. When you have cast on, you should have at least a 6in (15cm) length to sew in.

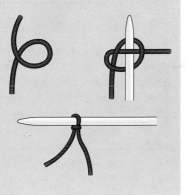

INTRODUCING KNIT STITCH

In knitting there are only two stitches to learn - knit stitch (k) and purl stitch (p). They are the foundation of all knitted fabrics. Once you have mastered these two simple stitches, by combining them in different ways, you will soon be knitting ribs, textures, cables and many more exciting fabrics.

English method *(yarn in the right hand)*

In knit stitch the yarn is held at the back of the work (the side facing away from you) and is made up of four steps.

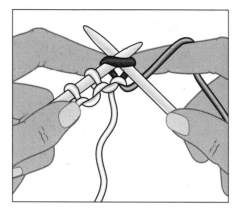

1 Hold the needle with the cast on stitches in your left hand, and insert the right-hand needle into the front of the stitch from left to right.

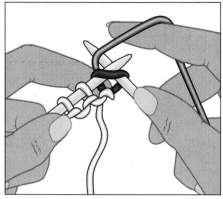

2 Pass the yarn under and around the right-hand needle.

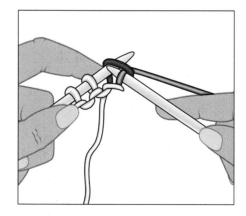

3 Pull the new loop on the right-hand needle through the stitch on the left-hand needle.

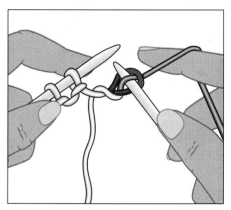

4 Slip the stitch off the left-hand needle. One knit stitch is completed.

To continue...
Repeat these four steps for each stitch on the left-hand needle. All the stitches on the left-hand needle will be transferred to the right-hand needle where the new row is formed. At the end of the row, swap the needle with the stitches into your left hand and the empty needle into your right hand, and work the next row in the same way.

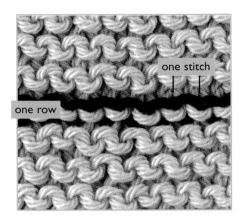

one stitch

one row

the result:

GARTER STITCH

knit every row

When you knit each row the fabric you make is called garter stitch (g st) and has rows of raised ridges on the front and back of the fabric. It looks the same on the back and the front so it is reversible. Garter stitch lies flat, is quite a thick fabric and does not curl at the edges. These qualities make it ideal for borders and collars, as well as for scarves and the main fabric of a garment.

Continental method *(yarn in the left hand)*

In this method the right-hand needle moves to catch the yarn; the yarn is held at the back of the work (the side facing away from you) and is released by the index finger of the left hand. This knit stitch is made up of four steps.

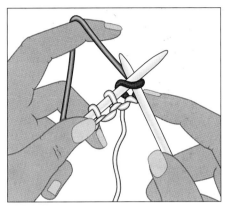

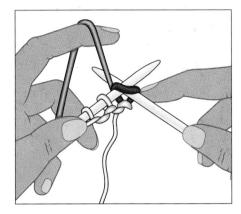

1 Hold the needle with the cast on stitches in your left hand and the yarn over your left index finger. Insert the right-hand needle into the front of the stitch from left to right.

2 Move the right-hand needle down and across the back of the yarn.

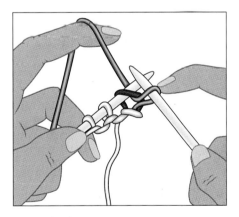

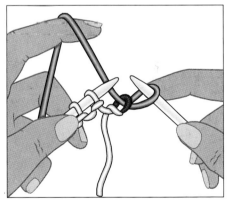

3 Pull the new loop on the right-hand needle through the stitch on the left-hand needle, using the right index finger to hold the new loop if needed.

4 Slip the stitch off the left-hand needle. One knit stitch is completed.

To continue...

Repeat these four steps for each stitch on the left-hand needle. All the stitches on the left-hand needle will be transferred to the right-hand needle where the new row is formed. At the end of the row, swap the needle with the stitches into your left hand and the empty needle into your right hand, and work the next row in the same way.

BINDING (CASTING) OFF

Bind (cast) off stitches when you have finished using them. This links stitches together to stop them unravelling and is the simplest method of binding (casting) off. See page 25 for advanced binding (casting) off.

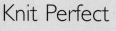

Knit Perfect

Like a cast on edge, it is important that a bind (cast) off edge is elastic. This means that it should not be so tight that it pulls the knitted fabric in. This is important when binding (casting) off a neckband, if it is too tight it will not stretch over your head and the edge may break, unravelling the stitches.

If you bind (cast) off too tightly, use a needle one or two sizes larger than that used for the knitted fabric. Always spend time undoing the edge and binding (casting) off again if it isn't right.

Bind (cast) off knitwise

This is the easiest method to bind (cast) off on a knit row.

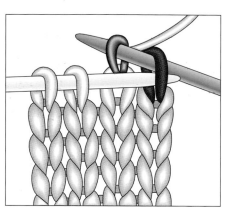

1 Knit two stitches, insert the tip of the left-hand needle into the front of the first stitch on the right-hand needle.

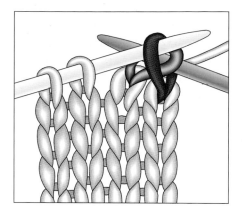

2 Lift this stitch over the second stitch and off the needle.

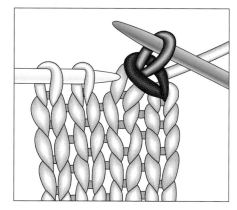

3 One stitch is left on the right-hand needle.

4 Knit the next stitch and lift the second stitch over this and off the needle. Continue in this way until one stitch remains on the right-hand needle.

To finish...

Cut the yarn (leaving a length long enough to sew in), thread the end through the last stitch and slip it off the needle. Pull the yarn end to tighten the stitch.

Bind (cast) off purlwise

To bind (cast) off on a purl row, simply purl the stitches instead of knitting them.

◀ KNIT SOMETHING NOW!

With what you have learnt so far – cast on, knit and bind (cast) off – you can easily complete this scarf, worked in one colour or in a simple striped pattern.

Plain scarf knitted in garter stitch in a bulky (chunky) wool yarn on size 11 (8mm/UK0) needles.
Striped scarf knitted in a fisherman (aran) merino wool yarn on size 7 (4.5mm/UK7) needles. Finished size for each scarf is 6in (15cm) wide by 62in (158cm) long. See page 129 for patterns.

INTRODUCING PURL STITCH

You may find purl stitch a little harder to learn than knit stitch. But really it is just the reverse of a knit stitch. If you purled every row, you would produce garter stitch (the same as if you knitted every row). It is not often that you will work every row in purl stitch; it is easier and faster to knit every row if you want garter stitch.

English method *(yarn in the right hand)*

In purl stitch the yarn is held at the front of the work (the side facing you) and is made up of four steps.

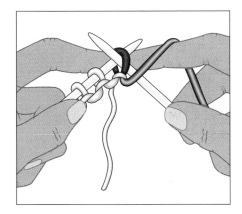

1 Hold the needle with the cast on stitches in your left hand, and insert the right-hand needle into the front of the stitch from right to left.

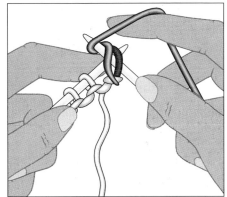

2 Pass the yarn over and around the right-hand needle.

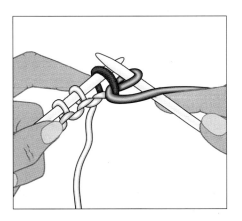

3 Pull the new loop on the right-hand needle through the stitch on the left-hand needle.

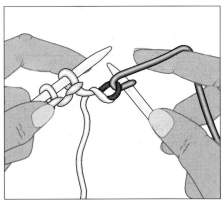

4 Slip the stitch off the left-hand needle. One stitch is completed.

To continue...
Repeat these four steps for each stitch on the left-hand needle. All the stitches on the left-hand needle will be transferred to the right-hand needle where the new purl row is formed. At the end of the row, swap the needle with the stitches into your left hand and the empty needle into your right hand, and work the next row in the same way.

introducing purl stitch

As with knit stitch there are two ways of holding the needles and yarn to work purl stitch. The left-hand index finger controls the yarn which is hooked through on to the right-hand needle.

Continental method *(yarn in the left hand)*

In purl stitch the yarn is held at the front of the work (the side facing you) and is made up of four steps.

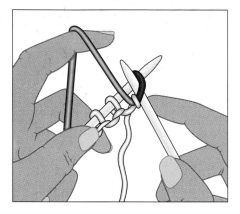

1 Hold the needle with the cast on stitches in your left hand, and insert the right-hand needle into the front of the stitch from right to left, keeping the yarn at the front of the work.

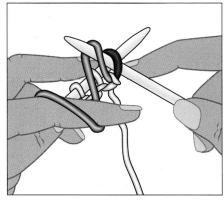

2 Move the right-hand needle from right to left behind the yarn and then from left to right in front of the yarn. Pull your left index finger down in front of the work to keep the yarn taut.

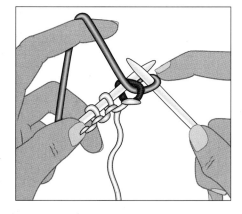

3 Pull the new loop on the right-hand needle through the stitch on the left-hand needle, using the right index finger to hold the new loop if needed.

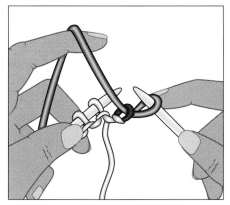

4 Slip the stitch off the left-hand needle. Return the left index finger to its position above the needle. One stitch is completed.

To continue...
Repeat these four steps for each stitch on the left-hand needle. All the stitches on the left-hand needle will be transferred to the right-hand needle where the new purl row is formed. At the end of the row, swap the needle with the stitches into your left hand and the empty needle into your right hand, and work the next row in the same way.

COMBINING KNIT AND PURL

If you work one row of knit stitches followed by one row of purl stitches, and repeat these two rows, you will produce stockinette (stocking) stitch (st st), the most widely used fabric in knitting. Work a row of knit stitches. At the end of the row, swap the needle with the stitches into your left hand and the empty needle into your right hand, and then work the next row in purl stitch.

In knitting instructions, stockinette (stocking) stitch is written as follows:
Row 1 (RS) Knit.
Row 2 Purl.
or the instructions may be:
Work in st st (1 row k, 1 row p), beg with a k row...

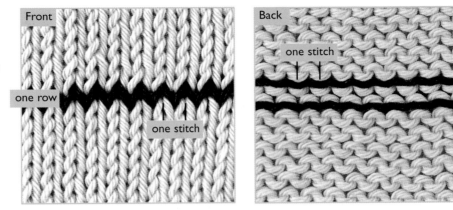

Front   one row   one stitch

Back   one stitch

the result:

STOCKINETTE STITCH
(stocking stitch)
knit one row, purl one row

The front or right side (RS) of stockinette (stocking) stitch is smooth or flat, and the back or wrong side (WS) has rows of raised ridges and is rough. If you lay a piece of stockinette (stocking) stitch down you will see that the side edges curl towards the back of the fabric whilst the cast on and bind (cast) off edges curl towards the front of the fabric. This is why a garment in stockinette (stocking) stitch usually has a rib or garter stitch edging.

If the back of the fabric is used as the right side it is called reverse stockinette (stocking) stitch (rev st st). This is commonly used as the background for cables and embossed knitting.

✓ Knit Perfect

In stockinette (stocking) stitch, to identify which row to work next, look at the fabric on the left-hand needle as though you were ready to start. If the smooth (knit) side is facing you, work a knit row. If the rough (purl) side is facing you, purl the next row. To count rows in stockinette (stocking) stitch either count the V's on the knit side or the top loops of the ridges on the purl side.

Knit and purl stitches can also be combined to make a wide range of textured fabrics; (see Stitch library page 89–100).

◄ KNIT SOMETHING NOW!

Once you have mastered the two basic stitches, and know how to combine them to make stockinette (stocking) stitch, you can make this handy little bag.

Striped bag knitted in stockinette (stocking) stitch using a sport (4ply) weight mercerized cotton yarn on size 3 (3.25mm/UK10) needles. Finished size is 6½ x 7in (17 x 18cm). See page 131 for pattern.

ADVANCED CASTING ON

Using the correct method of casting on and off is important, whether it is at the start of a piece of knitting, adding or removing stitches part way through or finishing off.

Knitting on

This simple method of casting on needs two needles. Begin by making a slip knot about 6in (15cm) from the end of the yarn and slip it on to a needle held in your left hand. This method produces a loose cast on edge, ideal for lace fabrics where a hard edge is not necessary.

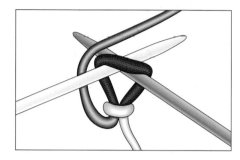

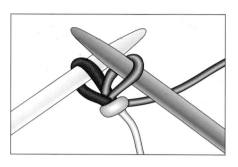

1 Insert the right-hand needle into the slip knot as though to knit it and wrap the yarn around the tip.

2 Pull a new loop through but do not slip the stitch off the left-hand needle.

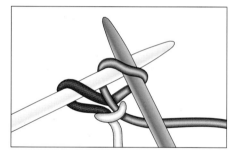

3 Place the loop on to the left-hand needle as shown by inserting the left-hand needle into the front of the loop from right to left as shown.

4 Insert the right-hand needle (as though to knit) into the stitch just made and wrap the yarn around the tip. Pull a new loop through and place it on to the left-hand needle.

Repeat step 4 until you have cast on the required number of stitches.

Cable cast on

Work the same as knitting on but instead of going into a stitch the needle goes between stitches. It should be worked quite loosely so the needle slips between stitches easily. This produces a rope-like edge used when working buttonholes where stitches are cast off on one row and cast on again on the next row (see page 69).

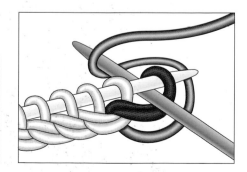

Cast on two stitches using the knitting on method. Insert the right-hand needle between the first and second stitches and wrap the yarn round the tip. When the new loop is pulled through between the stitches, place it on to the left-hand needle as for knitting on step 3.

Knitting on and Cable cast on...
These two methods are also used for casting on stitches at the beginning of a row, which usually happens in shaping a garment.

ADVANCED BINDING (CASTING) OFF

Picot bind (cast) off

This is a pretty, decorative finish used when the bind (cast) off edge is part of the design, for example across the top of a pocket or around a collar.

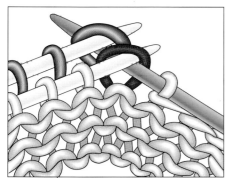

1 Using the simple bind (cast) off method cast off two stitches (see page 20).

2 Slip the stitch on the right-hand needle back to the left-hand needle and, using the cable cast on method, cast on two stitches (see left).

3 Bind (cast) off four stitches. These are the two stitches just cast on and the next two stitches of the bind (cast) off edge.

To continue...
Repeat steps 2 and 3 until only one stitch remains on the right-hand needle. Cut the yarn, pull it through the last stitch and draw up tightly.

The picots can be spaced wider apart by binding (casting) off five or more stitches.

Seam bind (cast) off

This is used to join two edges with the same number of stitches. It is often used for shoulder seams where the stitches have been left on stitch holders. You need three needles for this method.

1 Slip each set of stitches on to a needle, place together with right sides facing and hold in the left hand.

2 Insert the third (right-hand) needle through both sets of stitches and draw a loop through, knitting the stitches together. Repeat for the next set of two stitches.

Using the simple bind (cast) off method (see page 20), bind (cast) off stitches on the right-hand needle.

To finish...
With right sides together the bind (cast) off seam will be inside the garment; with wrong sides facing it will be a decorative seam on the outside as shown above.

Bind (cast) off in pattern

You should always bind (cast) off in the same stitch that you are using for the main fabric. On a knit row, you knit all the stitches when you bind (cast) off and on a purl row you purl all the stitches when you bind (cast) off. To cast off in rib, you must knit the knit stitches and purl the purl stitches of the rib. If you are working a pattern of cable stitches or lace, you would bind (cast) off in pattern; again knit the knit stitches and purl the purl stitches.

KNIT SOMETHING NOW! ▶

Use the techniques you have already learned together with more advanced methods which you will learn further on to make this simple sweater.

The flower top is knitted in worsted (DK) weight wool and cotton yarn on size 3 (3.25mm/UK10) and size 6 (4mm/UK8) needles. See page 130 for pattern.

INCREASING STITCHES

To shape knitting, stitches are increased or decreased. Increases are used to make a piece of knitting wider by adding more stitches, either on the ends of rows or within the knitting. Some increases are worked to be invisible whilst others are meant to be seen and are known as decorative increases. You can increase one stitch at a time or two or more.

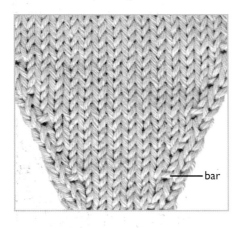
bar

Increasing one stitch (inc 1)

The easiest way to increase one stitch is to work into the front and back of the same stitch. This produces a small bar across the second (increase) stitch and is very visible. This makes counting the increases easier.

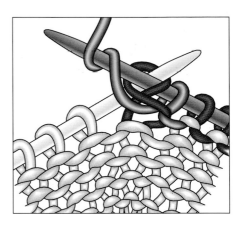

On a knit row knit into the front of the stitch as usual, do not slip the stitch off the left-hand needle but knit into it again through the back of the loop. Then slip the original stitch off the left-hand needle.

On a purl row purl into the front of the stitch as usual, do not slip the stitch off the left-hand needle but purl into it again through the back of the loop. Then slip the original stitch off the left-hand needle.

the result:

FULL FASHIONING

To make a neater edge when working increases at the beginning and end of rows, work the increase stitches a few stitches from the end. This leaves a continuous stitch up the edge of the fabric that makes sewing up easier. Because the made stitch lies to the left of the original stitch, at the beginning of a knit row you knit one stitch, then make the increase, but at the end of a knit row you work the increase into the third stitch from the end. The increase stitch lies between the second and third stitches at each end (see page 28–9 for more information on full fashioning).

On a purl row you work in exactly the same way; the bar will be in the correct position two stitches from either end.

KNIT SOMETHING NOW! ▶

This simple beret comes in three sizes, small, medium and large and is knitted in stockinette (stocking) stitch with a k1, p1 rib border.

Plain beret knitted in a worsted (DK) tweed wool yarn.
Two colour striped beret knitted in two colours of a worsted (DK) wool yarn on size 3 (3.25mm/UK10) and size 6 (4mm/UK8) needles. Finished head circumference measures 18 [20:22]in (45.5 [51:56]cm). See page 137 for pattern.

Make 1 (M1)

This is another way to increase one stitch and is often used when increasing stitches after a rib. The new stitch is made between two existing stitches using the horizontal thread that lies between the stitches – called the running thread. This is an invisible increase and is harder to see when counting.

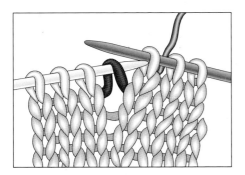

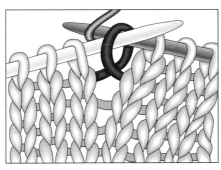

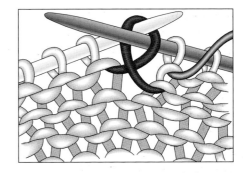

To twist the made stitch to the left
1 Knit to the point where the increase is to be made. Insert the tip of the left-hand needle under the running thread from front to back.

2 Knit this loop through the back to twist it. By twisting it you prevent a hole appearing where the made stitch is.

3 If you are working M1 on a purl row, you purl the loop through the back.

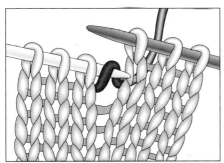

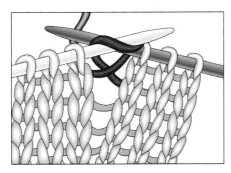

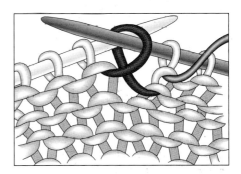

To twist the made stitch to the right
1 Knit to the point where the increase is to be made. Insert the tip of the left-hand needle under the running thread from back to front.

2 Knit this loop through the front to twist it.

3 If you are working M1 on a purl row, you purl the loop through the front.

the result:

INVISIBLE INCREASES

Being able to twist M1 to the right or left is useful when using this increase to shape a sleeve; the increases will be in pairs.
On a knit row, you knit two stitches, then work a M1 twisted to the right, knit to the last two stitches, then work a M1 twisted to the left.
On a purl row, purl two stitches and work a M1 twisted to the left, then purl to the last two stitches and work a M1 twisted to the right.

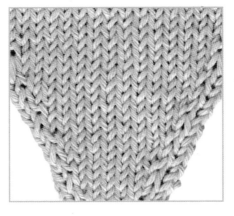

Increasing more than one stitch

To increase two stitches simply knit into the front, back and then the front again of the same stitch. When knitting bobbles (see page 42), you will sometimes make five, six or seven stitches out of one stitch in this way. For example, to make seven stitches the instructions would read (k into front and back of same st) 3 times, then k into front again.

DECREASING STITCHES

Decreasing is used at the ends of rows or within the knitted fabric to reduce the number of stitches being worked on. This means that you can shape your knitted fabric by making it narrower.

✓ Knit Perfect

Always read how to work a decrease very carefully. Some of them have similar abbreviations with only a slight difference between them.

In patterns the designer may use different abbreviations to those given here. Always check the detailed explanation of abbreviations.

▼ KNIT SOMETHING NOW!

The baby's bootees are worked in stockinette (stocking) stitch and shaped by using increases and decreases creatively.

Baby bootees knitted in a worsted (DK) merino yarn on size 6 (4mm/UK8) needles. See page 147 for pattern.

Decreasing one stitch

The simplest way to decrease one stitch is to knit or purl two stitches together (k2tog or p2tog). Both of these methods produce the same result on the front (knit side) of the work; the decrease slopes to the right.

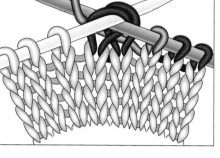 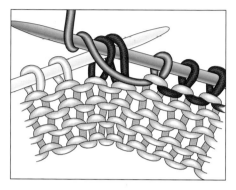

K2tog on a k row Knit to where the decrease is to be, insert the right-hand needle (as though to knit) through the next two stitches and knit them together as one stitch.

P2tog on a p row Purl to where the decrease is to be, insert the right-hand needle (as though to purl) through the next two stitches and purl them together as one stitch.

Decorative decreasing one stitch purlwise

Sometimes decreases are decorative, especially in lace knitting where they form part of the pattern. Then you have to be aware of whether the decrease slants right or left. Each decrease has an opposite and the two of them are called a pair. There is one way to work the decrease that is the pair to p2tog which slopes to the left when seen on the front (knit side) of the work. See page 32 for ways to slip stitches.

Slip one, slip one, purl two together through backs of loops (ssp or p2tog tbl)

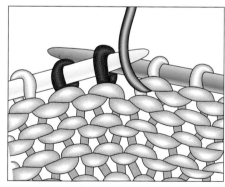 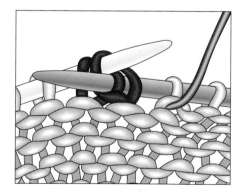

1 Slip two stitches knitwise, one at a time, from the left-hand needle to the right-hand needle (they will be twisted), pass these two stitches back to the left-hand needle in this twisted way.

2 Purl these two stitches together through the back loops.

Decorative decreasing one stitch knitwise

There are two ways to work the decrease that is the pair to k2tog. They both produce the same result and slope to the left. See page 32 for ways to slip stitches.

Slip one, slip one, knit two together (ssk or p2tog tbl)

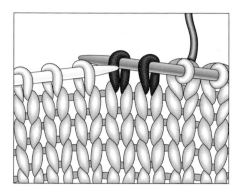 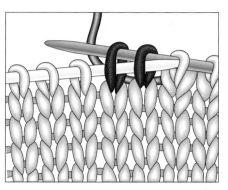

1 Slip two stitches knitwise one at a time from left-hand needle to right-hand needle.

2 Insert the left-hand needle from left to right through the fronts of these two stitches and knit together as one stitch.

Slip one, knit one, pass slipped stitch over (skpo)

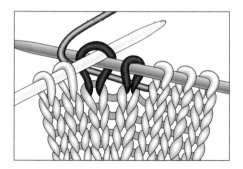 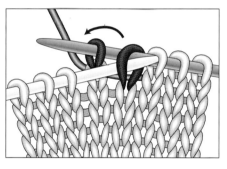

1 Insert the right-hand needle knitwise into the next stitch and slip it on to the right-hand needle without knitting it. Knit the next stitch.

2 With the tip of the left-hand needle, lift the slipped stitch over the knitted stitch and off the needle. This is like binding (casting) off one stitch.

Central decreasing

Slip two stitches knitwise, knit one, pass the two slipped stitches over (sl2tog-k1-psso)

Double decreases can also be worked where the two decreased stitches are arranged around a central stitch. Sk2po (see right) is a central decrease. To make a feature of the double decrease with its unbroken chain stitch running up the centre, work the central decrease as follows.

Insert the right-hand needle into the next two stitches as if to knit them together, slip them off together on to the right-hand needle without knitting them. Knit the next stitch. With the tip of the left-hand needle, lift the two slipped stitches together over the knitted stitch and off the needle.

the result:

FULL FASHIONED DECREASES

You can use decreases in full fashioning in the same way as increases.

Slope to the right
knit row – k2tog
purl row – p2tog

Slope to the left
knit row – ssk or skpo
purl row – ssp

Decreasing two stitches at once

The two simplest ways are to knit three stitches together (k3tog) or purl three stitches together (p3tog). These are worked the same as k2tog and p2tog, but worked over three stitches instead of two.

The pair to k3tog is slip one, knit two together, pass slipped stitch over (sk2po), which is worked in the same manner as skpo but k2tog instead of k1.

Alternatively, the pair can be worked like ssk but slip three stitches knitwise instead of two.

The pair to p3tog is worked like ssp but over three stitches instead of two.

RIBS

Ribs are the result of alternating columns of knit and purl stitches. The knit columns stand out at the front and the purl columns sink to the back. When you lay a piece of ribbing flat, you will only see the knit columns as they pull together and cover the purl columns. This means that ribbing is very elastic; you can pull it out horizontally and it will spring back. When used at the waist, neck and wrists of garments, the ribs will expand when you put it on and then spring back to fit snugly.

The number of stitches in a rib fabric can be even, for example knit 1, purl 1 (k1, p1), knit 2, purl 2 (k2, p2), knit 3, purl 3 (k3, p3) or it can be uneven, for example knit 2, purl 3 (k2, p3), knit 2, purl 4 (k2, p4). Work a few samples of rib in different combinations to see the elastic effect of ribbing.

✓ Knit Perfect

Ribs are usually worked on needles two sizes smaller than those used for stockinette (stocking) stitch, because the action of moving the yarn backwards and forwards between the knit and purl stitches can loosen the work. Try and keep a regular tension when working a rib pattern.

KNIT SOMETHING NOW! ▶

This snug winter scarf uses six different ribs. It will grow quickly and give you lots of practise in ribbing

Ribbed scarf is knitted in a bulky (chunky) yarn using size 10½(6.5mm/UK3) needles. Finished size is 6in (15cm) wide by 64in (162cm) long. See page 135 for pattern.

Single rib (k1, p1)

Cast on an odd number of stitches.

1 With the yarn at the back of the work, knit the first stitch.

2 Bring the yarn to the front of the work between the needles and purl the next stitch.

3 Take the yarn to the back of the work, and knit the next stitch.

Single rib – k1, p1

Double rib – k2, p2

To continue...

Repeat steps 2 and 3 to the end of the row. On the return row knit the knit stitches and purl the purl stitches.

Double rib (k2, p2) is worked the same, but cast on a multiple of four stitches plus two stitches and knit or purl two stitches each time.

the result:

SINGLE AND DOUBLE RIB
k1, p1, or k2, p2

When using ribs for garments, it is usual to start and finish each row with the same stitch so the rib looks balanced when the garment is sewn up. So for a knit 1, purl 1 rib you would cast on an odd number of stitches, and for a knit 2, purl 2 rib you would need to cast on a multiple of four stitches plus two stitches.

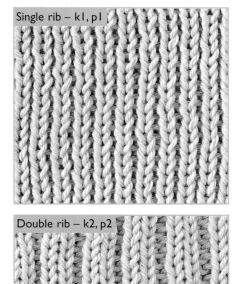

GAUGE (Tension)

At the beginning of any knitting pattern, the designer will state the gauge (tension) that you need to achieve and this is used to calculate the finished dimensions of the garment. It is a very important part of knitting and is the number of stitches and rows to 1in (2.5cm). If you do not get the correct gauge (tension) the garment will not be the correct size. More stitches to 1in (2.5cm) and the garment will be smaller; fewer stitches to 1in (2.5cm) and the garment will be bigger. A tight fitting sweater may end up big and baggy.

In knitting patterns, the gauge (tension) is given over 4in (10cm). For example, 22 stitches and 28 rows to 4in (10cm) measured over stockinette (stocking) stitch on size 6 (4mm/UK8) needles. You must work a square of fabric measuring at least 6in (15cm), using the stated yarn, needle size and stitch. You can then measure the fabric in the middle of the square, avoiding the edge stitches which will be distorted.

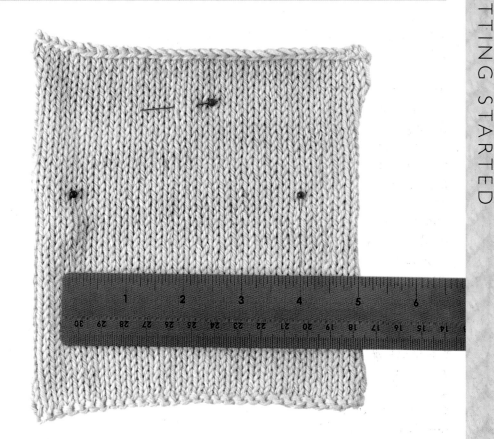

Knit Perfect

✓

Many knitters do not check their gauge (tension) because they think it is boring and a waste of time and yarn. They assume that they have the same gauge (tension) as the designer, but this is not necessarily the case.

Everyone holds the yarn at a different tension when they knit, this makes the stitches tighter or looser than someone else knitting exactly the same yarn on the same size needles.

Knitting a gauge (tension) square

To knit a gauge (tension) square for stockinette (stocking) stitch cast on the number of stitches stated for 4in (10cm) plus 10 extra stitches.

1 Work in stockinette (stocking) stitch for at least 6in (15cm) and then bind (cast) off loosely.

2 Steam or block the square in the way that you will use for your finished project (see page 66). The knitting pattern will tell you whether to block the pieces or not.

3 Lay the square on a flat surface without stretching it. Place a ruler horizontally on the square and place a pin four stitches in from the edge and place another at 4in (10cm) from the first pin.

4 Do the same for the rows by placing the ruler vertically, keeping away from the cast on and bind (cast) off edges, which may pull the fabric in.

5 Count the number of stitches and rows between the pins and this will be your gauge (tension):
Too many stitches means that your stitches are too small; you need to use a size larger needle to make the stitches bigger and so get fewer to 4in (10cm).
Too few stitches means your stitches are too big; you need to use a size smaller needle to make the stitches smaller and therefore get more to 4in (10cm).

6 Work more gauge (tension) squares until you achieve the gauge (tension) stated in the pattern.

If the gauge (tension) is quoted over a stitch pattern like a lace stitch, cast on enough stitches to work complete repeats. For aran patterns, cast on enough stitches to work all the different cables.

Checking your gauge (tension) will save you time spent unravelling your work and starting again, and it means the difference between a perfect garment and a disaster!

KNIT PERFECT

Here is some useful information and handy tips to improve the appearance of your knitting.

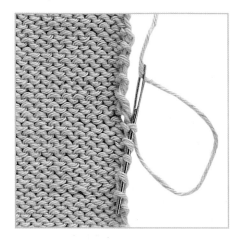

Joining a new ball

When you run out of yarn and need to start a new ball in the same colour or need to change to another colour, always start a new ball of yarn at the beginning of a row, at a seam edge where the ends can be woven in without showing on the front.

Simply drop the old yarn, wrap the new yarn around the needle and work a few stitches. Tie the two ends securely together at the beginning of the row so neither one will work its way free and unravel your stitches. When you've finished the piece, undo the knot and weave one end up the edge for a couple of inches, and then double back over a few stitches to secure the end.

Make sure you haven't pulled it too tightly and distorted the edge. Weave the other end down the edge using the same method. Use this method when knitting stripes and changing colours at the beginning of a row.

If you are coming to the end of a ball, to see if you have enough yarn to work one more row, lay the knitting flat and measure the yarn four times across the width. This will be sufficient to work one row of stockinette (stocking) stitch; textured and cabled fabric will need more yarn. When in doubt, join in a new ball of yarn to avoid running out of yarn halfway through and having to unravel stitches.

Knit Perfect

✔ Hairy yarns are sometimes difficult to unravel, the hairs become tangled into several stitches. Use a pair of sharp scissors to carefully cut the tangled hairs. Be careful not to cut the yarn completely. If the yarn is too damaged to re-use, cut it off and rejoin new yarn at the beginning of the row.

✔ If you snag a stitch in your knitted piece, a loop of yarn is pulled out drawing up several stitches tightly. Using a tapestry needle, ease the extra yarn back through the distorted stitches, one by one, starting with the stitch closest to the snag and yarn loop.

Slip stitches

Slipping stitches from one needle to another is part of many of the techniques already described and it is important to slip them correctly.

To slip a stitch, you pass it from one needle to the other without working into it. In the instructions you will usually be told how to slip the stitch, knitwise (kwise) or purlwise (pwise). To slip knitwise (sl1 kwise), insert the right-hand needle as if to knit and pull the stitch off the left-hand needle. This will twist the stitch as if you have worked it. To slip purlwise (sl1 pwise), insert the right-

hand needle as if to purl and pull the needle off the left-hand needle. The stitch will not be twisted.

Slipping either knitwise or purlwise makes a difference to the appearance of your work. In decreasing you always slip the stitch knitwise on a knit row and purlwise on a purl row, otherwise, when it is pulled over the other stitches in the decrease, it will appear to be twisted. When instructed to slip a stitch at the beginning of a row, to form a neat edge, slip knitwise on knit rows and purlwise on purl rows.

Stopping knitting

When you wish to stop knitting always finish the complete row. Finishing in the middle of a row will stretch the stitches and they may slide off the needle. If you need to put your knitting aside for several weeks or even months and do not have time to finish the piece beforehand mark on the pattern or

make a note of where you have got to. If you are working in a regular pattern like stockinette (stocking) stitch, when re-starting again it is worth unravelling a couple of rows and re-knitting them as stitches left over time on the needles can get stretched and leave an unsightly ridge where you stopped.

ABBREVIATIONS

Abbreviations are used to shorten techniques and words to make written knitting instructions easier to read and a manageable length. There are some standard abbreviations but others can vary. Always read the abbreviations on your pattern's knitting instructions carefully. The following are the most common abbreviations used throughout this book.

alt	alternate
approx	approximately
beg	begin/beginning
CC	contrast colour
cm	centimetre(s)
CN	cable needle
cont	continue
dec(s)	decrease(s)/decreasing
DK	double knitting
dpn	double-pointed needle
foll	following
g	gram
g st	garter stitch (k every row)
in(s)	inch(es)
inc(s)	increase(s)/increasing
k	knit
k2tog	knit 2 stitches together (1 stitch decreased)
k3tog	knit 3 stitches together (2 stitches decreased)
kwise	knitwise
LH	left hand
LT	left twist
m	metre(s)
mm	millimetre(s)
M1	make one (increase 1 stitch)
M1L	make one twisted to the left (increase 1 stitch)
M1R	make one twisted to the right (increase 1 stitch)
M1p	make one purlwise (increase 1 stitch)
MB	make a bobble
MC	main colour
oz	ounces
p	purl
patt(s)	pattern(s)
patt rep(s)	pattern repeat(s)
PB	place bead
PM	place marker
p2tog	purl 2 stitches together (1 stitch decreased)
p3tog	purl 3 stitches together (2 stitches decreased)
psso	pass slipped stitch over
p2sso	pass 2 slipped stitches over
pwise	purlwise

rem	remain/ing
rep(s)	repeat(s)
rev st st	reverse stockinette stitch (1 row p, 1 row k) (UK: reverse stocking stitch)
RH	right hand
rnd(s)	round(s)
RS	right side
RT	right twist
skpo	slip 1 stitch, knit 1 stitch, pass slipped stitch over (1 stitch decreased)
sk2po	slip 1 stitch, knit 2 stitches together, pass slipped stitch over (2 stitches decreased)
sl2tog-k1-psso	slip 2 stitches together, knit 1 stitch, pass 2 slipped stitches over (2 stitches decreased)
ssk	slip 2 stitches one at a time, knit 2 slipped stitches together (1 stitch decreased)
ssp	slip 2 stitches one at a time, purl 2 slipped stitches together through the back of the loops (1 stitch decreased)

sl	slip
sl st	slip stitch
sl 1	slip 1 stitch
sl 1k	slip 1 stitch knitwise
sl 1p	slip 1 stitch purlwise
st(s)	stitch(es)
st st	stockinette stitch (1 row k, 1 row p) (UK: stocking stitch)
tbl	through back of loop
tog	together
WS	wrong side
wyib	with yarn in back
wyif	with yarn in front
ybk	yarn to the back
yd(s)	yard(s)
yfwd	yarn forward
yo	yarn over
yrn	yarn round needle
yon	yarn over needle
*	repeat directions following * as many times as indicated or until end of row
[ ]	instructions in square brackets refer to larger sizes
( )	repeat instructions in round brackets the number of times indicated

Throughout the book US terms are given with UK terms in brackets. These are the most commonly used:

Instructions	US	UK
	bind off	cast off
	gauge	tension
	stockinette stitch	stocking stitch
	reverse stockinette stitch	reverse stocking stitch
	work even	work straight/work without shaping

Yarns	US	UK
	fingering/baby yarn	2ply/3ply
	sport weight	4ply
	worsted	DK
	fisherman/medium weight	aran
	bulky	chunky

Creative Options

In this section, you will build upon the techniques that you have learnt so far. You will see new ways of working stitches, such as lace knitting, using yarn overs and decreases decoratively. The sections on cables, twisted stitches and embossed knitting introduce manipulating stitches, twisting them and carrying them across the fabric, to add a three dimensional aspect to your knitting. Colour knitting is covered by the sections on two techniques; intarsia and fair isle knitting. There is a section on circular knitting and how to use four or more needles, or circular needles. Short rows are useful for shaping and can produce wonderful structural effects.

KNIT SOMETHING NOW! ▶

Knit a trio of lace sachets to hold pot pourri or lavender and practise three lace stitch patterns.

The **lace bags** are knitted in a sport (4ply) mercerized cotton yarn on size 2 (3mm/UK11) needles. See page 143 for the patterns.

LACE KNITTING

The general term used to cover eyelets, faggoting and lace is lace knitting. These form categories on their own, but many stitch patterns overlap between two or even three of them.

Eyelets are single holes worked in rows or in groups on a background of stockinette (stocking) stitch; for example, a drawstring can be threaded through a row of eyelets with three or four stitches between them.

Knitted faggoting is the same term as that used in embroidery and describes a line of horizontal or vertical holes, next to each other and separated by a few strands of thread. It is often used as an open insertion around a hem or cuff. All-over faggoting forms a net or mesh.

Lace is the most open variation where the holes and decreases are arranged to form patterns. A lace stitch pattern can be repeated as an all-over fabric or worked as an insertion on stockinette (stocking) stitch. The stitch and row repeat can vary from simple patterns of less than ten stitches and two rows up to complex patterns of 20 or 30 stitches and as many rows.

The holes in lace knitting are made by working a yarn over. This makes (increases) a stitch so it has to be accompanied by a decrease. The way you work a yarn over depends on the stitches either side of it. In patterns, where yarn over (yo) is given, you decide which yarn over method to use. Some patterns will tell you which one to use.

Working a yarn over

Between two knit stitches
(k1, yo, k1) or (k1, yfwd, k1)

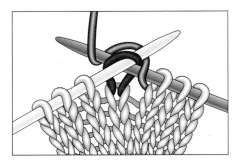

Bring the yarn forward (yfwd or yf) between the two needles. Knit the next stitch, taking the yarn over the right needle.

Between two purl stitches
(p1, yo, p1) or (p1, yrn, p1)

Take the yarn back over the right-hand needle and forward between the needles to bring yarn round needle (yrn). Purl the next stitch.

Between knit and purl stitches
(k1, yo, p1) or (k1, yfrn, p1)

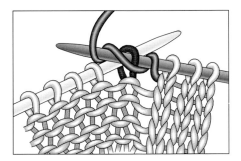

Bring the yarn forward between the two needles, take it back over the right-hand needle and forward again between the two needles – yarn forward and round needle (yfrn). Purl the next stitch.

Between purl and knit stitches
(p1, yo, k1) or (p1, yon, k1)

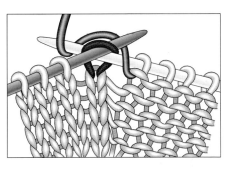

Take the yarn back over the right-hand needle – yarn over needle (yon). Knit the next stitch.

✓ Knit Perfect

When working a lace pattern you may find it helpful to place a marker (make several slip knot loops of a contrasting colour yarn) between each repeat, where the asterisks are, and slip them on every row. Then you can keep track of each small repeat instead of having to work back through a long row of stitches if you make a mistake.

lace knitting

At the edge of work

Sometimes you have to work a yarn over at the edge of the work, before the first stitch.

Multiple yarn overs
(yo twice)

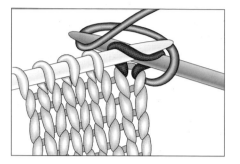

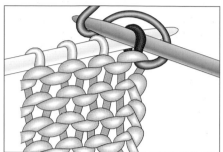

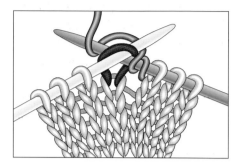

Before a knit stitch bring the yarn forward as if to purl, knit the first stitch bringing the yarn over the right needle as you do so.

Before a purl stitch take the yarn back as though to knit, purl the first stitch, bringing the yarn over the needle as you do so.

These are used to make bigger holes. Wrap the yarn around the needle twice. On the return row, you must knit then purl into the double yarn over.

✓ Knit Perfect

Decreases in lace stitches play a decorative part and the lace stitch pattern will tell you which decrease to work (see page 74).

the result:

SIMPLE LACE PATTERN

To see the lace pattern at its best the knitting needs to be stretched slightly to open it out and then blocked. Lace patterns look particularly good knitted in a smooth cotton yarn.

Working a lace stitch pattern

A simple lace pattern is written as follows:

Row 1 K1, * yfwd, k1, sk2po, k1, yfwd, k1; rep from * to end.
Row 2 P to end.
Row 3 K1, * k1, yfwd, sk2po, yfwd, k2; rep from * to end.
Row 4 P to end.

This pattern is worked over a multiple of six stitches plus one and over four rows. If you cast on 25 stitches this will give you four repeats of the pattern. The part you repeat is between the asterisks; so on row 1 you would begin with k1, then work a yfwd, k1, then work the decrease sk2po, k1, another yfwd, and then k1. The sk2po decreases the two stitches that you make by working the two yfwds. Go back to the asterisk and begin the repeat again with yfwd, k1, etc. Keep repeating the six stitches until you reach the end of the row. Count your stitches and make sure you still have 25; if you have more, you haven't worked the sk2po properly, if you have less you may have missed one of the yfwds. Row 2 is just a purl row. On row 3, begin with k1 and then work the repeat four times. Row 4 is a purl row. These four rows form the pattern and are repeated. So go back to row 1 and start again.

Shaping lace fabric

Placing markers for the lace pattern repeats is a good idea when you are shaping a piece of lace knitting for a garment. By marking the beginning of the first repeat and the end of the last repeat, you can increase stitches at the beginning and end of a row and keep the lace pattern correct. For more information on increasing into stitch patterns see page 74.

Blocking lace fabric

A lace pattern needs to be stretched slightly when blocking (see page 66). It needs to be opened out to show off the pattern of holes. By working decreases so often the fabric will be puckered. When working a gauge (tension) square, pull it out so that it lies flat and the holes are open. Do not over stretch it or it will be distorted.

FAIR ISLE

Authentic fair isle sweaters were worked as circular knitting so the right side of the knitting was always facing the knitter. This meant that the pattern was always visible and only knit stitches were used.

Because the knitting was circular there were no seams; armholes and the front openings of cardigans were cut after the knitting was finished. Extra stitches were added for this purpose and they were called steeks; the extra stitches were turned back after cutting and sewn down to prevent the stitches unravelling. Sleeves were picked up around the armholes and knitted down to the cuff, and shoulder seams were grafted.

Today the term fair isle knitting is used to describe the technique of knitting with two colours in one row and is used in flat as well as circular knitting.

Reading a chart

Fair isle patterns are worked from charts. One square represents one stitch and one line of squares represents one row. The rows will be numbered, knit rows (right side rows) will be odd numbers and are read from right to left; purl rows (wrong side rows) are even numbers and are read from left to right.

Start knitting from the bottom right-hand corner of the chart. The whole garment may not need to be charted; many fair isle patterns have a small repeat. The chart will tell you which stitches to repeat. On each side of the pattern repeat there may be extra stitches that are only worked once. These balance the pattern, to make sure that it is the same at both side seams.

Colour charts show the actual yarn colours whilst on black and white charts each colour is represented by a symbol. A key is given with the chart to show which symbol or colour represents which colour yarn.

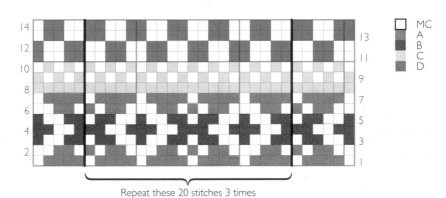

Repeat these 20 stitches 3 times

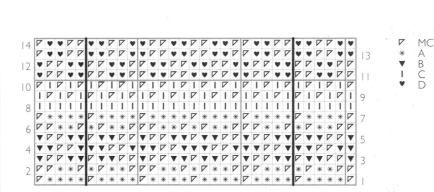

Repeat these 20 stitches 3 times

✓ Knit Perfect

In fair isle, the unused colour is loosely carried along the back of the work between stitches. Carrying the yarn between stitches is called stranding and you can strand yarn across if the pattern is small and the colours are changed frequently. However, if the yarn is to be stranded over five stitches or more, the loop will be too long and it will get snagged and distort the fabric. You must catch the loop in on the centre stitch of a long strand to prevent this. This is called weaving in.

✓ Knit Perfect

Practise knitting with both hands, it really is the easiest and fastest way of working. If you find the Continental method too awkward, adapt it to suit yourself. For example, try holding the yarn between the thumb and index finger.

Gauge (tension)

It is important in either stranding or weaving in that the yarn carried across the back is not pulled up too tightly. If it is, the knitted fabric will pucker and not lie flat. Keep spreading the stitches out on the needle to maintain the correct gauge (tension).

Fair isle knitting is easier and faster if you can learn to use both the right and left hands to hold the yarns. To do this you must practise the unfamiliar technique of either the English or Continental methods of knitting and purling (see page 16). If you find two-handed knitting awkward you can also hold both yarns in one hand (see right). If you find both of these methods difficult, you can hold only the working yarn, letting it drop to pick up the new yarn when you need to change colour but this is a very slow method of working.

Stranding

The loops formed by carrying the yarn between areas of colour are called floats. To get the floats to lie neatly and without lumps where the colours are changed and to prevent the yarns from becoming twisted together and tangled, one colour always lies above the other on the wrong side of the work. By keeping the back of the work neat in this way, the stitches on the front of the work will lie flat without puckering and without holes appearing between the colour changes. Never strand yarns over more than five stitches. In stranding, one colour must always be above the other on the back of the work. If they constantly change position, the fabric will be bulky and the yarns will tangle.

Using both hands

Hold the most frequently used colour (usually the background colour) in the right hand and the second colour in the left hand (see page 16 for the position of hands and yarns in the English and Continental methods). Whilst knitting, the right-hand colour crosses over the left-hand colour and it will always lie above the left-hand (second) colour.

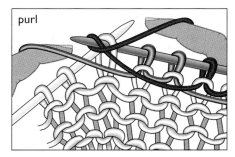

1 When knitting with the right-hand colour, keep the left-hand colour below the needle and out of the way of the working yarn.

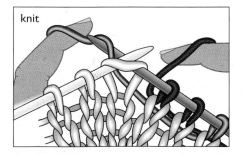
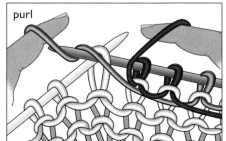

2 When knitting with the left-hand colour, keep the right-hand colour above the needle.

Knit Perfect

✓ There is no need to make bobbins for each colour of yarn. Just use the yarn straight from the ball.

✓ Turn the work clockwise at the end of a knit row and anti-clockwise at the end of a purl row. This action will prevent the yarns becoming tangled.

✓ Always carry both yarns to the beginning and end of the each row by catching the unused yarn into the first and last stitch. If you don't, the fabric here will be thinner than where both yarns are stranded across the back.

✓ As you work across the row, keep easing out the fabric to its correct width on the needle, so the floats or weaving are not pulled too tightly.

Both yarns in one hand

Hold both yarns together in the right hand. Have the working yarn over the index finger, knit or purl the required stitches then drop it and pick up the other colour on to the index finger. The predominant colour will always be picked up over the second colour and the second colour will always be picked up below the predominant colour. This will ensure that the floats of the predominant colour will always be above those of the second colour.

One yarn at a time

Drop one colour and pick up the new colour, making sure they don't become twisted and the floats are lying correctly. The predominant colour is always picked up over the second colour and the second colour is always picked up from below the other colour.

Weaving in

You must weave the floats in if they are stranded over five stitches or more. This is the same technique used to weave in ends in intarsia (see page 49). Refer to the diagrams and remember to weave the yarn in loosely without pulling up the stitches.

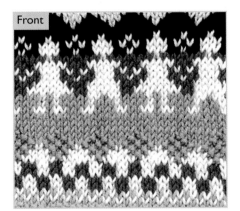
Front

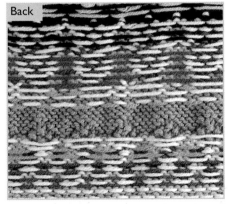
Back

the result:

FAIR ISLE KNITTING

The knitting should be smooth on the front with the yarn floats lying neatly across the back with one colour always above the other.

◄ KNIT SOMETHING NOW!

Using just two colours on each row does not limit the range of designs possible in traditional fair isle. This patch gives plenty of practise knitting with yarn held in both hands.

Fair isle baby blanket is knitted in a worsted (DK) wool/cotton yarn on size 6 (4mm/UK8) needles. See page 141 for pattern.

CABLES

Cables are simply a way of twisting two sets of stitches or carrying stitches across the fabric. There are two ways of moving the stitches; cabling and crossing. Stitches are cabled when all the stitches are knitted, but stitches are crossed when knit stitches are moved over a background of purl stitches. In patterns, cables are twisted to the back or front, while crossed stitches move right or left.

The two techniques to learn are moving the stitches at the back and moving them at the front. This is done by holding the stitches on a cable needle either at the back or the front of the work. This simple cable twists two sets of knit stitches, using four stitches.

Basic abbreviations for cables...

C4F   cable four front
C4B   cable four back
Cr4L   cross four left
Cr4R   cross four right

When following a pattern with cables, the designer will explain how to work the cables under special abbreviations at the start of the pattern.

Instead of twisting stitches to form cables, stitches can be crossed, carrying two knit stitches to the left or right, over a background of purl stitches.

Cable four front (C4F)

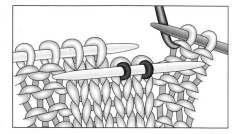

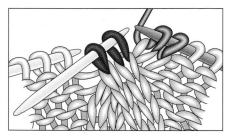

1 Slip the next two stitches from the left-hand needle on to a cable needle and hold at the front of the work.

2 Knit the next two stitches on the left-hand needle, then knit the two stitches from the cable needle.

Cable four back (C4B)

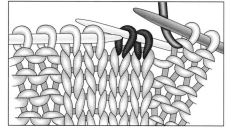

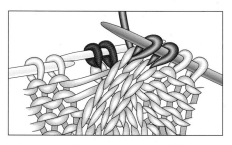

1 Slip the next two stitches from the left-hand needle on to a cable needle and hold at the back of the work.

2 Knit the next two stitches on the left-hand needle, then knit the two stitches from the cable needle.

More cables...
C6F or C6B is worked by slipping three stitches on to the cable needle and then knitting three stitches. C8F or C8B is worked with four stitches in each part of the cable. The more stitches there are in a cable, the more rows there are between twists. So C4F or C4B has three rows straight, C6F or C6B has five rows straight and so on. To make a looser cable, work more rows straight between twists.

Cross four left (Cr4L)

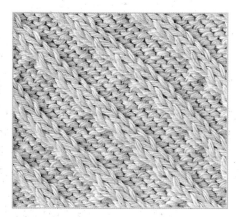

1 Slip the next two stitches from the left-hand needle on to a cable needle and hold at the front of the work.

2 Purl the next two stitches on the left-hand needle, then knit the 2 stitches from the cable needle.

Cross four right (Cr4R)

1 Slip the next two stitches from the left-hand needle on to a cable needle and hold at the back of the work.

2 Knit the next two stitches on the left-hand needle, then purl the two stitches from the cable needle.

the result:

CABLES AND CROSS STITCHES

The more stitches there are in a cable the more rows are worked between twists. Crossed stitches can move every right side row or with more rows worked between them.

More crossing cables...

Cr3L or Cr3R could be worked by moving the two knit stitches over one purl background stitch or by moving one knit stitch over two purl background stitches. Cr5L or Cr5R could be worked by moving two knit stitches over three purl background stitches or three knit stitches over two purl background stitches. In a pattern an explanation of the abbreviations used is given. Crossed stitches can be moved on every right side row or with straight rows in between.

✔ Knit Perfect

✔ Cable needles can be straight or they can have a kink in them to stop the stitches falling off. Try both kinds or, if you find the cable needle fiddly to work with because it is too short, try using a short double-pointed needle of the same size as those used for the main knitting. If you find working the stitches off the cable needle awkward, replace them on to the left-hand needle to work them.

✔ Use a row counter or make a mark for each row worked on a piece of paper to keep track of the rows between twists of the cable. To count the rows between twists of a cable, look for the row where you worked the twist; you will be able to identify this by following the path of the yarn from the last stitch of the cable to the first background stitch for a front cross cable or from the last background stitch to the first stitch of the cable for a back cross cable. On the row below this there will be no connecting strand of yarn between these same stitches. Count each strand for every row above the twist row.

▼ KNIT SOMETHING NOW!

This cable throw has each panel knitted separately so it is ideal for practising cables.

Cable throw knitted in four colours of a bulky (chunky) wool yarn on size 10½ (7mm/UK2) needles.
See page 132 for pattern.

EMBOSSED KNITTING

Embossed features are three dimensional, for example, popcorns and bobbles, both of which involve making extra stitches out of one stitch and are knitted independently of the background fabric. They also include bells and leaves, which are knitted into the background fabric.

Popcorn worked over four stitches

A popcorn is a small knot of stitches that are increased and immediately decreased.

1 To make four stitches from one stitch (knit into the front of the next stitch, then knit into the back of it) twice. Slip the original stitch from the left-hand needle.

2 With the tip of the left-hand needle, pull the second, third, and fourth stitches over the first stitch and off the needle. Work the stitch after the popcorn firmly to hold the popcorn in place at the front of the work.

Variations

Sometimes popcorn instructions will tell you to increase by (k1, p1) twice into the same stitch. Larger bobbles are made by increasing more stitches out of one stitch. You can work more or less rows of stockinette (stocking) stitch or work in reverse stockinette (stocking) stitch or garter stitch on these stitches. Decreases, too, can be worked in different ways, working a pair of decreases at each end of two rows or decreasing to three stitches and working a central decrease (see page 29).

Simple bobble of five stitches

A bobble is a round button of fabric, larger than a popcorn, made by increasing stitches and working a few rows on these stitches before decreasing. There are many ways to create a bobble and the pattern instructions will tell you the kind of bobble to work.

1 To make five stitches from one stitch (knit into the front of the next stitch, then knit into the back of it) twice, then knit into the front of the same stitch again. Slip the original stitch from the left-hand needle.

2 (Turn the work and purl these five stitches, turn the work and knit the same five stitches) twice.

3 To decrease the five stitches back to one stitch, with the tip of the left-hand needle, pull the second, third, fourth and fifth stitches over the first stitch and off the needle.

Bells

These small funnels of fabric, open at one end and knitted into the background fabric, look like small bells. Start by casting on stitches between two stitches of background fabric which is usually reverse stockinette (stocking) stitch and shape them by decreasing the cast on stitches over several rows.

Bell over 6 sts with 5 sts of rev st st each side.

Cast on 10 sts and work 2 rows in rev st st.
Row 1 (RS) P5, cast on 6 sts using the cable cast on method (see page 24), p5.
Row 2 K5, p the 6 sts just cast on, k5.
Row 3 P5, k6, p5.
Row 4 As row 2.
Row 5 P5, ssk, k2, k2tog, p5.
Row 6 K5, p4, k5.
Row 7 P5, ssk, k2tog, p5.
Row 8 K5, p2, k5.

Row 9 P5, k2tog, p5.
Row 10 K5, p1, k5.
Row 11 P4, p2tog (last st of bell and 1 st of rev st st), p5.
Row 12 K10.

The bell can be made bigger by casting on more stitches. Always shape the bell by working pairs of decreases (see pages 28–9). Bells can be worked singly, in rows or as an all-over pattern.

Leaves

Instead of the extra stitches being made all at once as for a bobble, two stitches at a time are increased on every right side row either side of a central stitch. They are usually created by a yarn over. The leaf is then decreased by working a pair of decreases on every right side row until three stitches remain, then a central decrease is worked to return to the original one stitch. The leaf is not worked separately but the extra stitches are worked into each row across the fabric. Leaves are usually worked on reverse stockinette (stocking) stitch or garter stitch.

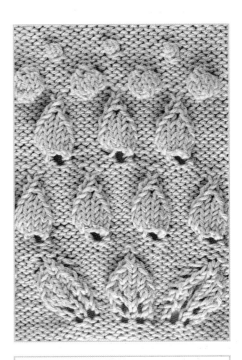

Simple leaf worked up to a width of 7 stitches with 5 sts of rev st st each side.

Cast on 11 sts and work 2 rows in rev st st.
Row 1 P5, yo, k1, yo, p5.
Row 2 K5, p3, k5.
Row 3 P5, k1, yo, k1, yo, k1, p5.
Row 4 K5, p5, k5.
Row 5 P5, k2, yo, k1, yo, k2, p5. The leaf now has 7 sts.
Row 6 K5, p7, k5.
Row 7 P5, ssk, k3, k2tog, p5.
Row 8 K5, p5, k5.

Row 9 P5, ssk, k1, k2tog, p5.
Row 10 K5, p3, k5.
Row 11 P5, sl2tog-k1-psso, p5.
Row 12 K to end.
Make a bigger leaf by working more increase rows. Make a more solid leaf by working M1 instead of yo. The leaf can be sloped to the right or left by working a decrease on one side in the rev st st and an increase on the other side in the rev st st.

the result:

EMBOSSED KNITTING
From the top the sample shows four stitch popcorns, five stitch bobbles, two rows of bells and a central leaf with leaves sloping to the left and right each side.

✓ Knit Perfect

Embossed features add great texture to a garment as an all-over pattern such as the Popcorn pattern on page 102 or the Boxed bobble pattern on page 103. Popcorns and bobbles are often added to cables, for example the Medallion bobble cable on page 109 and the Nosegay pattern on page 115. Combined with other stitches they contrast well with lace or knit and purl fabrics.

Here a single repeat of Norwegian fir lace from page 120 is used as a central panel between lines of popcorns on five stitches of stockinette (stocking) stitch and a panel of leaves worked on a background of seven stitches of reverse stockinette (stocking) stitch.

SHORT ROWS

Short rows are partially knitted rows; the work is turned before the row is completed and the same stitches are worked back across. This results in there being two more rows at one side of the fabric than at the other. Short row knitting is also called turning, or partial knitting.

The technique is commonly used for shaping sock heels, known as turning a heel. On each turning row one less stitch is worked and then, to turn the heel, you work one more stitch each turning row until you are back to your original number of stitches.

On a knit row

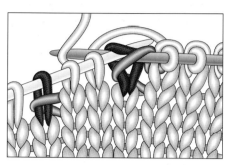

1 Knit to the turning point, slip the next stitch knitwise on to the right-hand needle and bring the yarn forward between the needles to the right side of the work.

2 Slip the slipped stitch back to the right-hand needle and take the yarn back to the knit position. Turn the work as though at the end of a row. The slipped stitch has been wrapped and it has a bar across it. Purl back across the row.

To hide the bar...
When you knit back over the turning point and the wrapped stitch you can knit it into the fabric to hide it. Work to the wrapped stitch. Insert the tip of the right-hand needle into the bar and the wrapped stitch, and knit them together. The bar will be knitted in and not show on the fabric. Alternatively you can leave the bar as it is.

Knit Perfect

✓ When you turn the work, a hole appears when all the stitches are worked over again. You can either leave this as a pattern feature or use the wrap method to cover it up.

✓ Wrapping the stitch does not work if you are only decreasing or increasing by one stitch on every turning row. To hide the hole in this case, slip the first stitch after the turn purlwise and then work the slip stitch together with the head of the stitch below when working back across the turn. This method can also be used instead of the wrap method.

On a purl row

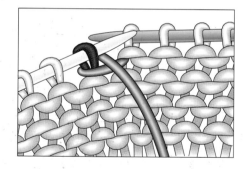
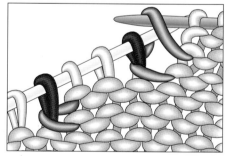

1 Purl to the turning point, slip the next stitch purlwise on to the right-hand needle and then take the yarn back between the needles to the right side of the work.

2 Slip the slipped stitch back to the right-hand needle and take the yarn back to the knit position. Turn the work as though at the end of a row. The slipped stitch has been wrapped and it has a bar across it. Purl back across the row.

To hide the bar...
Insert the tip of the right-hand needle into the back of the loop and place it on to the left-hand needle. Purl it and the wrapped stitched together.

Horizontal darts can also be worked in short rows to add shape to a garment. Work from the side edge to the tip of the dart and turn, then work back to three or four stitches from the side edge. Continue in this way, working three or four stitches further from the side seam each time until the dart is the required depth. Then work across all stitches.

Shoulder shaping can also be done using short rows. Binding (casting) off the stitches produces a stepped edge. Instead, turn the work before the stitches that are to be bound (cast) off. Repeat this on each bind (cast) off row. You will then have all the stitches still on the needle to bind (cast) off in one go or to join the shoulder seam by the three-needle seam bind (cast) off method (see page 25).

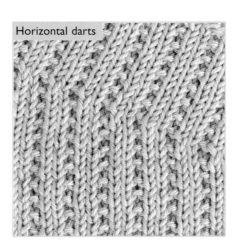

Horizontal darts

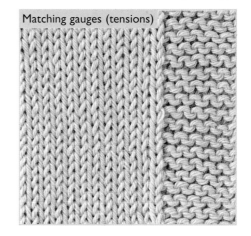

Shoulder shaping

Matching gauges (tensions) Short rows are also useful when knitting together two stitch patterns with different row gauges (tensions). For example, a garter stitch front border on a stockinette (stocking) stitch cardigan. You need to work six rows of garter stitch for every four rows of stockinette (stocking) stitch. Finish the row at the end of the garter stitch, turn and knit the garter stitches, turn and knit back across them. Then work across all stitches of the garment.

Matching gauges (tensions)

KNIT SOMETHING NOW! ▶

This sculptured cushion is worked in a pattern of points built up by short rows. The turns are not wrapped so the holes add a jagged edge to the points.

The short row cushion is knitted in a sport (4 ply) weight 100 per cent silk yarn on size 3 (3.25mm/UK10) needles. See page 136 for pattern.

TWISTED STITCHES

Single stitches can be twisted over each other without using a cable needle. As in cables, two knit stitches can be cabled to the right or the left. Twisted stitches can also be crossed (one knit stitch moving over a purl stitch) to the right or left.

Basic abbreviations for twisted stitches...

RT   twisted cables – right twist
LT   twisted cables – left twist
Cr2R crossed stitches – cross right
Cr2L crossed stitches – cross left

When following a pattern with twisted stitches, the designer will explain how to work the stitches under special abbreviations at the start of the pattern.

▲KNIT SOMETHING NOW!

A coaster featuring twisted stitches in the shape of hearts. Knit it together with a place mat with a pocket for cutlery – an ideal pair for outdoor eating.

Place mat and coaster knitted in a worsted (DK) wool yarn on size 6 (4mm/UK8) needles. See page 133 for pattern.

Twisted cables – right twist (RT)

1 Insert right-hand needle into second stitch on left-hand needle and knit it. Don't slip this stitch off the needle.

2 Knit the first stitch on the left-hand needle and slip both stitches on to the right-hand needle.

Twisted cables – left twist (LT)

 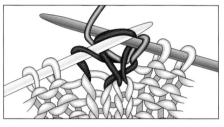

1 Insert right-hand needle into front of second stitch on left-hand needle, working behind the first stitch, and knit it. Don't slip this stitch off the needle.

2 Knit the first stitch on the left-hand needle and slip both stitches on to the right-hand needle.

Crossed stitches – cross right (Cr2R)

 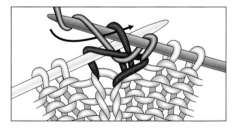

1 Insert right-hand needle into second stitch on the left-hand needle and knit it. Don't slip this stitch off the needle.

2 Purl the first stitch on the left-hand needle and slip both stitches on to the right-hand needle.

Crossed stitches – cross left (Cr2L)

1 Insert right-hand needle into back of second stitch on left-hand needle, working behind first stitch, and purl it. Don't slip this stitch off the needle.

2 Knit the first stitch on the left-hand needle and slip both stitches on to the right-hand needle.

INTARSIA

Intarsia is a technique of colour knitting suitable for large areas of colour where several blocks of different colours are worked in the same row. Unlike fair isle knitting where two colours are carried along the row to form a repeating pattern, intarsia knitting is characterized by single motifs, geometric patterns or pictures.

Intarsia uses a separate ball of yarn for each block of colour. The yarns are twisted together to link the areas of colour and prevent a hole. Most colourwork designs are worked in stockinette (stocking) stitch and it is only suitable for flat knitting; in circular knitting the yarns will always be at the end of the colour block and must be cut off and rejoined at the beginning. Intarsia patterns are worked from charts and often the whole garment will be charted (see page 37).

Bobbins

Each area of colour needs its own bobbin of yarn. You should never knit straight from the ball because with all the twisting, the yarn will become horribly tangled and the knitting becomes a chore. Working with bobbins you can pull out sufficient yarn to knit the stitches and then leave it hanging at the back of the work out of the way of the other yarns.

You can buy plastic bobbins and wrap a small amount of yarn on to each one but it is easy to make your own and cheaper if the intarsia design requires a lot of separate areas of colour. Leaving a long end, wind the yarn in a figure of eight around your thumb and little finger. Cut the yarn and use this cut end to tie a knot around the middle of the bobbin. Use the long end to pull the yarn from the middle of the bobbin. If the knotted end becomes loose around the bobbin as you pull yarn out, keep tightening it otherwise the bobbin will unravel.

Plan your knitting before you start. Work out how many bobbins of each colour you will need. If there are only a small number of stitches to be worked, cut a sufficient length of yarn, there is no need to wind it into a bobbin. Allow three times the width of stitches for the yarn needed to work those stitches.

Joining in a new colour

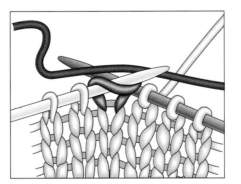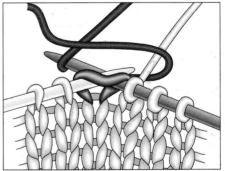

1 Insert the tip of the right-hand needle into the next stitch, place the cut end (4in/10cm from the end) of the new colour over the old colour and over the tip of the right-hand needle.

2 Take the working end of the new colour and knit the next stitch, pulling the cut end off the needle over the working end as the stitch is formed so it is not knitted in. Hold the cut end down against the back of the work.

To continue...
The old and new colours will be twisted together, preventing a hole and you can carry on using the new colour. Leave the cut end dangling to be sewn in later or continue weaving it in (see page 49).
    On a purl row, join in a new colour in the same way, twisting the yarns together on the wrong side of the work.

intarsia

Twisting yarns together

Once you've joined in all the colours that you need across the row, on the return row the yarns should be twisted to join the blocks of colour together. When you change colour, always pick up the new colour from under the old yarn. This is particularly important when the colours are changed at the same place in two or more rows. A line of loops will be formed on the wrong side of the work; these should not show through to the right side. Pull the yarns up firmly for the first stitch after twisting.

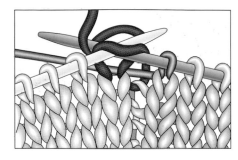

Twisting yarns on a knit row
Insert the tip of the right-hand needle into the next stitch, pull the old colour to the left, pick up the new colour and bring it up behind the old colour. Knit the next stitch. The two yarns are twisted together.

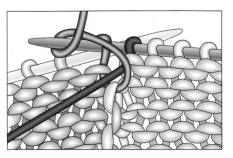

Twisting yarns on a purl row
Insert the tip of the right-hand needle into the next stitch, pull the old colour to the left, pick up the new colour and bring it up behind the old colour. Purl the next stitch. The two yarns are twisted together.

Carrying yarn

Sometimes you will need to begin a new colour several stitches before where you used it on the previous row. Work the next stitch with the new colour, twisting it with the old colour as before; do not pull the yarn too tightly across the back of the work, spread the stitches out to get the correct tension. This will result in a loop of the new colour laying across the back of the work. If it is only a couple of stitches, this will not be a problem. If it is over several stitches, and there is a long loop, you need to catch it into the knitting or it will snag during wear. If it is more than seven stitches, it is best to cut the yarn and join it in at the new position.

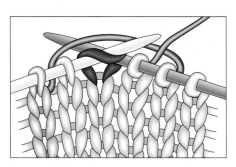

On a knit row
1 Knit two stitches in the new colour. Insert the tip of the right-hand needle into the next stitch, then pick up the long loop.

On a purl row
1 Purl two stitches in the new colour. Insert the tip of the right-hand needle into the next stitch, then pick up the long loop.

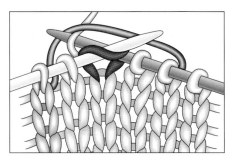

2 Wrap the yarn around as though to knit, then pull the long loop off the needle. Knit the stitch. The loop will be caught without appearing on the front of the work.

2 Wrap the yarn around as though to purl, then pull the long loop off the needle. Purl the stitch. The loop will be caught without appearing on the front of the work.

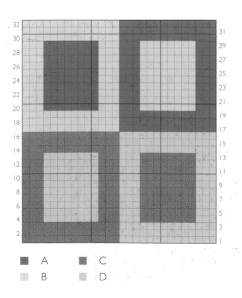

■ A ■ C
■ B ■ D

Using bobbins

Each area of colour on an intarsia chart needs a separate length of yarn. This simple block pattern shows the three bobbins needed to work the central square of each block using the intarsia method. Each bobbin is picked up in turn and used before being left to hang from a short length of yarn to prevent it becoming tangled with the others. When the centre square is completed, only one bobbin will be used to finish the block and the other two will be cut off and the ends sewn in neatly.

Weaving in yarn

In an intarsia design, you will get a lot of ends of yarn where areas of colour have begun or ended. It is important to weave in these ends either as you knit or stop knitting after every ten rows and sew them in. It gets rid of any ends that could tangle with working yarns, and if you leave it until the end it will seem a very long and arduous job. Sewing in the ends is neater but, if you have many yarn ends to finish, weaving them in as you go is faster.

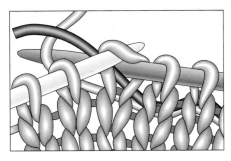

Weaving in ends on a knit row
1 Insert the tip of the right-hand needle into the next stitch, bring the cut end over the needle, wrap the yarn around the needle as though to knit.

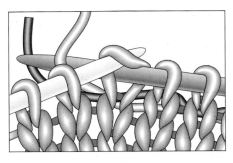

2 Pull the cut end off the needle and finish knitting the stitch. The cut end is caught into the knitted stitch.
Work the next stitch as normal then catch the cut end in as before. If you work alternately like this the cut end will lie above and below the row of stitches.

✓ ## Knit Perfect

Finish a piece of intarsia knitting by sewing in and cutting off any stray ends neatly. Where the two colours are twisted together, you will see a line of loops. Using a large-eyed tapestry needle, darn in the end along this line in one direction and then back again for a few stitches.

Block the piece (see page 66) and push any distorted stitches back into place with the end of a tapestry needle.

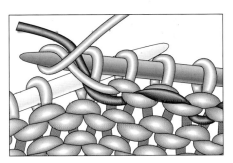

Weaving in ends on a purl row
1 Insert the tip of the right-hand needle into the next stitch, bring the cut end over the needle, wrap the yarn around the needle as though to purl.

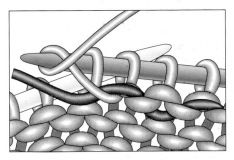

2 Pull the cut end off the needle and finish purling the stitch. The cut end is caught into the purled stitch.
Work the next stitch as normal then catch the cut end in as before. If you work alternately like this the cut end will lie above and below the row of stitches.

KNIT SOMETHING NOW! ▶

Practise using the intarsia method of colour knitting by making this colourful cushion.

Intarsia cushion knitted in a worsted (DK) wool yarn on size 6 (4mm/UK8) needles. See page 154 for pattern.

CIRCULAR KNITTING on double-pointed needles

Flat knitting is knitted in rows, working back and forth, moving the stitches from one needle to the other. Circular knitting is knitted in rounds, working round and round without turning the work.

✓ Knit Perfect

✓ The first round is awkward; the needles not being used dangle and get in the way. When you have worked a few rounds the fabric helps hold the needles in shape and knitting will become easier.

✓ For maximum control, always use the correct length of needle for what you are knitting; short needles for a small number of stitches such as for gloves, and longer needles for garments.

✓ To avoid a gap at the beginning of the first round, use the tail end of the yarn and the working yarn together to work the first few stitches. Or cast on one extra stitch at the end of the cast on, slip it on to the first needle and knit it together with the first stitch.

✓ Avoid gaps at the change over between needles by pulling the yarn up tightly, or work a couple of extra stitches from the next needle on each round. This will vary the position of the change over and avoid a ladder of looser stitches forming.

✓ Double-pointed needles are also used for knitting circles and squares (see page 52) or seamless garments. Use five needles to knit a square, with the stitches divided between the four sides.

Working on four needles

Use a set of four double-pointed needles, adding the stitches at one end and taking them off at the other. Cast the stitches on to one needle and then divide them evenly between three of the needles. For example, if you need to cast on 66 sts, there will be 22 sts on each needle; if you need to cast on 68 sts, there will be 23 sts on two of the needles and 22 on the third. The fourth needle is the working needle.

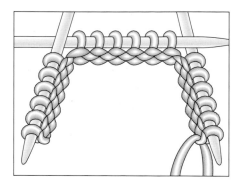

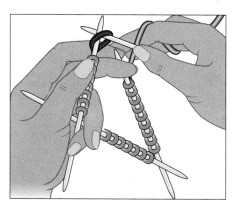

Arrange the needles into a triangle, making sure the cast on edge faces inwards and is not twisted. Place a marker between the last and first cast on stitches to identify the beginning of the round. Slip this marker on every round. Knit the first stitch, pulling up the yarn firmly so there is no gap between the third and first needle. Knit across the rest of the stitches on the first needle. As this needle is now empty, it becomes the working needle.

To continue...

Knit the stitches from the second needle, then use the new working needle to knit the stitches from the third needle. One round has been completed. Continue in this way, working in rounds and creating a tube of fabric. By knitting each round you will produce stockinette (stocking) stitch. To produce garter stitch, you will need to knit one round and then purl one round.

CIRCULAR KNITTING on circular needles

A circular needle can be used in place of double-pointed needles. The length of flexible nylon wire fixed between two short needles comes in several lengths. The longer ones are suitable for large garments and the shorter ones are ideal for small projects like hats.

✓ Knit Perfect

✓ To uncoil circular needles, immerse them in hot water for a few minutes to straighten them out.

✓ Circular needles are also useful for knitting backwards and forwards for flat knitting. It is easier to work a large number of stitches (such as for a throw) on circular needles because all the weight of the fabric is held in front of you, on your lap, rather than at the end of long straight needles.

Cast on the required number of stitches on to one of the needle ends. Spread them evenly around the needle, making sure the cast on edge faces inwards and is not twisted. The stitches should lie closely together and not be pulled too far apart. If the stitches are stretched when the needles are joined, you will need to use a shorter needle.

To identify the beginning of the round, place a marker in a contrast colour yarn between the last and first cast on stitch and slip this on every row.

Bring the two needles together and knit the first stitch, pulling up the yarn to prevent a gap. Continue knitting each cast on stitch to reach the marker. One round has been completed.

KNIT SOMETHING NOW! ▶

The mittens are worked in one colour on four needles with the faces worked flat on two needles and sewn on after. Work pairs of tigers, bears, dogs or cats.

Fun children's mittens are knitted in a worsted (DK) wool yarn on size 3 (3.25mm/UK10) double-pointed needles for the rib and size 6 (4mm/UK8) double-pointed needles. See page 134 for pattern.

Exploring Choices

These advanced techniques will add excitement and individuality to your knitting. Three techniques – medallion knitting, entrelac and mitred squares – show you how to work creatively with shapes. Embellish your knitting using beads, looped knitting, smocking or embroidery stitches. Alter the knitted fabric by fulling. Sections guide you through reading a knitting pattern, explaining abbreviations and commonly used phrases. A sweater pattern is explained stage by stage, from the first stitches cast on, tips on shaping sleeves and neck, and how to alter a pattern to fit you. A section on making up includes various seams to professionally finish your garment. Finishing details include tassels and cords, flowers and leaves, how to make buttons and add an edging.

▼ KNIT SOMETHING NOW!

A textured throw worked in traditional Garden Plot squares sewn together to form larger squares.

The throw is knitted in a worsted (DK) weight cotton yarn on size 6 (4mm/UK8) needles. See page 138 for pattern.

MEDALLION KNITTING

Medallions are individually knitted patches, sewn together to form larger items like throws, cushions and bedspreads or garments. It is a form of patchwork knitting. Large single medallions can be used as the two sides of a bag, a small rug or the top of a beret. Most medallions, whether circles, ovals or squares, are knitted with five double-pointed needles from the centre out, with rows of increases arranged to form the shape. Circles have rows of at least eight increases evenly spaced, whilst a square will have eight increases worked in pairs at four corners. Increases are usually worked on every alternate row. Squares can also be worked on two needles by increasing from one corner and then decreasing to the opposite corner.

Basic circle (see sample opposite)

Cast on 8 sts and arrange on 4 needles.
Round 1 and every following alternate round Knit.
Round 2 (increase round) Knit into front and back of every st. 16 sts.
Round 4 (K1, knit into front and back of next st) 8 times. 24 sts.
Round 6 (K2, knit into front and back of next st) 8 times. 32 sts.
Continue in this way, working one more stitch between increases on every increase round. Keep laying the circle down as you work to make sure it is flat; too many increases over too few rounds will make the fabric wavy. To stop this work another knit round between increase rounds. When circle is the required size, cast off loosely.

✓ Knit Perfect

✓ Block the medallions to shape (see page 66).

✓ Use a multicoloured yarn to work medallions. In circular knitting, purl every alternate round for garter stitch. Mix garter stitch ridges with stockinette (stocking) stitch ridges. Use alternating ridges of stockinette (stocking) stitch and reverse stockinette (stocking) stitch or garter stitch for the square knitted on two needles.

✓ Work the increases in another way; as a yarn over or use an invisible increase like M1.

✓ Keep laying the medallion flat as you work to make sure it isn't becoming wavy. Add more straight rounds between increase rounds if it is.

Basic square

Cast on 8 sts and arrange on 4 needles.
Round 1 and every foll alt round Knit.
Round 2 (increase round) Knit into front and back of every st. 16 sts.
Round 4 (Knit into front and back of next st, k2, knit into back and front of next st) 4 times. 24 sts.
Round 6 (Knit into front and back of next st, k4, knit into back and front of next st) 4 times. 32 sts.
Continue in this way, working two more stitches between increases on every increase round. Check frequently to make sure the square is lying flat and if not work another knit round between increase rounds. When the square is the required size, cast off loosely. Knit two large squares for a bag or cushion. Work several small squares and join them together for a throw or bedspread.

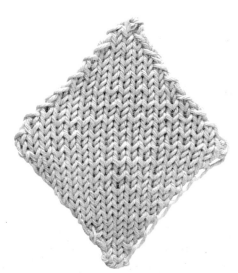

More circles...

A circle knitted like this can be used in different ways. A small circle makes the top of a beret. Continue working in rounds and make a small circular rug or join two circles together for a cushion or an unusual bag.

Because the eight increases are worked in the same place on each round, the shape will be octagonal rather than a true circle. The bigger you knit the circle, the more pronounced this shape will be. At this point, work 16 increases in the increase row by dividing the stitches between increases in two.

For example, after working the round (k14, knit into front and back of next st) 8 times, there will be 16 stitches between increases. The next round will be (k7, knit into front and back of next st) 16 times. Work three knit rounds between increase rows.

Square on two needles

An increase is worked before the first stitch on every row (see page 36).
Cast on 3 stitches.
Row 1 Purl.
Row 2 (RS) Yo, k3.
Row 3 Yo, p4.
Row 4 Yo, k5.
Row 5 Yo, p6.
Continue in this way until the side of the square is the required length, ending with a WS row. A decrease is now worked at the start of every row (see page 28–9)
Next row Ssk, k to end.
Next row P2tog, p to end.
Continue to decrease until 3 sts remain, sk2po. Fasten off.

Depending on the gauge (tension), the square may be more of a diamond. Block it to shape or work in a pattern that has more rows to the 4in (10cm). A traditional use of this square is called Garden Plot or Grandmother's Garden where several different patterns are worked. When the squares are sewn together, the diagonal patterns across the square form diamonds (see page 138).

BEADED KNITTING

In beaded knitting, beads (or sequins) are used on stockinette (stocking) stitch to form a pattern, or they are incorporated into a lace, cable or texture pattern. (It should not be confused with bead knitting, a technique that involves working different colour beads together to form a pattern, and where no knitted fabric is visible.)

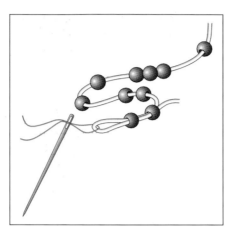

Thread the beads on to the ball of yarn before starting the knitting, the pattern instructions will tell you how many. To do this, choose a needle that will pass easily through the hole in the bead, and thread it with the two ends of a loop of sewing cotton. Thread the end of the yarn through the cotton loop. Now thread the beads on to the needle, pulling them down the sewing cotton and on to the yarn. Unwind sufficient yarn from the ball to accommodate the number of beads to be used and then rewind the ball to start knitting the item.

Knit Perfect

✓ Beads should have a large enough hole to slide on to the yarn without being forced. If the fit is too tight, the yarn will wear and fray.

✓ Match the beads to the yarn; use small, light beads with a delicate yarn and larger beads with a harder wearing, thicker yarn.

✓ The fabric should be knitted tightly enough so that the beads won't slip between the stitches to the wrong side. Always knit the stitches either side of the bead firmly.

The slip stitch method

Add the beads on a right side row so they hang horizontally. This is usually referred to in pattern instructions as place bead (PB).

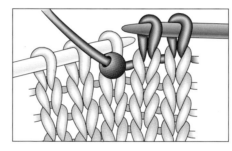

1 On a right side row, work to the position of the bead, knitting the last stitch worked firmly. Bring the yarn to the front of the work and push a bead down the yarn so that it rests next to the last stitch worked.

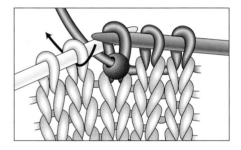

2 Slip the next stitch purlwise. Take the yarn back to the wrong side of the work and knit the next stitch firmly.

KNIT SOMETHING NOW! ▶

A stunning evening bag knitted in gold yarn is decorated with bronze beads. The simple lace pattern is enhanced with the beads used in a diamond pattern.

Beaded bag knitted in a sport (4ply) lurex yarn on size 3 (3.25mm/UK10) needles. See page 139 for pattern.

LOOPED KNITTING

A border of looped knitting makes a mock fur fabric for the collar and cuffs on a garment. As an all-over fabric, it can be used to make soft toys or, with the loops cut, a pile rug. The base fabric is garter stitch; a row of twisted knit stitches knitted through the back of the loop (k1 tbl) is followed by a row of loop stitches.

The pattern is a two row repeat with the loops made on the wrong side row and all the stitches are knitted through the back of the stitch on the right side row. Knitting the first and last stitches of the loop row through the back of the stitch makes the edges more stable for making up.

Row 1 Work a row of (k1tbl) twisted stitches.
Row 2 K1 tbl, then make loop as follows:

1 Knit into the back of the next stitch, do not slip stitch off the left-hand needle.

2 Insert the tip of the right-hand needle into the front of the same stitch and knit the stitch by passing the yarn anti-clockwise around the index finger of the left hand and then round the needle. Slip the stitch off the left-hand needle.

3 Insert the tip of the left-hand needle through the front of the two stitches just worked and knit them together. Pull the loop on the index finger gently to tighten the stitch. Remove finger. Repeat steps 1-3 for every stitch across the row to the last stitch, k1 tbl. These two rows form the pattern.

For flatter loops...
The fabric produced has loops on every alternate row and the loops will stand up. By adding more twisted knit rows between the loop rows the loops will lie flatter.

the result:

LOOPS AND CUT PILE

A sample of looped knitting showing half the loops intact and the other half cut to create a pile. The twisted stitches which prevent the loops or pile being pulled out show on the back of the fabric.

▶ KNIT
SOMETHING NOW!

A really woolly sheep uses the loop stitch to great effect!

Sheep toy knitted in a worsted (DK) weight wool yarn on size 3 (3.25mm/UK10) needles.
See page 140 for pattern.

ENTRELAC

Another way to work patchwork knitting is entrelac. In entrelac (a French word, which is pronounced on-tra-lak) the squares are knitted diagonally in rows; one row of squares being completed and the next row worked in the opposite direction on top. The knitted piece is started at the bottom from a cast-on edge and finished at the top. The squares can be worked in stockinette (stocking) stitch, as well as in lace, cable or textured stitches. If two colours are used, one for each alternate row, a woven effect is achieved, as shown here. In entrelac the stitches of all the squares in one row will be on the needles.

Each square has twice as many rows as stitches. The written instructions for entrelac can appear to be confusing so to learn how easy this technique is, work the following sample. The squares are eight stitches wide and the piece is three squares wide.

To begin, a foundation row of base triangles is worked. These are built up by short rows from the cast on stitches (see page 44). There is no need to work the wrapped stitch.

Base row of triangles

Cast on 24 sts loosely using the knitting on method (see page 24).

right side

First base triangle
Rows 1 and 2 K2 and turn, p1, sl 1 purlwise (pwise) and turn.
Rows 3 and 4 K3 and turn, p2, sl 1 pwise and turn.
Rows 5 and 6 K4 and turn, p3, sl 1 pwise and turn.
Rows 7 and 8 K5 and turn, p4, sl 1 pwise and turn.
Rows 9 and 10 K6 and turn, p5, sl 1 pwise and turn.
Rows 11 and 12 K7 and turn, p6, sl 1 pwise and turn.
Row 13 K8 and do not turn.
The first triangle is completed.

> **To continue...**
> Leave these eight stitches on the right-hand needle and work the second triangle over the next eight stitches. The third triangle is then worked over the following eight stitches. There will be 24 stitches on the right-hand needle. Turn at the end of this row of triangles to begin the return row of squares.

Purl row of squares

To make the sides of the piece straight, you need a side edge triangle.

wrong side

** Left side edge triangle
Rows 1 and 2 P2 and turn, k2 and turn.
Rows 3 and 4 P into front and back of first st (to shape side edge), p2tog (last st of triangle and next st on right-hand needle to join the pieces together) and turn, k3 and turn.
Rows 5 and 6 P into front and back of first st (p1 fb), p1, p2tog and turn, k4 and turn.
Rows 7 and 8 P1 fb, p2, p2tog and turn, k5 and turn.
Rows 9 and 10 P1 fb, p3, p2tog and turn, k6 and turn.
Rows 11 and 12 P1 fb, p4, p2tog and turn, k7 and turn.
Row 13 P1 fb, p5, p2tog and do not turn. All 8 sts of the base triangle have been used. Leave the 8 sts of the side triangle on the right-hand needle.

Square
With the right-hand needle and wrong side of the work facing, pick up and purl 8 sts evenly along the next edge of the base triangle and turn.
Rows 1 and 2 K7, sl 1 pwise and turn, p7 (including sl st of previous row), p2tog (last st of square and next st on right-hand needle to join pieces together) and turn. Repeat these 2 rows 6 times more.
Rows 15 and 16 K7, sl 1 pwise and turn, p7, p2tog and do not turn. All 8 sts of the base triangle have been used. Leave the 8 sts of this square on the right-hand needle. Work the second square over the next 8 sts.
To make this side edge straight, you need to work a right side edge triangle.

Right side edge triangle

With the right-hand needle and wrong side of the work facing, pick up and purl 8 sts evenly along the next edge of the base triangle and turn.

Rows 1 and 2 K7, sl 1 pwise and turn, p6 (including sl st of previous row), p2tog (to shape side edge) and turn.
Rows 3 and 4 K6, sl 1 pwise and turn, p5, p2tog and turn.
Rows 5 and 6 K5, sl 1 pwise and turn, p4, p2tog and turn.
Rows 7 and 8 K4, sl 1 pwise and turn, p3, p2tog and turn.
Rows 9 and 10 K3, sl 1 pwise and turn, p2, p2tog and turn.
Rows 11 and 12 K2, sl 1 pwise and turn, p1, p2tog.
Rows 13 and 14 K1, sl 1 pwise and turn, p2tog and turn. All sts are on the left-hand needle ready for the next row of squares. **

Knit row of squares

On this row, there are no side triangles to work.

right side

First square

Slip the first st on to the right-hand needle then with the right side of the work facing, pick up and knit 7 sts evenly along the edge of the right side triangle and turn. 8 sts.
Rows 1 and 2 P7, sl 1 purlwise and turn, k7 (including sl st of previous row), ssk (last st of square and next st on left-hand needle to join pieces together) and turn.
Rep these 2 rows 6 times more.
Rows 15 and 16 P7, sl 1 purlwise and turn, k7, ssk and do not turn.
All sts of the square in the row below have been used.

Second and third squares

With right-hand needle and right side of work facing, pick up and knit 8 sts along edge of next square in row below and turn.
Work as given for first square. Then work a third square the same. Turn.
Work a purl row of squares from ** to ** again, working into the squares of the previous row instead of the base triangles. To finish the piece, a row of triangles has to be worked to give a straight top edge.

Top row of triangles

With right side of work facing, slip the first st on to the right-hand needle then pick up and knit 7 sts along edge of first square and turn. 8 sts.

Rows 1 and 2 P8 and turn, k7, ssk (last st of square and next st on right-hand needle to join the pieces) and turn.
Rows 3 and 4 P6, p2tog (to shape top edge) and turn, k6, ssk and turn.
Rows 5 and 6 P5, p2tog and turn, k5, ssk and turn.
Rows 7 and 8 P4, p2tog and turn, k4, ssk and turn.
Rows 9 and 10 P3, p2tog and turn, k3, ssk and turn.
Rows 11 and 12 P2, p2tog and turn, k2, ssk and turn.
Rows 13 and 14 P1, p2tog and turn, k1, ssk and turn.
Rows 15 and 16 P2tog and turn, ssk and do not turn. Leave this st on right-hand needle.
Repeat this top triangle twice more across the top of the piece. Cut yarn and thread through last stitch to fasten off.

Knit Perfect

✔ The number of stitches to cast on equals the number of stitches in each square multiplied by the number of squares. Cast on more or less stitches to make the squares bigger or smaller.

✔ Always start with the base row of triangles, then repeat the purl row of squares and the knit row of squares to form the main fabric, ending with a purl row to work the top triangles across.

✔ The woven effect of entrelac can be emphasised by working in two colours; work the knit rows of squares in one colour and the purl rows of squares in another. The squares can also be worked in any stitch; try knitting them in cable patterns, textured stitch patterns like moss or garter stitch, or a lace pattern.

✔ Slipping the edge stitches purlwise makes it easier to pick up stitches; pick them up through both loops of the edge stitch. Edge stitches are explained more fully in mitred squares, see page 58.

MITRED SQUARES

Another patchwork knitting technique is mitred squares (also known as domino knitting). Each square is worked individually and the stitches for the next square are picked up from any side of the first square. It requires little or no sewing up. The shape of the squares is achieved by decreasing into the centre, hence the name of mitred squares. In mitred squares only the stitches of one square will be on the needles at any time.

This is a technique best learnt by working it and this example is a group of four basic garter stitch squares.

Basic mitred square

Cast on 19 sts loosely using the knitting on method (see page 24).
Row 1 and every foll WS row K to last st, sl 1 purlwise with yarn in front of the work (wyif).
Row 2 (RS) K8, sl 1-k2tog-psso, k7, sl 1 pwise wyif. 17 sts.
Row 4 K7, sl 1-k2tog-psso, k6, sl 1 pwise wyif. 15 sts.
Row 6 K6, sl 1-k2tog-psso, k5, sl 1 pwise wyif. 13 sts.
Row 8 K5, sl 1-k2tog-psso, k4, sl 1 pwise wyif. 11 sts.
Row 10 K4, sl 1-k2tog-psso, k3, sl 1 pwise wyif. 9 sts.
Row 12 K3, sl 1-k2tog-psso, k2, sl 1 pwise wyif. 7 sts.
Row 14 K2, sl 1-k2tog-psso, k1, sl 1 pwise wyif. 5 sts.
Row 16 K1, sl 1-k2tog-psso, sl 1 pwise wyif. 3 sts.
Row 18 Sl 1-k2tog-psso. Cut yarn and thread through last st to fasten off.
One square is completed. By slipping the last stitch of every row, a line of edge stitches is created along two sides of the square. These make it much easier to pick up stitches for the next square.

Second square

To work the next square, with the right-hand needle and right side of work facing, pick up and knit 9 sts along the side of the first square through both loops of the edge stitches, pick up 1 st at the corner then cast on 9 sts (using knitting on method). 19 sts. Complete as given for basic mitred square.

Third square

Cast on 9 sts, then pick up and knit 10 sts (1 corner st and 9 other sts) along edge of first square through both loops of the edge stitches. Complete as given for basic mitred square.

Fourth square

With the right-hand needle, pick up and knit 9 sts along side of square three, pick up and knit 1 st at corner then pick up and knit 9 sts along side of second square. 19 sts. Complete as given for basic mitred square.

the result:

MITRED SQUARE

This sample knitted in garter stitch shows all the techniques needed to work mitred squares and to join them together. The basic square can be any number of stitches, as long as it is an odd number. Work the squares in stockinette (stocking) stitch by working the WS rows as purl rows. Moss stitch works well over the odd number of stitches; just repeat k1, p1 across all rows. Whichever stitch you use, always remember to keep working the edge stitches in the same way; slip the last stitch purlwise with the yarn at the front of the work and knit the slipped stitch on the return row.

fourth square

second square

third square

first square

Designing with mitred squares

The basic square forms a mitred corner; work two together and a rectangle is formed. Work three together and an L shape is made; work four together and a complete mitred square is made. For a rectangle, cast on twice the number of stitches for the basic square (2 x 19 sts = 38 sts), for an L shape cast on three times the stitches and for a complete square cast on four times the stitches. Place a slip marker every 19 stitches to show you where one square ends and the next begins. Work each 19 stitches as a basic square; do not work a slip stitch on the inside edges of the individual squares; work it to match the main fabric.

To complete the square, either sew it closed or pick up stitches along each edge towards the middle and use the three needle seam bind (cast) off (see page 25).

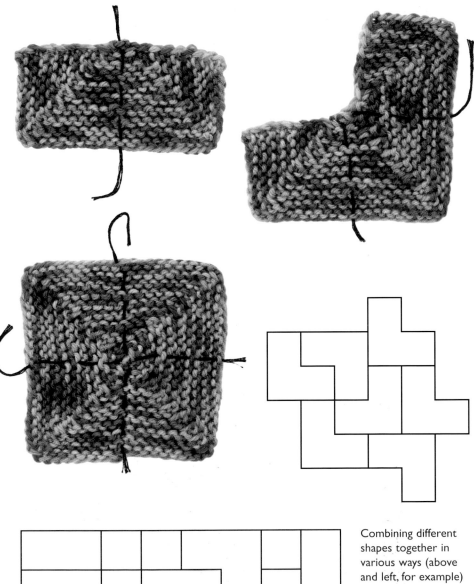

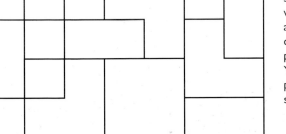

Combining different shapes together in various ways (above and left, for example) can make interesting patchwork patterns. You can plan it on paper first or just start knitting.

Knit Perfect

✓ The edge stitches are important; whatever fabric you are working, slip the last stitch purlwise with the yarn at the front of the work and knit the slipped stitch on the return row. If the penultimate stitch is a knit, you will have to bring the yarn forward between the needles. If it is a purl stitch, the yarn will be in the correct position. Always knit the slipped stitch on the next row, the yarn will be in the knit position to remind you.

✓ Mitred squares look best when worked in many colours. Either choose a multi-coloured yarn or make your own by tying yard (metre) lengths of different coloured yarns together. It is a great way to use up leftover yarn.

✓ With a multi-coloured yarn it is unnecessary to cut the yarn between each square. Use the last stitch of one square as the first stitch of the next. Keeping one yarn going makes the placement of the squares more random and your knitted piece will grow organically rather than in a planned manner.

✓ Weave any ends in as you go (see page 49).

✓ Try a different decrease, instead of sl 1-k2tog-psso work sk2po or, for an unbroken chain stitch running up the centre, sl2tog-k1-psso.

FULLING

Fulling is the process of washing woollen fabric to produce a felt-like fabric. It is often mistakenly called felting, which is worked on carded unspun wool, whilst fulling is worked on a finished fabric. Fulled fabric is soft, spongy and has a brushed appearance; any garment that is fulled will be more dense and warmer than one that is not.

Fulling can only be worked on yarns that are 100 per cent wool; it doesn't work on synthetics, cotton or wools that have been treated to be machine washable. The treatment withstands exactly the changes that are needed to full a garment. During fulling, the wool expands, fibres mesh together and individual stitches close up so it is hard to see fulled stitches. The finished fabric will also shrink by up to 10 per cent in length and width.

Hand or machine fulling?

The two methods for fulling a fabric are by hand or washing machine. By hand offers the most control, you can stop and check the fabric at every stage. By machine is less hard work, and you can full a number of items together, but it is not as easy to control. There is no single recipe for fulling, each yarn reacts differently and may be easier or harder to full. To experiment, knit several identical samples in the yarn you are using making a note of needle size and gauge (tension). Keep one sample aside to compare with the fulled samples.

Hand fulling

Fulling depends on extremes of temperature, from hot to cold, agitation by kneading and the use of laundry soap or soap flakes. Do not use detergent or washing powder. Dissolve the soap flakes in hot water and immerse one of the samples.

Start kneading the fabric without pulling, stretching or rubbing the knitting together. Remove the sample from the water frequently to check the fulling process. Rinse the soap out in cold water and pull the sample gently. If the stitches still move apart easily, continue the fulling. Keep up the temperature of the hot water. Stop when the fabric is dense and has a fuzzy appearance. Rinse the soap out and squeeze to remove excess water. Roll the sample up in a towel to soak up any remaining moisture and then lay it out flat, away from direct heat, to dry. Make a note of how long it took.

Try another sample but rinse it more often in cold water or knead it in hotter water. These things will make a difference to how quickly the sample fulls. Overwork one of the samples until it is matted and distorted to see the difference between correct fulling and matting. Keep notes of everything you do as you do it.

✔ Knit Perfect

✔ Always test samples of coloured knitting such as fair isle and intarsia to make sure all the yarns are colourfast.

✔ Fulling only works on 100 per cent wool; work a sample before you knit your project to make sure your yarn will full.

✔ Fulled fabric can be cut and sewn like a woven fabric. The stitches will not fray or unravel. Garments that are too large can be taken in with darts or tucks or shortened by cutting off the bottom edge and finishing it with blanket stitch.

✔ Start by hand fulling, it is easier to control. It will be more work but you will not run the risk of ruining your project in the washing machine. Wear gloves to protect your hands from the hot water and soap.

✔ Brush the surface of the knitting when dry with a stiff brush; use a gently pulling or lifting action rather than a vigorous back and forwards motion.

Machine fulling

Wash the samples with soap in a full load. They need friction to be fulled correctly so add towels to fill the machine. Run them through on the shortest hot wash/cold rinse cycle but do not spin dry. Remove from the machine whenever possible during the cycle to check their progress. If they haven't fulled correctly, take one sample out and put the others through the same cycle again. Repeat until you have achieved the effect you want. By removing samples at each stage, you have a record of when the perfect fulling moment happens.

Fulling garments

Garments will not behave in exactly the same way as the samples. There is more fabric and there are seams, both factors will alter the fulling process. Use your sample results as a guide only and check at every stage of the process because fulling is irreversible.

When the garment has fulled correctly, lay it out flat and pull it into shape, straightening the seams. Fulled garments are usually more figure hugging so try it on when it is almost dry. Gently pull the armhole seams so the sleeves sit correctly and arrange the neckband. Pull evenly around the edge of the body and sleeves for the correct length. Remove carefully and lay out flat to dry.

the result:

TEST SAMPLES
These three samples were all knitted in stockinette (stocking) stitch over the same number of stitches and rows. The first one (1) has not been fulled, the second (2) has been fulled the correct amount and the third (3) has been distorted and matted rather than fulled.

KNIT SOMETHING NOW! ▼

The lavender sachets and covered clothes hanger are ideal for your first fulling projects.

The **scented sachets** and **hanger cover** are knitted in a 2ply jumper weight 100 per cent shetland wool yarn on size 3 (3.25mm/UK10) needles. See page 142 for pattern.

SMOCKING

Smocking can be worked very successfully on ribbed fabric. Like smocking on a woven fabric, it pulls in the knitted fabric in a decorative manner. The smocking stitches can be worked in the same yarn as the main fabric, in a contrasting colour or in embroidery threads which have a larger range of colours for coloured smocking patterns. Make sure the smocking thread is colourfast and washes to the same instructions as the knitted yarn.

The rib should not be too wide or the resulting bunching of fabric will be too bulky, especially in thick yarns. A (p3, k1) rib or (p4, k1) rib is ideal.

Smocking stitch on (p3, k1) rib

Work from left to right and in a zigzag manner. The smocking stitches should be equally spaced on every 4th row. (Note: the artwork shows the stitches not tightened so the path of the needle can clearly be seen.)

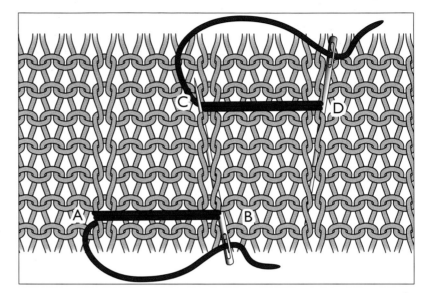

1 Bring the needle with the smocking thread up at A, having secured it on the wrong side by running it through the edge of the knit rib with a few backstitches. Follow the row across and take it under the stitch at B from right to left. Take the needle across the front of the work between the knit stitches and take it under the knit stitch at A from left to right. Pull the stitch tight so the ribs lie next to each other without distorting them and work two more stitches the same, finishing with the needle down at B.

2 Count 4 rows up from B and bring the needle up at C. Follow the row across and take it under the knit stitch at D from right to left. Work two more stitches the same, pulling them tight as before and finishing with the needle down at D. Take the needle back down to the previous smocking row, 4 rows below. Repeat these two smocking rows across the rib fabric and up to the top of the piece.

Ribbed fabrics for smocking

(p3, k1) rib

Cast on a multiple of 4 sts plus 3 sts.
Row 1 P3, * k1, p3; rep from * to end.
Row 2 K3, * p1, k3; rep from * to end.
These 2 rows form the rib pattern and are repeated.

(p4, k1) rib

Cast on a multiple of 5 sts plus 4 sts.
Row 1 P4, * k1, p4; rep from * to end.
Row 2 K4, * p1, k4; rep from * to end.
These 2 rows form the rib pattern and are repeated.

the result:

SMOCKED RIB

The embroidery thread can be a contrast colour as shown here, or the same colour as the knitting. Careful counting of the stitches and rows is essential for the smocking to look even.

✓ Knit Perfect

When the knitted fabric is smocked it will loose some of its elasticity, so is not suitable for close-fitting cuffs and lower edge ribs on garments.

There are also honeycomb stitches that are smocked while being knitted (see Stitch library page 102–3).

READING KNITTING PATTERNS

A knitting pattern tells you how to knit and make up a knitted project. There are two styles of instructions; a pattern that tells you what to do row by row, and a pattern that has shorter written instructions with a chart. If each row of a garment was written down row by row the knitting pattern would probably fill a small book, so the instructions use shorthand phrases and abbreviations. The abbreviations are listed on the pattern with an explanation of what they mean. Many are commonly used, such as k and p (see page 33). Others refer to special stitches, like C4F, and these are explained in the technique or patterns.

Common shorthand phrases

cont as set/cont as established
instead of repeating the same instructions over and over, you must continue to work as previously told. For example: **Row 1** K. **Row 2** P. Cont in st st as set.

keeping patt correct
continue with a stitch pattern, keeping it correctly worked over the correct amount of stitches, whilst doing something that may interfere with the stitch pattern (see page 74).

at the same time
two things must be done at the same time. For example, decreasing at an armhole edge and decreasing at a neck edge.

work straight/work even
continue without increasing or decreasing.

work as given for
to avoid repeating instructions. For example, the front is often worked as given for the back up to a certain point.

reversing all shaping
shaping is given for one piece and the other piece must be shaped to be a mirror image of it. For example, the left and right side of the neck, or the left and right front of a cardigan.

Sizes

Knitting patterns are usually written in more than one size, with the smallest size first (outside the brackets) and the remaining sizes inside square brackets, separated by colons. The largest size is at the end. For example, if the sizes are S [M:L:XL], the chest measurements could be 30 [32:34:36] in (76 [82:87:92] cm). Your size will always appear in the same place in the bracket; instructions for the first size will always be first, for the second size they will be second, etc. If a pattern is written in both imperial and metric measurements, stick to one or the other; some imperial to metric measurements are not exact conversions.

Reading size instructions

Square brackets are used within the instructions to indicate the number of stitches and rows to be worked, or how many times a pattern is repeated, for each size. For example, cast on 90 [92:94:96] sts, or work patt 1 [2:3:4] times. If a zero appears for your size do not work the instruction it is referring to. For example, dec 3 [0:1:2] sts. If only one figure appears then it refers to all sizes. Read through the pattern and underline or highlight your size in the square brackets.

Size diagrams

Knitting patterns should have a drawing of the knitted pieces with their finished measurements. These help to decide which size is best for you or if you need to alter things like body or sleeve length. They also show the shape of the pieces and make the written instructions clearer. If your pattern does not have size diagrams, it is a good idea to draw your own, using the finished measurements given and adding any others by using the gauge (tension) information.

Reading a stitch chart

A knitting pattern may contain a stitch chart which is similar to a colour pattern. A stitch chart is an illustration of a cable, a lace pattern or a texture pattern with each stitch being represented by a symbol, which usually reflects the texture of the stitch. A knit stitch often appears as a blank square, whilst a purl stitch is a dot or horizontal dash. The key tells you what each symbol means. Imagine looking at the right side of a knitted piece; each symbol represents the stitch as it appears on the right side of the work. A whole garment may be charted like this or just one repeat of the stitch pattern. Each square is one stitch on your needle. Decreases are shown after they have been worked and so appear as one square. Yarn overs are shown as a new stitch and so occupy one square. Beginning at the bottom right-hand corner, right side rows are read from right to left and wrong side rows from left to right. Colour charts are covered on page 37.

Stitch chart with symbols

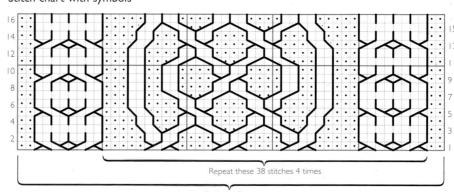

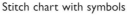
Repeat these 38 stitches 4 times

Back and Front

C4F		Cr3L
C4B		Cr3R
Cr4L		· p on RS rows, k on WS rows
Cr4R		☐ k on RS rows, p on WS rows

Cable abbreviations...
See pages 40–41 for Cables and a guide to the abbreviations.

KNITTING A GARMENT

Reading through a knitting pattern for the first time can seem a bit daunting. There's a lot of information given but it also assumes you know a lot, too. Use this pattern as a guide to knitting a garment, from choosing the yarn to sewing it up. This is a pattern for a close-fitting stockinette (stocking) stitch sweater with waist shaping, set in sleeves and a turtleneck. The instructions as they would appear in a knitting pattern are set in boxes, the text below explains what is meant.

Order of knitting...
The written instructions take you through the construction of a garment piece by piece. Garments are usually knitted in the same order, back, front and sleeves, and often one piece will contain cross-references to another which has already been knitted, if they are both worked the same. For example, for a front it might say work in rib as given for back. When the main pieces have been worked, the finishing is done. The pieces are blocked and the garment is made up with any other details like neckband, pockets or button bands added.

Sizes

To fit bust	30/32 [34/36:38/40]in (76/82 [87/92:97/102] cm)
Actual size	36 [40:44]in (92 [102:112]cm)
Length	22½ [23:23½]in (57 [58.5:60]cm)
Sleeve length	20½ [21:21½]in (52 [53.5:54.5]cm)

First decide which size you are going to make. The important measurement is the actual size, measured as the finished width under the arm. Different designers add different amounts of ease to the bust/chest measurement, depending on the style of the garment. So look at the actual size rather than the size ranges which are often there only as a guide. Refer to the size diagrams that are a sketch of the finished pieces needed to make up the garment. Check that the sleeve and body lengths are right for you. If they are too long or too short, make alterations to the body or sleeve shaping (see page 72). Go through the pattern and underline or highlight all the instructions in the brackets for your size.

Materials

Debbie Bliss Merino DK (100% Merino Wool – 109yds/100m per 1¾oz /50g ball)
10 [11:12] × 1¾oz/50g balls in colour 213 Light Blue

Always try to use the yarn recommended by the designer, especially novelty yarns which sometimes have a gauge (tension) all of their own. However, if the spinner discontinues a yarn, or it is a standard thickness, then another yarn can be substituted (see page 128).

The type of yarn used to knit the projects in this book are given in the pattern, together with the yardages and tension. The actual yarn used is given on page 158 with suppliers listed on page 159.

Needles

1 pair size 3 (3.25mm/UK10) needles.
1 pair size 6 (4mm/UK8) needles.

These are the recommended sizes of needles to use. They will give you the gauge (tension) that the garment has been calculated from.

Gauge (tension)

22 sts and 28 rows to 4in (10cm) measured over stockinette (stocking) stitch on size 6 (4mm/UK8) needles.

Work a gauge (tension) square before you begin knitting (see page 31).

Back

Using size 3 (3.25mm/UK10) needles, cast on 101 [113:123] sts.
Row 1 (RS) K1, * p1, k1; rep from * to end.
Row 2 P1, * k1, p1; rep from * to end.
Rep these 2 rows until rib measures 2in (5cm) from beg, ending with a WS row.
Change to size 6 (4mm/UK8) needles and work 10 rows in st st.

Patterns vary, some have an increase row worked evenly over the last rib row. When the rib is complete, pick up one of the larger needles and knit the stitches off the smaller needle. Remember to discard both the smaller needles when you pick up the other larger needle. If the pattern does not tell you, always start stockinette (stocking) stitch (1 row k, 1 row p) with a knit (right side) row.

Side shaping

Working in st st, dec 1 st at each end of next and every foll 8th row to 91 [103:113] sts.

From the size diagrams, you can see that the side edges are shaped into the waist. One stitch is decreased at each side on the next row, then work seven rows without shaping and decrease on the next row, work another seven rows and decrease on the next row until you reach the stitch total for your size. You can decrease by working two stitches together at the edge or you could work the decreases as full fashioning. These decorative decreases will add an elegant finish to the garment (see page 28–9). A full fashioning decrease row would be k3, ssk, k to last 5 sts, k2tog, k3.

Work straight until back measures 10in (25cm) from beg, ending with a p row.
Inc 1 st at each end of next and every foll 6th row to 99 [111:121] sts.

Several rows are worked at the waist without shaping and then the back is increased out again for the bust measurement. One stitch is increased at each end of the next row, then work five rows without shaping and increase on the next row, work another five rows

straight and increase on the next row until you reach the stitch total for your size. You can full fashion the increases to match the decreases (see page 27). A full fashioning increase row would be k2, knit into front and back of next st, k to last 4 sts, knit into front and back of next st, k3.

Work straight until back measures 14in (35.5cm) from beg, ending with a p row.

Lay the work on a flat smooth surface, not on your lap or the carpet as they can cling to the knitting and you won't get a true measurement. Use a tape measure and place it vertically slightly in from the edge of the piece to get an accurate measurement. Measure from the cast on edge to the needles.

Shape armholes

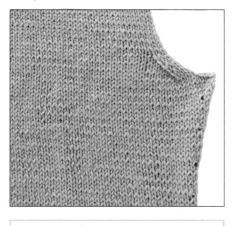

Bind (cast) off 5 [6:7] sts at beg of next 2 rows. Dec 1 st at each end of every row to 79 [85:91] sts.

Use the same method to decrease as you used for the shaping to the waist.

Work straight until armhole measures 7½ [8:8½]in (19 [20.5:21.5]cm), ending with a p row.

Shape shoulders

Bind (cast) off 6 [7:8] sts at beg of next 4 rows then 6 sts at beg of next 2 rows. Bind (cast) off rem 43 [45:47] sts.

Front

Work as given for back until front is 16 rows less than back to shoulder shaping, ending with a p row.

Instead of repeating all the same instructions, work exactly as you did for the back, using the same methods of decreasing and increasing. In many patterns this is given as a measurement. Make sure you work the same number of straight rows at the waist and below the underarm. On the back, place a marker 16 rows down from the first row of bind (cast) off stitches at the shoulders. Count the number of rows from the last decrease at the armhole to this marker, and work the same number of rows on the front. Sewing the garment together is made much easier if the side and armhole seams have the same number of rows.

Shape neck

Next row K29 [31:33] sts, join in a 2nd ball of yarn and bind (cast) off centre 21 [23:25] sts, k to end. Working both sides at the same time, dec 1 st at neck edge on foll 11 rows. 18 [20:22] sts at each side. Work 4 rows straight, ending at armhole edge (work 1 row more on left side of neck).

Patterns vary on how they tell you to work the neck shaping. This pattern tells you to work both sides at the same time, by joining in a second ball of yarn. Working both sides at once ensures that they will be the same. In some other patterns, the left side is worked first and the right side is worked as a mirror image of it. Use the same method as before to decrease.

knitting a garment

Shape shoulders

Bind (cast) off 6[7:8] sts at beg of next and foll alt row. Work I row then cast off rem 6 sts.

Sleeves

Using size 3 (3.25mm/UK10) needles, cast on 45 [47:49] sts and work 2in (5cm) in rib as given for back.

You can work the sleeves one at a time. But you can also work both sleeves at the same time on the same needles, like the neck shaping. By doing this, you will know that you have worked all the shaping in exactly the same way. Cast on two sets of stitches, with a ball of yarn for each, and work across the first sleeve, pick up the new yarn and work the same row across the second sleeve.

Change to size 6 (4mm/UK8) needles and work in st st, inc I st at each end of 5th and every foll 11th [10th:9th] row to 67 [71:77] sts.

Work 4 rows straight in st st and then increase I st at each end of next row. Work 10 [9:8] rows straight and then increase on the next row. Use the same method for the increases as before.

Work straight until sleeve measures 20½ [21:21½] in (52 [53.5:54.5] cm), ending with a p row.

Shape cap

Bind (cast) off 5 [6:7] sts at beg of next 2 rows. Dec I st at each end of next 3 rows, then on foll 3 alt rows, and then on every foll 4th row to 41 [41:45] sts. Dec I st at each end of every foll alt row to 25 sts, and then on foll 2 rows, ending with a p row. Bind (cast) off 4 sts at beg of next 2 rows, then rem 13 sts.

The top of a set-in sleeve is shaped in a curve to fit into the armhole. Read the instructions carefully and use a pencil and paper to keep a tally of the straight rows and decreases. Use the same method to decrease as before.

Finishing

Sew in all ends of yarn, by weaving up the edges of the pieces. Block pieces to measurements.

Blocking is the process of pinning out the garment pieces to their finished measurements and then setting the fabric shape by steam or wet pressing. Fair isle and intarsia designs can look crumpled when they come off the needle and improve immensely with careful pressing. Lace is stretched out to reveal its full glory and heavy cabled fabrics lie flatter. Always refer to the washing and pressing instructions on the ball band to help you decide which method to use. Blocking is done on a soft surface that you can stick pins into and that won't spoil if it gets damp. Ironing boards are ideal for small pieces, but large garment pieces need more room to lie flat. You can make a blocking board from a folded blanket covered with a towel or sheet.

Using rust proof pins, pin the knitted pieces out, wrong side up, on the blocking board, using the measurements given on the size diagrams. Pin out the width and length first and then the other measurements. Place a pin every 1in (2.5cm) or so to hold the edges straight. Do not pin out the ribs. If you press these they will loose their elasticity.

Wet pressing Wet a clean cloth and wring out the excess water until it is just damp. Place it over the pinned out piece (avoiding the ribs) and leave to dry away from direct heat. When the cloth is completely dry, remove it. Make sure the knitted pieces are also dry before you take out the pins and remove them from the board.

Steam pressing Lay a clean cloth over the pinned out piece to protect it. Set the steam iron on an appropriate heat setting for the yarn. Hold the iron close to the surface of the knitting without touching it. Do not press the iron on to the knitted fabric or steam the ribs. Let the steam penetrate the fabric. Remove the cloth and allow the fabric to dry before unpinning. Some yarns will not stand the high temperature needed for steaming so always check the ball band first. Synthetic yarns should never be steamed.

Making up

Join right shoulder seam.

For a neat finish, use mattress stitch to join all the seams (see page 70).

Neckband

Using size 3 (3.25mm/UK10) needles, pick up and k22 sts down left side of neck, 21 [23:25] sts across front neck, 22 sts up right side of neck and 42 [44:46] sts across back neck.
107 [111:115] sts.
Work 5in (12.5cm) rib as given for back. Bind (cast) off loosely in rib.

To pick up stitches neatly see page 68.

Join shoulder and neckband seam. Set in sleeves. Join side and sleeve seams.

To set the sleeve into the armhole, pin the centre of the sleeve cap to the shoulder seam and each end to the beginning of the armhole shaping. Sew both sets of bound (cast) off stitches together at the beginning of the sleeve and armhole shaping. Pin the remaining sleeve cap around the armhole, easing any fullness in evenly.

Size diagrams

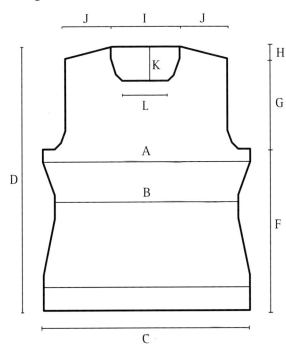

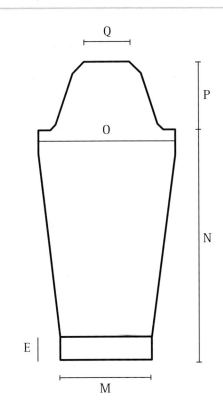

Size diagram measurements

A 18 [20:22]in (46 [51:56]cm)
B 16½ [18½:20½]in (42 [47:52]cm)
C 18½ [20½:22½]in (47 [52:57]cm)
D 22½ [23:23½]in 57 [58.5:60]cm)
E 2in (5cm)
F 14in (35.5cm)
G 7½ [8:8½]in (19 [20.5:21.5]cm)
H 1in (2.5cm)
I 8 [8¼:8½]in (20.5 [21:21.5] cm)
J 3¼ [3½:4]in (8.5 [9:10]cm)
K 3in (7.5cm)
L 4 [4¼:4½]in (10 [11:11.5]cm)
M 8 [8½:9]in (20.5 [21.5:23.5]cm)
N 20½ [21:21½]in (52 [53.5:54.5]cm)
O 12 [13:14]in (30.5 [33:35.5]cm)
P 5½ [6:6½]in (14 [15:16.5]cm)
Q 4in (10cm)

KNIT SOMETHING NOW! ▶

This basic sweater pattern can be used as the basis for various adaptations such as adding a central lace or cable panel.

Turtleneck fitted sweater knitted in worsted (DK) weight merino wool on size 6 (4mm/UK8) needles. See pages 64–7 for pattern.

OTHER GARMENT DETAILS

It is the finishing details which can make all the difference to the look of a garment – picking up stitches evenly, sewing up invisibly and making the correct size buttonholes all give the final professional touch.

Picking up stitches

When you add a neckband, button band or any type of border to another knitted piece, you pick up the stitches for it evenly along the edge using one needle. With the right side of the work facing, the needle is held in the right hand and inserted through the edge stitches, the left hand holding the work. A new ball of yarn is joined and is wrapped around the needle and a loop is pulled through. One stitch has been knitted on to the needle. Use a size smaller needle than that used for the main piece.

✓ Knit Perfect

Knitting patterns will usually tell you how many stitches to pick up. You must pick up the stitches evenly; begin and end at the edges and space the remaining stitches equally along the edge.

Using a tape measure and with the work laid out flat, place a marker (length of yarn or a safety pin) in the centre of the edge, divide each half in half again and place a marker, and then halve each quarter and place a marker, dividing the edge into eight equal sections. Divide the number of stitches to be picked up by eight. Count the number of rows or stitches in each section and work the picked up stitches evenly between them.

For example, each section has ten rows and you have to pick up eight stitches. Pick up a stitch in each of the first four rows, miss a row then pick up a stitch in each of the next four rows, miss a row, then go on to the next section.

Work the stitches in the last section so that there is a stitch picked up in each of the last four rows, for example, one stitch in each of first two rows, miss a row, one stitch in each of next two rows, miss a row, one stitch in each of last four rows.

On a horizontal bound (cast) off edge

Hold the work in your left hand. With a needle and the yarn in your right hand, insert the needle into the centre of the first stitch in the row below the bound (cast) off edge. Wrap the yarn knitwise around the needle and draw through a loop. Continue in this way, inserting the needle through the centre of the stitch.

On a vertical edge
(for example, the front of a cardigan)

Hold the work in your left hand. With a needle and the yarn in your right hand, insert the needle between the first and second stitches at the beginning of the first row, wrap the yarn around knitwise and pull through a stitch. Continue up the edge, inserting the needle between the stitches on each row, taking in one stitch. If you are using a thick yarn, where one stitch may measure ½in (1.5cm) or more, insert the needle through the centre of the edge stitch, taking in only half a stitch to reduce bulk.

On a shaped edge
(for example, neck shaping)

Use the above methods for picking up stitches along the straight edges of the neck. On the shaped part, insert the needle into the centre of the stitches one row below the decreasing. Do not pick up along the edge as this will result in holes. If you have to pick up extra stitches to cover a gap, for example, between the bind (cast) off stitches and the shaping, decrease these stitches on the next row.

Buttonholes

A knitting pattern will tell you to work the button band before the buttonhole band. This is because you can use the button band to work out how many buttons you need and how they will be spaced. Lie the piece flat and place a pin at the position of the top and bottom buttons. These should be ½in (1.5cm) from the ends. Using a tape measure, place pins to mark the positions of the remaining buttons. Make sure they are spaced evenly by counting the rows or stitches between the pins. To decide on the size of buttonhole to use, work a few samples of different buttonholes on a sample of the border stitch. Small garments like lacy cardigans or summer tops will look better with several small buttons than a few large ones, while a heavy cabled garment is better with fewer, larger buttons.

For small buttons

Make the buttonhole using a yarn over with a corresponding decrease. On a band worked in rib or moss stitch, try to space the buttonholes so that the yarn over is worked in place of the purl stitch and the decrease is worked with the knit stitch on top. For example, opposite the button marker, on a right side row, work a k1, yo, k2tog. This will give a neater finish.

For large buttons

Work the buttonhole by binding (casting) off two or three stitches on a right side row and then casting them back on in the next row.

For example, on a band picked up and worked horizontally along the edge of a cardigan, you would work to one stitch before the marker, bind (cast) off three stitches, work to one stitch before the next marker and work another buttonhole and so on to the end of the row. The marker marks the centre of the buttonhole, so by working to one stitch before the marker, the centre of the buttonhole will be in the right position. On the next row, work to the bound (cast) off stitches, turn the work and cast on three stitches using the cable cast on method (see page 24). Before placing the final stitch on the left-hand needle, bring the yarn to the front between the needles; this stops a loop being formed which makes the buttonhole look untidy. Don't cast on too tightly, the stitches need to be as elastic and as wide as those on the bound (cast) off edge. Turn the work back and continue across the row to the next buttonhole. It looks neater if you plan to work the buttonholes in the same place in the rib. For example, bind (cast) off three stitches over k1, p1, k1 each time.

To sew on buttons, either use the same yarn, if it is thin enough to go through the button, or use a strong sewing thread in a matching colour.

Knit Perfect

✔ If the knitting pattern does *not* tell you how many stitches to pick up, measure the length of the edge and multiply it by the stitch gauge (tension) of the border to be knitted. You can get this from measuring the border if it has already been used on the garment, or by knitting a piece of the border as though it were for a gauge (tension) sample. Place markers every 1in (2.5cm) along the edge and pick up the number of stitches in 1in (2.5cm) of the border.

Practise by picking up stitches along the edge of the gauge (tension) square worked for the main fabric.

For example, if the edge measures 10in (25cm) and the stitch gauge (tension) of the border is 4 stitches to 1in (2.5cm), you would place markers every 1in (2.5cm) and pick up 4 stitches between them for a total of 40 stitches.

✔ If you pick up too few stitches for a neckband, button band or border, it will pull or gather up the main fabric. If you have too many stitches, the neckband, button band or border will be fluted and will not lie flat. Work out your stitches carefully before you begin and always unravel and start again if it does not look right.

A badly knitted border will spoil a well-knitted garment.

other garment details

Sewing up

Whenever possible sew the pieces together with the yarn they are knitted from. If the yarn is something that will break easily or has a pile, like chenille, use a plain yarn in a matching colour. Check that it will wash the same as the knitting yarn. Do not use the long ends left after knitting the pieces; always sew these in before seaming. If you have to unpick the garment for any reason, the ends may start to unravel the knitting. Use a tapestry needle and an 18in (45cm) length of yarn. The action of taking the yarn through the work too frequently can fray it.

Mattress stitch

To get an invisible seam use mattress stitch. This is worked from the right side, making it easier to match patterns such as fair isle, and shaping details, like on a sleeve. Place the two pieces to be joined side by side on a flat surface.

Secure the yarn by weaving it down the edge of one of the pieces, bringing it to the front on the first row between the corner stitch and the second stitch. On the opposite edge, insert the needle from back to front on the first row between the corner stitch and the second stitch. Take the needle back to the first edge and insert it from back to front through the same hole. Pull the yarn up tight to draw the pieces together.

Joining two pieces of stockinette (stocking) stitch

Work row by row and use for vertical seams like side and sleeve seams. Secure the yarn as given above. Take the needle across to the opposite side and insert it into the first row again from front to back, take it under the horizontal strand of the row above and pull the yarn through. Take the needle across to the other edge, insert the needle into the first row again from front to back and take it under the horizontal strands of the two rows above. Pull the yarn through. Insert the needle into the first edge again, in the same hole that the yarn came out of and take it under the horizontal strands of the two rows above. Continue zigzagging between the edges, working under two rows each time. Pull the yarn up every few stitches to draw the seam together; not too tightly, the seam should not pucker the fabric.

Joining ribs

This is worked row by row. In k1, p1 rib work through the centre of the first stitch so that half a stitch is taken up on each side. Work under one row at a time. Pull the seam together and a whole stitch will be formed, so the rib is not interrupted by the seam. In k2, p2 rib work as given for st st, taking up a whole stitch to keep the rib correct.

Joining two pieces of reverse stockinette (stocking) stitch

Work row by row and use for vertical seams like side and sleeve seams. Join the lower edges and work as above but instead of working under two strands, work under one strand only. Insert the needle from front to back under the horizontal strand of the row above and pull the yarn through. Take the needle across to the other edge and insert it from front to back under the top loop of the second stitch. Take the needle back to the other edge and work under the strand of the row above. Continue in this way, inserting the needle under the top loop of the second stitch on one edge and under the horizontal strand between the first and second stitches on the other edge. One side of the seam takes in one and half stitches and the other takes in one stitch but this weaves the rev st st together so the seam is invisible.

Joining two pieces of garter stitch

This is worked row by row the same way as for reverse stockinette (stocking) stitch, working under the top loop of a stitch on one side and the horizontal strand between stitches on the other side.

Joining two bound (cast) off edges

Work stitch by stitch and use for shoulder seams. Lay the two pieces, one above the other, with the bound (cast) off edges together. Weave the yarn through a few stitches on the bottom piece to secure it. Bring the needle to the front through the centre of the first stitch of the row below the bound (cast) off edge. Take the needle up to the top piece and insert the needle through the centre of the first stitch and bring it out in the centre of the next stitch. Take the needle back down to the bottom piece and insert it into the same hole, and bring it up in the centre of the next stitch. Take the needle back to the top piece and insert the needle into the same hole and bring it out in the centre of the next stitch. Pull the yarn up tight to hide the bound (cast) off edges. Continue in this way, and the seam will resemble a new row of stitches.

Joining bound (cast) off stitches to rows

Use for sewing a sleeve into an armhole. Lay the pieces flat with the edges together. Secure the end of the yarn to the bound (cast) off edge. Bring the needle out through the centre of the first stitch of the row below the bound (cast) off edge. Take the needle up to the row piece and insert it under one horizontal strand between the first and second stitches. Insert the needle into the same place on the bound (cast) off piece and bring it out through the centre of the next stitch. Continue in this way, pulling the yarn tight to close the seam. There are usually more rows than stitches so one stitch cannot always be sewn to one row. Pin the pieces together carefully and pick up two horizontal strands every so often to take in the extras rows.

Sewing in a sleeve

Whatever style of sleeve a garment has, it is sewn in after joining shoulder seams but before joining side and sleeve seams.

Dropped shoulders

Dropped shoulders On garments with dropped shoulders there is no armhole shaping to sew the sleeve into. Bind (cast) off the sleeve top in one row. Lay the joined front and back pieces flat, measure half of the top of the sleeve measurement (information found on the size diagrams) down from the shoulder seam on each side edge and place a marker. Pin the centre of the bound (cast) off edge of the sleeve to the shoulder seam. Pin each end of the top of the sleeve to the markers. Pin the rest of the sleeve top between the markers and sew evenly in position, making sure the seam is straight.

Square set-in sleeves

Square set-in sleeves The sleeve top is bound (cast) off in one row like a dropped shoulder, but a square armhole is created by casting off a few stitches. Match the centre of the sleeve top to the shoulder seam. Pin each end into the corner of the armhole and sew the sleeve top into place. Then sew the ends of the sleeve horizontally against the bound (cast) off edges of the armhole.

ADAPTING A PATTERN

Not everyone is a standard size but knitting patterns assume they are and that by following the instructions slavishly the garment will fit perfectly. It is disappointing to spend time knitting a sweater which you never wear because the sleeves are too long or the body just that bit too short to be comfortable. Many patterns provide a diagram of the knitted pieces with measurements. Check these carefully against your own measurements to ensure a perfect fit. If the pattern doesn't have a diagram you will need to draw your own. It is worth the effort for a sweater that fits.

✓ Knit Perfect

✓ To work out the stitches and rows per inch (cm), divide the gauge (tension) by 4 (10). For example, 18 sts and 24 rows to 4in (10cm) = 4.5 sts and 6 rows to 1in (1.8 sts and 2.4 rows to 1cm).

✓ It is important to work in only imperial or metric measurements, do not use both together.

✓ If you find the maths too daunting, chart the garment on to graph paper. Chart the sleeve as per the instructions and then you will be able to see how many increases are made up each side. Chart any side shaping on the front or back. It is always easier to see the shape of the garment rather than try to visualize it from written instructions.

Sleeve length

The important measurement is from the centre of the back of your neck to your wrist (or where you want the cuff to end). Place one end of a tape measure on the bone at the back of your neck, extend your arm and measure to your wrist bone. On the garment diagram add the measurements for the back neck and both shoulders together and then divide this by two. This is the measurement from the centre back neck to the top of the sleeve. Take this measurement from your neck to wrist measurement and this will be the sleeve length. For example, the back neck plus shoulders = 18in (46cm), divide by 2 = 9in (23cm). Your neck to wrist measurement is 30in (76cm), so 30in (76cm) minus 9in (23cm) = 21in (53cm) sleeve length. Compare this to the sleeve length measurement given on the diagram.

> **To make the sleeve longer…**
> simply work more rows after the shaping until the sleeve measures the correct length.
>
> **To make the sleeve shorter…**
> is trickier. A sleeve is increased evenly up its length to get to the required width at the top to fit into the armhole. If you follow the instructions but stop when you reach your required sleeve length you may not have increased enough stitches and your sleeve will be too narrow to fit into the armhole.
> Calculate the required increases as described below.

Charting a shorter sleeve

Chart your sleeve on graph paper to work out how to space the increases to fit them into your shorter length. On graph paper, one square represents one stitch. Draw a line centrally at the bottom of the sheet, the number of stitches after you have worked the cuff and any increase row. Mark the centre. To work out how many rows you have to work the increases over, take the

length of the cuff from the sleeve length and multiply this by the number of rows per inch (cm). For example, if your sleeve length is 21in (53.5cm) with a cuff of 2in (5cm) the length of the sleeve without the cuff is 19in (48.5cm). Multiply this by the row tension, for example, 6 rows to 1in (2.4 rows to 1cm) = 114 rows (115.2 rows). Round any fractions down to an even number. Count 114 rows from the cuff line and draw a line for the top of the sleeve. Draw a vertical line from the centre of the cuff line to the top line. Count out half the number of stitches after all the increases each side from this central line.

Take the number of cuff stitches (56) from the sleeve top stitches (98) making 42 stitches which means 21 stitches have to be increased at each side of the sleeve. Divide the number of rows by the number of increases, 114 divided by 21 = 5.4, rounded down to 5.

Mark the first increase on the fifth row and then on every following fifth row until the width is reached. Then draw a straight line from the last increase to the top. There should be at least 1in (2.5cm) straight after the last increase. Work from this chart to knit the new shorter sleeve length.

Garment length

If there is no armhole shaping, just work the length that you require to the shoulder shaping. For a garment with armhole shaping, you need to alter the length before reaching the armhole. The armhole length must remain as in the instructions as the sleeve shaping has been worked out to fit into that armhole. If the garment has shaping from the waist to the bust, draw a chart to work out the increases as described for working out a shorter sleeve.

Adding colour motifs

Using the instructions for the plain sweater, chart the main pieces of the garment on to graph paper. Use the same outline for both the back and front, with the neck shaping drawn in for the front, and chart one sleeve. It is now easy to draw in any colour motifs or fair isle patterns that you want to add.

Adding a cable panel

You can add a cable panel to the plain sweater pattern on page 144. To be in proportion, a cable panel should measure about one third of the width of the front. Any smaller than this and it will look lost and have no impact. Any bigger and it will dominate and become an all-over fabric instead of a panel.

Designing the panel

To design your panel choose cables from the Stitch library (see pages 108–16). Start with a central feature cable, something bold or intricate, and then add complimentary but smaller cables each side. For example, the centre cable may have three stitches in each of the strands and uses C6F and C6B to cross the strands so it would look better with six stitch cables each side rather than thinner four stitch cables.

Chart the cables on graph paper with two stitches of reverse stockinette (stocking) stitch each side of the cables.

For example, the sweater shown here is a size 38in (96.5cm) with an actual chest measurement of 44in (112cm). The front measures 22in (56cm) therefore the panel should be about 7in (18cm).

Knitting the garment

Knit the back of the garment. Using the same needles you used to get the stockinette (stocking) stitch tension, cast on the required number of stitches for the cable panel you have designed plus at least three stitches each side for stockinette (stocking) stitch. Knit a gauge (tension) square of the cable panel. Lay it out flat and measure the cables and the reverse stockinette (stocking) stitch

each side. Do not include the stockinette (stocking) stitch. If it is over a third of the width of the back, use fewer stitches between the cables, but no less than two because each cable should have room to lie against reverse stockinette (stocking) stitch. If it is too narrow, add another smaller cable on each side.

When you were knitting the cable panel gauge (tension) piece you will have noticed that you need more stitches to get a panel which is the same width of stockinette (stocking) stitch. Cables pull the knitted fabric together and the reverse stockinette (stocking) stitch acts a bit like a rib, rolling under the edges of the cables.

Lay the back of the garment flat on a table with the right side towards you. Using a ruler, measure the width of the cable panel in the middle of the fabric along one row and place a pin at each side. Count the number of stitches across the row between the pins. This is the number of stitches of stockinette (stocking) stitch that will be replaced by the stitches of the cable panel.

For this example, the cable panel measures 7½in (19cm) and has 58 stitches (see sample below). The same width of stockinette (stocking) stitch has 33 stitches.

To calculate the number of stitches needed for the front of the sweater, subtract the number of stockinette (stocking) stitches and add on the number of cable panel stitches. Take away the number of stitches cast on for the rib (this must stay the same as the

▲ KNIT SOMETHING NOW!

Add a cable panel or colour motifs to this simple sweater.

Cable panel sweater knitted in fisherman (aran) merino wool on size 6 (4mm/UK8) and size 8 (5mm/UK6) needles. See page 145 for pattern.

back) to work out how many stitches to increase evenly on the last rib row.

For example, the back of the sweater has 99 stitches; to place the panel in the middle, 99 sts minus 33 sts to be removed = 66 sts, so there will be 33 sts of stockinette (stocking) stitch each side of the cable panel of 58 sts. For the front, there needs to be a total of 66 sts + 58 sts = 124 sts. The rib of the sweater is worked on 99 sts. The number of increase stitches from the rib to the front stitches is 124 sts minus 99 sts = 25 sts. These increase sts are usually worked into the last row of the rib.

To place increases (M1) evenly in a row, calculate as follows: divide the number of increases minus one, into the number of stitches in the row for the number of stitches between increases.

In this example, 25 incs minus 1 = 24 incs, then 99 sts divided by 24 incs = 4.125 sts, round down to 4 sts, which will leave 3 sts to be worked at the sides. The increase row is rib 2, M1, (rib 4, M1) 24 times, rib 1. 124 sts.

Measure the cable panel and the reverse stockinette (stocking) stitch each side.

KNITTING A PATTERNED GARMENT

Increasing and decreasing to shape a piece of stockinette (stocking) stitch is straightforward. Each stitch is either knitted or purled. In stitch patterns with a repeat of two or more stitches, an increased stitch must be worked in pattern to keep the pattern correct.

To shape a sleeve, a knitting pattern will instruct you to increase one stitch into pattern at each end of every, say, 6th row but will not tell you how to work the stitch you have made. The increases are worked at the ends of the rows using inc 1, but not the full fashioning method (see page 26). There are two ways to keep track of increases, working them into pattern successfully: charting, which is the easiest, and using markers.

✓ Knit Perfect

A good knitting pattern should be written so that any shaping into the stitch pattern will look well designed. Some instructions, however, can result in half a cable or an incomplete lace stitch repeat being worked at each side of the neck or armhole. If this looks like it is going to happen, add or take off one stitch more than instructed to get the pattern lying nicely into the shaping.

Don't alter it by more than one stitch in bulky (chunky) yarn or a couple of stitches in worsted (DK) yarn. At the neck shaping, make a note of what you have done, so more or less stitches are picked up for the neckband.

Charting

Chart the outline of the sleeve on to graph paper (see below). Beginning at the bottom right-hand corner, plot the rows of the stitch pattern as given in the knitting instructions, using symbols to represent the stitches (see page 63 and the Stitch library). This helps you identify the pattern repeat. The lace cardigan on this page is knitted in a pattern with a six stitch repeat, plus one stitch at the end to balance it.

Lace pattern

Row 1 K1, * yfwd, k1, sk2po, k1, yfwd, k1; rep from * to end.
Row 2 P to end.
Row 3 K2, * yfwd, sk2po, yfwd, k3; rep from * to end, ending last rep with k2.
Row 4 P to end.
These 4 rows form the lace pattern.

Plot the lace pattern across the bottom of the sleeve and the first and last repeats up to the top of the sleeve. Now fill in what pattern stitches you can in the increased stitches at each side. Use this method for cables, texture stitches as well as lace stitches but remember that in a lace pattern, a yarn over increase must be accompanied by a decrease. If there are not sufficient stitches to work both, wait until you have increased enough stitches to do so. Rather than work a long panel of stockinette (stocking) stitch before you can work a complete pattern repeat, it is sometimes possible to change the decrease. There is a double decrease in this pattern and by changing it to a single decrease, like ssk, half a pattern repeat can be worked. Use the same method for cables or texture stitches.

Decreases can be charted in the same way. For example, a neck is shaped by decreasing on every row. Chart the outline of the front of the garment with the neck shaping and plot in the stitch pattern. The knitting pattern will tell you which stitch pattern row you should finish before beginning to shape the neck.

Chart for lace pattern on sleeve showing increases

Chart for cable pattern on sleeve showing increases

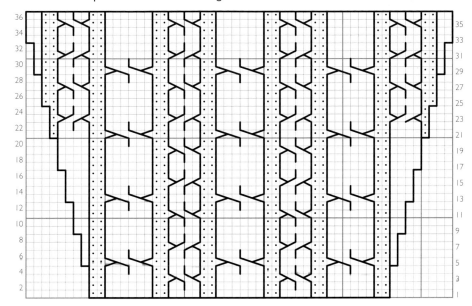

Chart for lace pattern on front showing neck and shoulder shaping

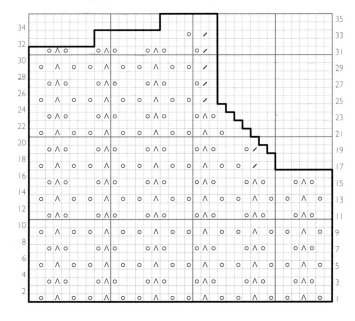

Working with markers

Work the first increases at each end of the row, placing markers between the new stitches and the original stitches. Continue in pattern, slipping the markers on every row and working the increases into stockinette (stocking) stitch. Wait until you have sufficient new stitches next to the marker to work a complete pattern repeat. A half pattern repeat could be worked if the pattern will allow (see charting method left). When a whole repeat has been worked, move the marker out to begin a new pattern repeat.

Before working the first decreases place a marker one pattern repeat in from the edges to be shaped. Work this pattern repeat until there are insufficient stitches to work it correctly. Work the remaining stitches in stockinette (stocking) stitches until they, too, are decreased. Move the marker one pattern repeat in and continue to decrease over these stitches.

KNIT SOMETHING NOW! ▶

Knit this cardigan to practise shaping over a lace pattern. Draw your own chart and plot the pattern before you start any shaping.

Lace cardigan knitted in worsted (DK) weight merino wool on size 6 (4mm/UK8) needles. See page 146 for pattern.

TASSELS, FRINGES AND CORDS

Adding fringing and cords made from complementary yarns to your garments and soft furnishings provides the finishing touch. They are quick and easy to make.

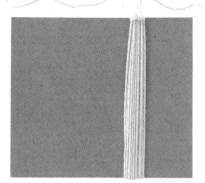

Tassels

Wrap the yarn loosely around a piece of card the required length of the tassel. Thread a long length of yarn under the strands at the top, fold in half and secure tightly with a knot, leaving two long ends. Cut the wrapped strands at the bottom and remove the cardboard. Thread one long end on to a tapestry needle, insert it through the top of the strands and bring out 1in (2.5cm) below. Wrap the yarn several times around the tassel. Pass the needle through the middle of the wrapped strands to secure the long end, then insert the needle again and pull it back through the top. Use these ends to sew the tassel in place. Trim the bottom of the tassel neatly.

Plain fringe

Wrap yarn loosely around a piece of cardboard the required length of the fringe. Cut the wrapped strands at the bottom and remove the cardboard. Fold several lengths in half and, using a crochet or rug hook, pull the strands through the edge of the knitted piece from front to back by catching the fold with the hook. Pass the ends through the folded loop and pull to tighten the knot. Space each bunch of strands evenly along the edge. Trim the bottom of the fringe neatly to the finished length required.

Knotted fringe

Work the fringe as given left with an even number of strands in each bunch. Take half the strands from one bunch and half the strands from the next and tie them together. Continue across the fringe, making sure the knots are in line. The extra knot will take up yarn so make the strands longer than the desired finished length. Try working another row of knots below, combining the original bunches again.

✓ Knit Perfect

On a multi-coloured garment, instead of a one colour fringe, try using equal amounts of every colour yarn used in each bunch (see example, left).

Knitted cord

This long tube, sometimes called an I-cord, is knitted on two double-pointed needles, using two sizes smaller than normally used for the yarn.

Cast on four stitches and knit one row. Do not turn the work but instead push the stitches to the other end of the needle. Swap the right-hand needle with the left-hand needle, pull up the yarn and knit the four stitches again. Repeat for every row. By pulling the yarn up at the end of the row, the edges of the knitting are pulled together and a tube is formed. Cast on three stitches for a finer cord, and five stitches for a thicker one. Piping cord can be threaded through the knitted cord for a firmer edging for cushions or as the handle for a bag.

The intarsia cushion (see page 154) uses a knitted cord to trim the edges.

Twisted cord

Strands of yarn twisted together will form a cord. The more strands you use, the thicker the cord will be. Cut lengths of yarn three times the finished length required and tie them together with a knot at each end. Hook one end over a doorknob or hook, and holding the other knotted end, stand back so that the strands are taut. Insert a pencil into the end and wind it to twist the strands. Keep the strands taut as you wind, twisting until the cord starts to fold up and twist around itself. Keeping the cord taut, remove the end from the doorknob and bring both knotted ends together. The cord will twist around itself. Ask someone to hold the middle or hang a weight from a hook on the middle of the cord to hold it taut as it twists. Small tassels can be made at either end by knotting the strands, cutting the looped end and then untying the knots from the other end. A textured cord is made by combining different yarns or colours.

The heart sachet (see page 142) is hung up by a twisted cord loop.

Hold the strands taut as you twist

Bring the knotted ends together for a double twist

EDGINGS

Edgings can be added to garments instead of ribs or added to knitted items like throws (see page 138). They can be knitted separately, worked from the cast-on edge with the main fabric worked up from them or added to an edge by picking up stitches from a finished piece. Knitted edgings can also trim woven fabric garments, or used on household items. See the stitch library page 125–7 for more edgings.

✓ Knit Perfect

✓ For a simple delicate edging which looks great around collars, work a picot bind (cast) off (see page 25) or pick up and knit sts along an edge and then bind (cast) off.

✓ Have a look in antique shops for old garments, table linen and bed linen. A lot of these will have knitted lace edgings. White cotton lace edgings add a romantic look to ordinary bed linen. Choose one from the Stitch library (see page 125–7). Use a yarn with the same washing instructions as the bed linen. Wash both to make sure they don't shrink before sewing the edging on. Add edgings around ready-made cushions and throws.

✓ Lengths of knitted lace were traditionally used to decorate shelf edges. Soften the bottom edge of roller blinds by sewing on a picot point or frilled edging.

✓ Add the ruffled or frilled edging to the ends of a plain scarf. Use the same colour yarn or a contrasting one.

Ruffled edging worked first

Cast on a number of sts divisible by 6 plus 5 close to the finished number of sts required plus 10 sts for every 6 sts. For example, if 50 is the finished number of sts required, cast on 53 sts (8 × 6 + 5) plus 80 sts (8 × 10). The three extra stitches will be decreased evenly across the first row of the main fabric after knitting the ruffle.

Row 1 (WS) K5, * p11, k5; rep from * to end.
Row 2 P5, * k2tog, k7, ssk, p5; rep from * to end.
Row 3 K5, * p9, k5; rep from * to end.
Row 4 P5, * k2tog, k5, ssk, p5; rep from * to end.
Cont in this way, dec 1 st at each side of knit sts on every RS row and work 2 purl sts less in each repeat on every WS row until 3 knit sts remain for each ruffle, ending with a WS row.
Next row P5, * sl2tog-k1-psso, p5; rep from * to end.
Next row K5, * p1, k5; rep from * to end.
Cont in main fabric, dec 3 sts evenly for required number of sts on first row.

Ruffled edging worked at the end

Work before binding (casting) off the stitches of main piece or pick up and knit stitches along the edge of the main piece (see page 68). A multiple of 6 stitches plus 5 is required so increase stitches to get patt rep. The M1 stitches are made to the right and left (see page 27).

Row 1 (RS) P5, * k1, p5; rep from * to end.
Row 2 K5, * p1, k5; rep from * to end.
Row 3 P5, * M1R, k1, M1L, p5; rep from * to end.
Row 4 K5, * p3, k5; rep from * to end.
Row 5 P5, * M1R, k3, M1L, p5; rep from * to end.
Cont in this way, inc 1 st at each side of k sts on RS rows and work the extras sts as p sts on WS rows until there are 11 knit sts for each ruffle, ending with a WS row. Bind (cast) off loosely in patt.

Frilled edging

This edging is always worked first or as
a separate border and sewn on.
Cast on four times the finished number
of stitches required.
Row 1 * K2, lift first of these 2 sts over
second and off the needle; rep from *
to end. (Half the number of sts remain.)
Row 2 * P2tog; rep from * to end.
(Finished number of sts.)
Cont in main fabric of garment or cast off.

Double frill

You will need three needles. Work a frilled
edging as above followed by 8 rows of st
st (ending with a WS row), leave sts on
the needle. On another needle, work a
second frill followed by 2 rows of st st
(ending with a WS row). Place the two
needles together with the short frill over
the longer frill and both right sides facing
the front. Join together by knitting through
both sets of sts (see page 25).

points of equal size

two sizes of points, one increased
to 18 sts and the other to 12 sts

Picot point edging

Each point is worked separately, the
stitches left on a spare needle and then
joined together at the top by working
across all stitches. They can be any size and
different sizes worked alternately make
for a wave effect. Work in moss stitch or
a stitch pattern instead of garter stitch.
Sew beads or tassels on to the points.
Cast on 2 sts.
Row 1 K2.
Row 2 Yo, k2.
Row 3 Yo, k3.
Row 4 Yo, k4.

Cont in this way until the required even
number of sts is reached, having worked
an even number of incs. Cut yarn and
push the sts to the end of the needle.
Cast on 2 sts on to the other needle
and work another point. Continue in this
way until there are the required number
of points. Do not cut the yarn after the
last point, use it to knit across all the
points. Either work a few rows of garter
stitch and cast off or continue into the
main fabric.

Cable edging

Work as a separate border and sew
on to main piece or pick up and knit
stitches from edging for main fabric.
Add 2 sts and 2 plain rows more for a
six stitch cable version.
Cast on 8 sts.
Row 1 (RS) P3, k4, p1.
Row 2 K1, p4, k3.
Row 3 P3, C4F, p1.
Row 4 K1, p4, k3.
Rep these 4 rows until edging is
required length.

BUTTONS

Finishing a knitted project by making your own buttons will make it really individual. You can cover buttons in knitted fabric using the same yarn as the main piece and then embroider them or stitch on some beads. Make bobble buttons by running a gathering thread around a circle of fabric and stuff. Dorset buttons are a traditional thread button; work in yarn or use embroidery threads for their range of colours.

Covered buttons

You can use self-cover buttons, which are available in kits, or a plain flat button with a shank. Self-cover buttons are made from metal or plastic and come in two pieces, the part you cover and the back plate to secure the covering fabric. There will also be a pattern outline of a circle to use as a guide for the size of the fabric. If you are using an ordinary button, cut a pattern in thin card by drawing a circle with a diameter of twice the width of the button. For example, a 1in (2.5cm) diameter button would have a pattern 2in (5cm) in diameter. For the knitted cover, use a worsted (DK) yarn or finer, otherwise the fabric will be too bulky to fit around the button. The fabric has to be tight and firm so use needles two or three sizes smaller than normal.

Front, showing embellishment

Back, showing gathered thread

Embellishing and finishing

The fabric can be embroidered or beaded at this point but do not add anything too close to the edges which will be folded under and not seen. Don't make the fabric too lumpy on the wrong side. Run a gathering thread around the edge, place the button in the middle and pull the thread up tightly. (If the covered button shows through the knitting, cover the top with a circle of thin fabric.) Adjust the folds of fabric and make a few extra stitches through the folds to sew them together. Secure the end of the thread. The back plate of the self-cover button is unnecessary and probably will not fit unless the knitting is very fine.

Tension square

Work a small gauge (tension) square using the smaller needles. Lay the button pattern on to the square and place pins on all four sides so you can count the number of stitches and rows. Divide the number of rows by three. Working in stockinette (stocking) stitch, cast on half the number of stitches and work one third of the rows, increasing into the first and last stitch of every second row until all the stitches for the required width have been added. Work straight for a third of the rows and then decrease over the same number of rows back to the original number of stitches. Bind (cast) off and leave a long end for gathering. Use the card pattern as a guide while you are knitting. The cover will be octagonal rather than a true circle.

Bobble buttons

Work the fabric shape in the same way as the covered buttons. Run a gathering thread around the edge, pull up and stuff firmly with toy stuffing. Gather up tightly and secure the end of the thread.

Dorset thread buttons

These buttons are worked in yarn around a metal or plastic ring. The ring is covered with closely worked blanket stitch (see page 84) and weaving through crossing spokes fills the centre. Use sport (4ply) yarn, crochet thread or embroidery threads to make the buttons in one colour or in a different colour for each stage. The button is attached by working stitches through the centre at the back.

1 Thread a tapestry needle with a long length of yarn, and work blanket stitch around the ring, covering the end of the yarn with the first few stitches to secure it. Make sure the stitches lie close together and that the ring is entirely covered. Work a small stitch into the top of the first stitch to join. Twist the blanket stitch around so that the horizontal loops face towards the centre.

2 Put the ring on to a piece of paper and divide it into six sections by placing a mark opposite the last stitch worked and spacing another four marks evenly around the ring. Starting at the last stitch worked, where the thread is still joined, number the marks from 1 to 6. Make a spoke by taking the thread across the centre of the ring to 4 and inserting the needle into the horizontal loop from front to back. Take the thread across the back of the ring to 5 and insert the needle from back to front. Take the thread across the ring to 2 and insert it from front to back. Take the thread up at 3 and then down at 6 for the final spoke.

3 Bring the yarn at the back of the ring to the centre where the spokes meet. Work a small cross to bind them together. Working clockwise, take the needle under the first two spokes, back over the second spoke and then under the second and third spokes, forming a small backstitch on the second spoke. Take the needle under the third and fourth, then under the fourth and fifth and so on. As you work out from the centre, pull the backstitches gently to tighten the weaving. Continue weaving until the centre is completely filled. Secure the thread and cut off neatly.

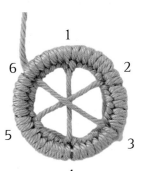

◀ KNIT SOMETHING NOW!

A covered button embroidered with roses (see page 85) is used as an unusual closure for a notebook.

The **rose button** is knitted in sport (4ply) weight mercerized cotton on size 2 (3mm/UK11) needles. See page 148 for pattern.

FLOWERS AND LEAVES

Knitted flowers and leaves are great for adding to plain garments or for scattering across a throw or cushion. Work in fine silky yarns for glamour, velvet chenille for luxury, or crisp cotton yarns that hold their shape well. If knitted in 100 per cent wool, the fabric can be fulled (see page 60). Embellish the edges of the leaves or petals with beads or embroidery.

Basic leaf

Cast on 3 sts and purl 1 row.
Row 1 (RS) K1, yfwd, k1, yfwd, k1. 5 sts.
Row 2 and every foll WS row Purl.
Row 3 K2, yfwd, k1, yfwd, k2. 7 sts.
Row 5 K3, yfwd, k1, yfwd, k3. 9 sts.
Row 7 K4, yfwd, k1, yfwd, k4. 11 sts.
Row 9 Ssk, k7, k2tog. 9 sts.
Row 11 Ssk, k5, k2tog. 7 sts.
Row 13 Ssk, k3, k2tog. 5 sts.
Row 15 Ssk, k1, k2tog. 3 sts.
Row 17 Sk2po.
Cut yarn and pull through last st. Make the leaf larger by adding extra increase rows. If you want a more solid leaf, work M1 instead of yfwd. Work the leaf in garter stitch instead of stockinette (stocking) stitch by working each WS row as a knit row. Make five leaves and arrange them in a circle with cast on points together at the centre to make a flower.

Daisy

These flowers look great worked in 4ply cotton yarn using size 2(3mm/UK11) needles, although they can be worked in any thickness or texture of yarn. Try a mohair or brushed yarn for a soft flower, or metallic or rayon yarns for a funky flower. Fill the centre with French knots (see page 84) or a button.
Cast on 2 sts.
** **Row 1** Knit into front and back of first st, k1.
Row 2 and every foll WS row K to end.
Row 3 Knit into front and back of first st, k2.
Cont in g st, inc into first st of every RS row until there are 6 sts, ending with a WS row.
Next row Bind (cast) off 4 sts, k2.
Next row K to end. **
One petal completed.
Work from ** to ** four more times.
Bind (cast) off rem 2 sts.
Run a gathering thread along the straight edge. Join the first petal to the last at cast on and bind (cast) off edges, forming a circle. Pull up the gathers until the daisy lies flat. Secure the thread. Make the petals bigger by working more increase rows. Make more petals and form into a spiral with two or more layers of petals.

Rose

Use a worsted (DK) yarn or thinner and a size smaller needle than normal, 3 (3.25mm/UK10), to make a firm fabric. Cast on 80 sts and knit 1 row.
Work 1in (2.5cm) st st, beg with a k row.
Dec row (K2tog) 40 times. 40 sts.
Dec row (P2tog) 20 times. 20 sts.
Dec row (K2tog) 10 times. 10 sts.
Cut yarn, leaving a long length. Thread yarn on to a tapestry needle and thread through sts on needle, taking them off the needle one by one. Pull up into gathers. Form the rose by twisting it round and round from the centre with right side of fabric facing outwards. Pull the rose into shape as you go, letting the fabric roll over in some places. Work a few stitches through all layers at the bottom to hold them in place.
　For a smaller rose, cast on fewer stitches and work less straight rows before decreasing as above.

▼ KNIT SOMETHING NOW!

A rose with two leaves has been fulled after knitting and makes an attractive brooch. The lavender sachet below right is trimmed with a leaf edging.

The **brooch** is knitted in 2ply jumper weight shetland wool and the leaf edging is knitted in sport (4ply) weight mercerized cotton. See page 148 for pattern.

EMBROIDERY

Embroidery should be done when the knitting has been completed and the pieces blocked but before the garment has been made up. You can use decorative stitches to add embellishments to any knitted fabric, although stockinette (stocking) stitch is the ideal base. The knitted stitches form a grid to work over and act as a guide for spacing embroidery stitches.

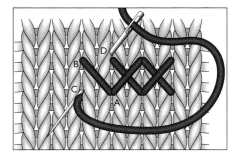

Cross stitch

Stockinette (stocking) stitch forms the grid for working cross stitch. They are worked over one stitch and one row, or on a fine knitted fabric, two stitches and two rows. Insert the needle between the stitches and make sure the top diagonal always goes in the same direction.

Bring the needle up at A then down at B, back up at C and then down at D. One stitch completed. Use this method for individual stitches or different colours.

For a horizontal or vertical line of cross stitches, work one diagonal of each stitch and then work back to complete the cross.

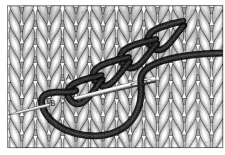

Chain stitch

Bring the needle out at A. In one movement, push the needle down in the same place and bring it out at B for the next stitch, looping the thread under the needle tip.

▼ KNIT SOMETHING NOW!

These drawstring bags are worked in knit and purl stitches. The bag on the right is embroidered using cross stitch (see above), and the other has delicate ribbon roses sewn on (see page 85).

Drawstring bags knitted in worsted (DK) cotton yarn on size 6 (4mm/UK8) needles and embroidered with DMC Stranded Cotton. See page 149 for pattern.

embroidery

Knit Perfect

✔ Use embroidery threads, tapestry wools or knitting yarn. The thread should be the same or slightly thicker than the knitted yarn. Too thin and it will sink into the fabric; too thick and it will distort the knitting. Check the threads are colourfast and will not shrink when washed. Work an embroidered sample and wash it if you are not certain.

✔ To transfer a pattern to the knitted fabric, draw it on tissue paper and tack into place on the knitted piece. Stitch through the paper and the knitted fabric. When completed, carefully cut or tear away the paper. On lightweight knitted fabric tack a piece of sew-on interfacing on to the wrong side and use it as a backing for the embroidery. Do not use iron-on interfacing as this may ruin the knitted fabric.

✔ Use a large-eyed blunt tapestry needle for embroidery. Work the embroidery stitches loosely, don't pull too tightly or the knitted fabric will pucker. Keep laying the piece flat to check for stretching or pulling. To begin the embroidery, weave the end of the thread through a few knitted stitches on the back of the fabric, working back through the thread to secure it; if you start with a knot, it may come undone during wear and knots make the wrong side lumpy.

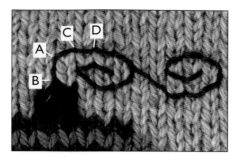

Backstitch

A continuous line used for outlining, for flower stems or for adding details.

To begin bring the needle up at A. Take the needle down at B and then up at C, down at A and up at D.

Lazy daisy stitch

Individual chain stitches worked around a centre to create the petals of a flower. The loops are fastened with a small stitch.

Bring the needle out at A. In one movement, push the needle down in the same place and bring it out at B, looping the thread under the needle tip. Take the needle back down at B, working over the loop, and bring it up at A for the next stitch.

French knot

Can be worked as the centre of lazy daisy stitch.

Bring the needle up and wind the yarn twice around the needle. Take the needle back down half a stitch away. Hold the loops around the needle with your finger tip to keep them in place whilst pulling the thread through to the back.

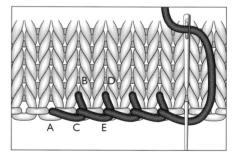

Blanket stitch

Use as a decorative edging along a garment, to sew on a patch pocket or appliqué shape, or to reinforce buttonholes. Often used to neaten raw edges, it can be worked from left to right or from right to left.

Bring the needle out at A. In one movement, take it down at B and back up at C, looping the thread under the needle tip. The next stitch is worked to the right, down at D and up at E. The horizontal threads should lie on the edge of the fabric.

Swiss darning or duplicate stitch

This stitch looks as though it has been knitted into the fabric; it follows the line of the yarn for the knit stitch on the right side of stockinette (stocking) stitch. It is used to embroider small areas of colour that would be tedious to knit, or to work a colour pattern instead of using fair isle or intarsia techniques. It is also useful for correcting mistakes in fair isle or intarsia. Use the same thickness of yarn used for the knitting. Take care to insert the needle between the strands and not to split the knitted stitches. The stitches will appear slightly raised on the surface of the knitting.

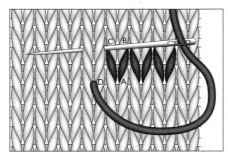

Horizontal stitches

Work from right to left, bringing the needle out at the base of the stitch (A). In one movement, take the thread around the top of the stitch by taking the needle down at B and up at C. In one movement, take the needle down at the base of the stitch (A) and up at the base of the next stitch (D). Continue across the row.

Vertical stitches

Work from bottom to top, bringing the needle out at the base of the stitch (A). Take the thread around the top of the stitch (B and C) and back down at the base (A). This time bring the needle up at the base of the stitch above and continue up the line of knitted stitches.

Rose stitch

Use a thin yarn or embroidery thread for the straight stitches and a thicker yarn or ribbon for the weaving through them that will cover the straight stitches.

Work five straight stitches in a circle the size of the rose required, all radiating from the central point. Thread the needle with the ribbon (or thick yarn) and bring it up through the centre hole. Going round and round from the centre outwards weave under and over the straight stitches until they are completely covered.

KNIT SOMETHING NOW! ▶

Mounted on ready-made greetings cards, these simple knitted patches are swiss darned with a heart for Valentine's Day and a tree for Christmas.

Valentine and **Christmas tree card** knitted in sport (4ply) mercerized cotton yarn on size 2 (3mm/UK11) needles and swiss darned with 12ply silk embroidery thread. See page 151 for pattern.

CORRECTING MISTAKES

When you are a beginner or are knitting fast, it is easy to work stitches incorrectly; splitting the yarn, dropping stitches off the needle, or not completing the stitch properly are common mistakes that are easily rectified. Twisting a cable the wrong way or working a colour pattern incorrectly are more serious errors. This is why it is important to inspect your knitting every few rows to save yourself the trouble of unpicking and re-knitting.

Dropped stitches

The sooner you spot that you have dropped a stitch the easier it is to rectify the mistake. Get into the habit of checking your knitting every few rows.

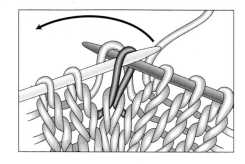

Knit stitch one row below
Insert the right needle through the front of the dropped stitch and then pick up the strand of yarn behind it. With the tip of the left needle, pass the stitch over the strand and off the needle.

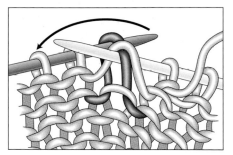

Purl stitch one row below
Insert the right needle through the back of the dropped stitch and then pick up the yarn strand in front of it. With the left needle, pass the stitch over the loop and off the needle.

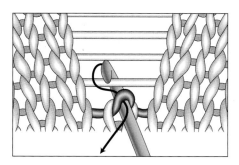

Stitch several rows below
If the stitch has run down a few rows, but no more than 4 rows, either repeat the instructions given for each row (making sure that you use the correct yarn strand for each row), or use a crochet hook. Insert the hook through the front of the dropped stitch, catch the yarn strand and pull through the stitch. Repeat for all the rows. For a purl stitch, work a knit stitch on the opposite side. If more than one stitch has been dropped, slip the others on to a safety pin to stop them running any further, while you pick them up one by one.
If you dropped a stitch and did not notice it until quite a few rows later, the only solution is to unravel your work back to that point. If you try to pick it up, the yarn strands will not be long enough to work the stitches to the correct tension. The picked up stitches will be tight and will show up badly.

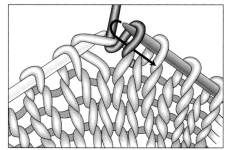

Unravelling one row
If the error occurred in stitches that you have just worked on the right needle. There is no need to take the work off the needle, just unravel, stitch-by-stitch, back to the error.

Insert the left needle into the stitch below from the front, drop the stitch off the right needle and pull the yarn. Repeat this for each stitch back to the error. Work in the same way for purl stitches.

✓ Knit Perfect

✓ When you spot an error quite a few rows back, mark the row with a coloured thread.

✓ If you are pulling back a complicated pattern, make a note of how many rows are pulled back and mark it on your pattern. Then you will start with the correct pattern row when you resume knitting.

✓ Put stitches back on to a size smaller needle, it will slip through the stitches easier. Remember to pick up the correct size needle when you start knitting.

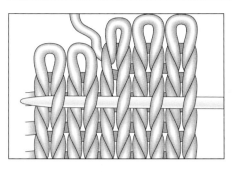

Unravelling several rows

Take the work off the needles, gather it up into one hand and unravel each row carefully to the row above the error. Do not be tempted to lay the work out flat to do this as the stitches are more likely to unravel beyond the row you are unravelling. Replace the stitches on to the needle and then unravel the last row as given left.

If you are using a slippery yarn or one that will not unravel easily, such as a hairy yarn, or if you are nervous about dropping stitches, you can pick up stitches in the row below the error before unravelling, as follows. Take a spare needle smaller than that used for the knitting and weave it through the first loop and over the second loop of each stitch on the row below the mistake (shown above).

If you are working a cable or lace pattern, pick the nearest row without too much patterning and where you can see the stitches clearly. Pull back the stitches above the spare needle. Slip the stitches back on to the correct size needles, making sure they are not twisted and lie correctly for the next row.

Split yarn

If you have split the yarn while working a stitch, go back and re-work it. The split yarn will show up on the surface of the work. Unravel the stitch by inserting the left-hand needle through the front, drop the stitch off the right-hand needle and pull the yarn. Rework the stitch with the yarn strand as given for dropped stitches.

Incomplete stitches

These occur where you have wrapped the yarn around the needle but it has not been pulled through the old stitch to form a new stitch. The yarn strand will be on the needle next to the unworked stitch. Work the stitch properly with the yarn strand as given for dropped stitches.

Colour patterns

If you have missed a few stitches or part of the pattern in a fair isle, use duplicate stitch to correct the errors (see page 85). If you have missed out a few rows or a whole section of pattern, either unravel the work back to the row before the error, or use the grafting method given right, and below in the Knit Perfect box.

Cables

It is easy to twist a cable the wrong way. If it was done in the previous few rows, unravel the cable stitches only and reknit by using the long loops of yarn released by unravelling. If the error is a long way down the piece or if by correcting it as above, it becomes really noticeable, it can only really be solved satisfactorily by unravelling the work back and reworking the whole piece again.

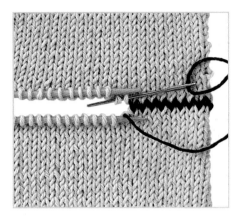

Grafting

Grafting is joining two sets of stitches by imitating a row of knitted stitches. It is often used in place of a seam, where a seam would show or be too bulky. It is easiest to work on stockinette (stocking) stitch. Use a tapestry needle and matching yarn. Two sets of stitches are left on needles.

1 Lay them edge to edge, and working from right to left, insert the tapestry needle from the back of the work through the first st on the lower edge.
2 Insert the tapestry needle from the back through the first stitch of the other edge and pull the yarn through.
3 Insert the tapestry needle into the first stitch of the lower edge again from front to back this time and then through the next stitch from back to front. Pull the yarn through.
4 Insert the tapestry needle into the first stitch of the upper edge again from front to back and then through the next stitch from back to front. Pull the yarn through. Continue as set, forming a row of new stitches, pulling the yarn through at the same gauge (tension) as the rest of the knitting.

✓ Knit Perfect

A mistake made in a fair isle panel can be altered through grafting, by reknitting the rows with the mistake. Thread a size smaller needle through the stitches of a one colour row above the mistake and another needle through the stitches of a one colour row below the mistake. Cut the yarn in the middle of the mistake row and pull back the knitting to the two needles. Your knitting will be in two pieces with the stitches caught on two needles. Knit the fair isle pattern rows up and the two sets of stitches can now be grafted together.

Stitch Library

This library of over 100 different stitches is presented in seven sections. The first section shows the great variety of fabrics that can be made simply by working knit and purl stitches (pages 89–96), beginning with moss stitch and including basketweave and check patterns, and on to stars and hearts. Next is a selection of traditional gansey or guernsey stitches (pages 97–100), which combine in panels to produce the famous fishermen's sweaters of the British Isles. Texture stitches follow (pages 101–5) to make your knitting three dimensional. The section on rib stitches (pages 106–7) presents lace ribs as well as ribs suitable for aran sweaters and brioche stitch which produces a thick, cosy fabric. A wide variety of cables is next (pages 108–16), ranging from simple four stitch cables to the more elaborate celtic cable and twisting vine cables. The next section of lace stitches (pages 117–24) includes traditional stitches used in Shetland shawls like Horseshoe lace and Crest of the Wave, as well as openwork leaves and diamonds. The final section is a selection of edgings (pages 125-7) from small delicate trims through to the wider and more open Cobweb frill, all of which can add a special finish to your knitting. Many of these stitches have been used in the projects but you can substitute others when you gain in experience.

KNIT SOMETHING NOW! ▶

Combine a variety of stitches from the stitch library to create a sampler cushion cover.

The **patchwork cushion** is knitted in worsted (DK) weight cotton yarn on size 6 (4mm/UK8) needles. See page 150 for pattern.

KNIT AND PURL STITCHES

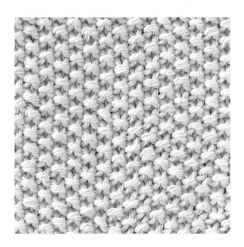

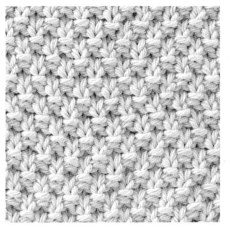

Moss Stitch (reversible)

On an odd number of stitches.
Row 1 K1, * p1, k1; rep from * to end.
Repeat this row.

On an even number of stitches.
Row 1 * K1, p1; rep from * to end.
Row 2 * P1, k1; rep from * to end.
Repeat these 2 rows.

Double Moss Stitch
(reversible)

On an odd number of stitches.
Row 1 K1, * p1, k1; rep from * to end.
Row 2 P1, * k1, p1; rep from * to end.
Row 3 As row 2.
Row 4 As row 1.
Repeat these 4 rows.

On an even number of stitches.
Row 1 * K1, p1; rep from * to end.
Row 2 As row 1.
Row 3 * P1, k1; rep from * to end.
Row 4 As row 3.
Repeat these 4 rows.

Double Moss Stitch and Rib Check (reversible)

Multiple of 12 sts plus 7.
Row 1 * (P1, k1) 3 times, p2, (k1, p1) twice; rep from * to last 7 sts, (p1, k1) 3 times, p1.
Row 2 K1, (p1, k1) 3 times, * (k1, p1) twice, k2, (p1, k1) 3 times; rep from * to end.
Row 3 P1, * k1, p1; rep from * to end.
Row 4 K1, * p1, k1; rep from * to end.
Row 5 As row 1.
Row 6 As row 2.
Row 7 * P2, k1, p1, k1, p2, (k1, p1) twice, k1; rep from * to last 7 sts, p2, k1, p1, k1, p2.
Row 8 K2, p1, k1, p1, k2, * (p1, k1) twice, p1, k2, p1, k1, p1, k2; rep from * to end.
Row 9 As row 3.
Row 10 As row 4.
Row 11 As row 7.
Row 12 As row 8.
Repeat these 12 rows.

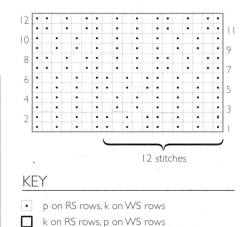

12 stitches

KEY

- • p on RS rows, k on WS rows
- ☐ k on RS rows, p on WS rows

Stitch library charts

Stitch charts have been included for most of the stitches in the library, apart from those where increasing and decreasing a number of stitches makes a chart difficult to follow.

You can use the stitch charts to design your own garments, work out increases and decreases in pattern (see page 74-5), design your own cable panels (see page 73) or put together gansey sweater designs. See page 63 for how to read charts.

KNIT AND PURL STITCHES

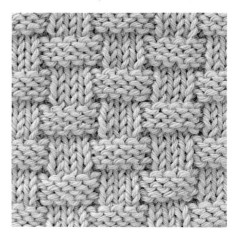

Two Stitch Check

(reversible)

Multiple of 4 sts plus 2.
Row 1 K2, * p2, k2; rep from * to end.
Row 2 P2, * k2, p2; rep from * to end.
Row 3 As row 2.
Row 4 As row 1.
Repeat these 4 rows.

Four Stitch Check

(reversible)

Multiple of 8 sts.
Rows 1, 2, 3 and 4 * K4, p4; rep from * to end.
Rows 5, 6, 7 and 8 * P4, k4; rep from * to end.
Repeat these 8 rows.

Basketweave

Multiple of 8 sts plus 5.
Row 1 (RS) Knit.
Row 2 * K5, p3; rep from * to last 5 sts, k5.
Row 3 P5, * k3, p5; rep from * to end.
Row 4 As row 2.
Row 5 Knit.
Row 6 K1, p3, k1, * k4, p3, k1; rep from * to end.
Row 7 * P1, k3, p4; rep from * to last 5 sts, p1, k3, p1.
Row 8 As row 6.
Repeat these 8 rows.

4 stitches

8 stitches

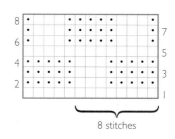

8 stitches

KEY

• p on RS rows, k on WS rows
□ k on RS rows, p on WS rows

KNIT AND PURL STITCHES

Double Basketweave

Multiple of 18 sts plus 10.
Row 1 (RS) Knit.
Row 2 P10, * p1, k2, p2, k2, p11; rep from * to end.
Row 3 * K1, p8, (k2, p2) twice, k1; rep from * to last 10 sts, k1, p8, k1.
Row 4 P1, k8, p1, * p1, (k2, p2) twice, k8, p1; rep from * to end.
Row 5 * K11, p2, k2, p2, k1; rep from * to last 10 sts, k10.
Row 6 As row 2.
Row 7 As row 3.
Row 8 As row 4.
Row 9 As row 5.
Row 10 Purl.
Row 11 * (K2, p2) twice, k10; rep from * to last 10 sts, k2, (p2, k2) twice.
Row 12 P2, (k2, p2) twice, * k8, p2, (k2, p2) twice; rep from * to end.
Row 13 * K2, (p2, k2) twice, p8; rep from * to last 10 sts, k2, (p2, k2) twice.
Row 14 P2, (k2, p2) twice, * p10, (k2, p2) twice; rep from * to end.
Row 15 As row 11.
Row 16 As row 12.
Row 17 As row 13.
Row 18 As row 14.
Repeat these 18 rows.

Pennant

Multiple of 7 sts plus 1.
Row 1 (RS) K1, * p1, k6; rep from * to end.
Row 2 * P5, k2; rep from * to last st, p1.
Row 3 K1, * p3, k4; rep from * to end.
Row 4 * P3, k4; rep from * to last st, p1.
Row 5 K1, * p5, k2; rep from * to end.
Row 6 P1, * k6, p1; rep from * to end.
Repeat these 6 rows.

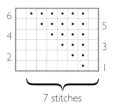

7 stitches

Pyramid

Multiple of 6 sts plus 1.
Row 1 (RS) * K1, p5; rep from * to last st, k1.
Row 2 P1, * k5, p1; rep from * to end.
Row 3 * K2, p3, k1; rep from * to last st, k1.
Row 4 P1, * p1, k3, p2; rep from * to end.
Row 5 * K3, p1, k2; rep from * to last st, k1.
Row 6 P1, * p2, k1, p3; rep from * to end.
Row 7 P3, k1, p2; rep from * to last st, p1.
Row 8 K1, * k2, p1, k3; rep from * to end.
Row 9 * P2, k3, p1; rep from * to last st, p1.
Row 10 K1, * k1, p3, k2; rep from * to end.
Row 11 * P1, k5; rep from * to last st, p1.
Row 12 K1, * p5, k1; rep from * to end.
Repeat these 12 rows.

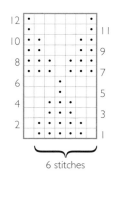

6 stitches

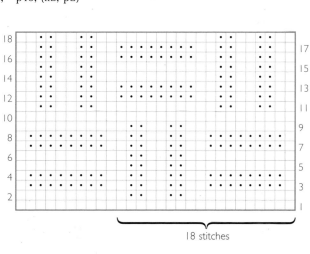

18 stitches

KEY

- • p on RS rows, k on WS rows
- ☐ k on RS rows, p on WS rows

KNIT AND PURL STITCHES

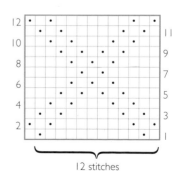

Moss Stitch Diamonds

Multiple of 6 sts plus 1.
Row 1 (RS) * K3, p1, k2; rep from * to last st, k1.
Row 2 P1, * (p1, k1) twice, p2; rep from * to end.
Rows 3, 4 and 5 * K1, p1; rep from * to last st, k1.
Row 6 As row 2.
Repeat these 6 rows.

Moss Stitch Rib

Multiple of 10 sts plus 1.
Row 1 (RS) * K4, p1, k1, p1, k3; rep from * to last st, k1.
Row 2 P1, * p2, (k1, p3) twice; rep from * to end.
Row 3 * K2, (p1, k1) 4 times; rep from * to last st, k1.
Row 4 P1, * k1, p1, k1, p3, (k1, p1) twice; rep from * to end.
Row 5 As row 3.
Row 6 As row 2.
Repeat these 6 rows.

King Charles Brocade

Multiple of 12 sts plus 1.
Row 1 (RS) *K1, p1, k9, p1; rep from * to last st, k1.
Row 2 K1, * p1, k1, p7, k1, p1, k1; rep from * to end.
Row 3 * (K1, p1) twice, k5, p1, k1, p1; rep from * to last st, k1.
Row 4 P1, * (p1, k1) twice, p3, k1, p1, k1, p2; rep from * to end.
Row 5 * K3, p1, (k1, p1) 3 times, k2; rep from * to last st, k1.
Row 6 P1, * p3, k1, (p1, k1) twice, p4; rep from * to end.
Row 7 * K5, p1, k1, p1, k4; rep from * to last st, k1.
Row 8 As row 6.
Row 9 As row 5.
Row 10 As row 4.
Row 11 As row 3.
Row 12 As row 2.
Repeat these 12 rows.

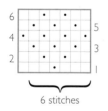

6 stitches

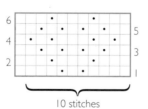

10 stitches

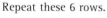

12 stitches

KEY

- p on RS rows, k on WS rows
- k on RS rows, p on WS rows

KNIT AND PURL STITCHES

Stepped Diamonds

Multiple of 12 sts plus 2.
Row 1 (RS) * P2, k10; rep from * to last 2 sts, p2.
Row 2 K2, * p10, k2; rep from * to end.
Row 3 * K2, p2, k6, p2; rep from * to last 2 sts, k2.
Row 4 P2, * k2, p6, k2, p2; rep from * to end.
Row 5 * K4, p2, k2, p2, k2; rep from * to last 2 sts, k2.
Row 6 P2, * (p2, k2) twice, p4; rep from * to end.
Row 7 * K6, p2, k4; rep from * to last 2 sts, k2.
Row 8 P2, * p4, k2, p6; rep from * to end.
Row 9 As row 5.
Row 10 As row 6.
Row 11 As row 3.
Row 12 As row 4.
Repeat these 12 rows.

Mock Cable

(reversible)

Multiple of 10 sts.
Row 1 * P4, k1, p1, k4; rep from * to end.
Row 2 *P3, k2, p2, k3; rep from * to end.
Row 3 * P2, k2, p1, k1, p2, k2; rep from * to end.
Row 4 * P1, (k2, p2) twice, k1; rep from * to end.
Row 5 * K2, p3, k3, p2; rep from * to end.
Row 6 * K1, p4, k4, p1; rep from * to end.
Repeat these 6 rows.

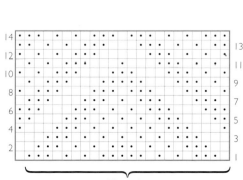

10 stitches

Moss Stitch Chevron

Multiple of 22 sts plus 1.
Row 1 (RS) * K1, p3, k1, (p1, k1) twice, p5, k1, (p1, k1) twice, p3; rep from * to last st, k1.
Row 2 P1, * p1, k3, p1, (k1, p1) twice, k3, p1, (k1, p1) twice, k3, p2; rep from * to end.
Row 3 * K3, p3, k1, (p1, k1) 5 times, p3, k2; rep from * to last st, k1.
Row 4 K1, * p3, k3, p1, (k1, p1) 4 times, k3, p3, k1; rep from * to end.
Row 5 * P2, k3, p3, k1, (p1, k1) 3 times, p3, k3, p1; rep from * to last st, p1.
Row 6 K1, * k2, p3, k3, p1, (k1, p1) twice, k3, p3, k3; rep from * to end.
Row 7 * K1, p3, k3, p3, k1, p1, k1, p3, k3, p3; rep from * to last st, k1.
Row 8 K1, * p1, k3, p3, k3, p1, k3, p3, k3, p1, k1; rep from * to end.
Row 9 * K1, p1, k1, p3, k3, p5, k3, p3, k1, p1; rep from * to last st, k1.
Row 10 K1, * p1, k1, p1, (k3, p3) twice, k3, (p1, k1) twice; rep from * to end.
Row 11 * K1, (p1, k1) twice, p3, k3, p1, k3, p3, (k1, p1) twice; rep from * to last st, k1.
Row 12 K1, * p1, (k1, p1) twice, k3, p5, k3, (p1, k1) 3 times; rep from * to end.
Row 13 * P2, k1, (p1, k1) twice, p3, k3, p3, (k1, p1) 3 times; rep from * to last st, p1.
Row 14 K1, * k2, p1, (k1, p1) twice, k3, p1, k3, p1, (k1, p1) twice, k3; rep from * to end.
Repeat these 14 rows.

KEY

•	p on RS rows, k on WS rows
☐	k on RS rows, p on WS rows

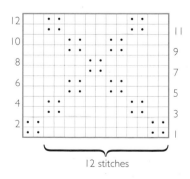

12 stitches

22 stitches

KNIT AND PURL STITCHES

Small Gingham

(reversible)

Multiple of 10 sts plus 5.
Row 1 * P5, k1, (p1, k1) twice; rep from * to last 5 sts, p5.
Row 2 K5, * (k1, p1) twice, k6; rep from * to end.
Rows 3 to 6 Repeat rows 1 and 2 twice more.
Row 7 * (k1, p1) twice, k6; rep from * to last 5 sts, (k1, p1) twice, k1.
Row 8 K1, (p1, k1) twice, * p5, k1, (p1, k1) twice; rep from * to end.
Rows 9 to 12 Repeat rows 7 and 8 twice more.
Repeat these 12 rows.

Gingham Check

Multiple of 14 sts plus 9.
Row 1 (RS) * (K1, p1) 4 times, k1, p5; rep from * to last 9 sts, (k1, p1) 4 times, k1.
Row 2 (K1, p1) 4 times, k1, * k6, (p1, k1) 4 times; rep from * to end.
Rows 3 to 5 Repeat rows 1 and 2 once more then row 1 again.
Row 6 P9, * (p1, k1) twice, p10; rep from * to end.
Row 7 * K9, (p1, k1) twice, p1; rep from * to last 9 sts, k9.
Rows 8 to 15 Repeat rows 6 and 7 four times more.
Row 16 As row 6.
Repeat these 16 rows.

Heart Squares

Multiple of 14 sts plus 1.
Row 1 (RS) * P1, k1; rep from * to last st, p1.
Row 2 Purl.
Row 3 * P1, k6; rep from * to last st, p1.
Row 4 P1, * p5, k3, p6; rep from * to end.
Row 5 * P1, k4, p2, k1, p2, k4; rep from * to last st, p1.
Row 6 P1, * (p3, k2) twice, p4; rep from * to end.
Row 7 * P1, k2, p2, k5, p2, k2; rep from * to last st, p1.
Row 8 P1, * p1, k2, p3, k1, p3, k2, p2; rep from * to end.
Row 9 * P1, k1, p2, k2, p3, k2, p2, k1; rep from * to last st, p1.
Row 10 P1, * p2, k4, p1, k4, p3; rep from * to end.
Row 11 * P1, (k3, p2) twice, k3; rep from * to last st, p1.
Row 12 Purl.
Repeat these 12 rows.

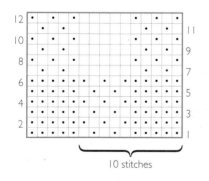

10 stitches

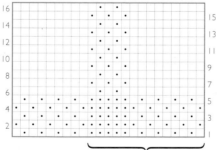

14 stitches

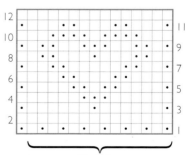

14 stitches

KEY

• p on RS rows, k on WS rows
☐ k on RS rows, p on WS rows

KNIT AND PURL STITCHES

Star in a Square

Multiple of 24 sts plus 1.
Row 1 (RS) * P1, k1; rep from * to last st, p1.
Row 2 Purl.
Row 3 * P1, k23; rep from * to last st, p1.
Row 4 P1, * (p7, k1) twice, p8; rep from * to end.
Row 5 * P1, k8, p1, k5, p1, k8; rep from * to last st, p1.
Row 6 P1, * p7, k1, p1, k1, p3, k1, p1, k1, p8; rep from * to end.
Row 7 * P1, k8, p1, (k1, p1) 3 times, k8; rep from * to last st, p1.
Row 8 P1, * p7, k1, (p1, k1) 4 times, p8; rep from * to end.

Row 9 * P1, k2, p1, (k1, p1) twice, k9, p1, (k1, p1) twice, k2; rep from * to last st, p1.
Row 10 P1, * p3, k1, p1, k1, p11, k1, p1, k1, p4; rep from * to end.
Row 11 * P1, k4, p1, k1, (p1, k4) twice, p1, k1, p1, k4; rep from * to last st, p1.
Row 12 P1, * p5, k1, p4, k3, p4, k1, p6; rep from * to end.
Row 13 * P1, k6, p1, k2, p5, k2, p1, k6; rep from * to last st, p1.
Row 14 As row 12
Row 15 As row 11.
Rows 16 to 23 Work from row 10 back to row 3.
Row 24 Purl.
Repeat these 24 rows.

Tumbling Blocks

Multiple of 10 sts.
Row 1 * K1, p1; rep from * to end.
Row 2 * P1, k1, p1, k2, p2, k1, p1, k1; rep from * to end.
Row 3 * K1, p1, k3, p3, k1, p1; rep from * to end.
Row 4 * P1, k4, p4, k1; rep from * to end.
Row 5 * K5, p5; rep from * to end.
Rows 6 to 8 Repeat row 5, 3 times more.
Row 9 * K4, p1, k1, p4; rep from * to end.
Row 10 * K3, (p1, k1) twice, p3; rep from * to end.
Row 11 * K2, (p1, k1) 3 times, p2; rep from * to end.
Row 12 * K1, p1; rep from * to end.
Row 13 * P1, k1; rep from * to end.
Row 14 * P2, (k1, p1) 3 times, k2; rep from * to end.
Row 15 * P3, (k1, p1) twice, k3; rep from * to end.
Row 16 * P4, k1, p1, k4; rep from * to end.
Row 17 * P5, k5; rep from * to end.
Rows 18 to 20 Repeat row 17, 3 times more.
Row 21 * K1, p4, k4, p1; rep from * to end.

Row 22 * P1, k1, p3, k3, p1, k1; rep from * to end.
Row 23 * K1, p1, k1, p2, k2, p1, k1, p1; rep from * to end.
Row 24 * P1, k1; rep from * to end.
Repeat these 24 rows.

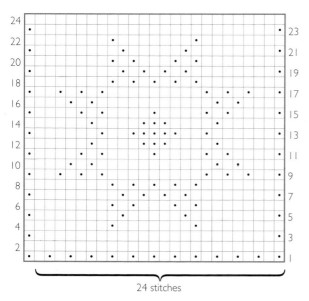

24 stitches

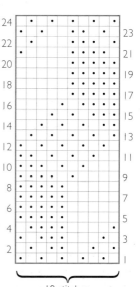

10 stitches

KNIT AND PURL STITCHES

Star in a Diamond

Multiple of 32 sts plus 1.

Row 1 (RS) * P1, (k1, p1) 3 times, k9, p1, k9, (p1, k1) 3 times; rep from * to last st, p1.

Row 2 P1, * k1, (p1, k1) 3 times, p7, k1, p1, k1, p7, (k1, p1) 4 times; rep from * to end.

Row 3 * P1, (k1, p1) 4 times, k5, p1, k3, p1, k5, (p1, k1) 4 times; rep from * to last st, p1.

Row 4 P1, * k1, (p1, k1) 4 times, p3, k1, p5, k1, p3, (k1, p1) 5 times; rep from * to end.

Row 5 * P1, (k1, p1) 6 times, k7, (p1, k1) 6 times; rep from * to last st, p1.

Row 6 P1, * k1, p1, k1, p7, k1, p9, k1, p7, (k1, p1) twice; rep from * to end.

Row 7 * P1, (k1, p1) twice, k5, p1, k1, p1, k7, p1, k1, p1, k5, (p1, k1) twice; rep from * to last st, p1.

Row 8 P1, * k1, p1, k1, p5, k1, p3, k1, p5, k1, p3, k1, p5, (k1, p1) twice; rep from * to end.

Row 9 * K2, p1, k1, p1, (k3, p1) twice, k1, p1, k3, p1, k1, (p1, k3) twice, (p1, k1) twice; rep from * to last st, k1.

Row 10 P1, * p2, k1, p3, k1, p5, (k1, p1) 3 times, k1, p5, (k1, p3) twice; rep from * to end.

Row 11 * K4, p1, k1, p1, k5, p1, (k1, p1) 4 times, k5, p1, k1, p1, k3; rep from * to last st, k1.

Row 12 P1, * p4, k1, p7, k1, (p1, k1) 3 times, p7, k1, p5; rep from * to end.

Row 13 * K4, p1, (k1, p1) 12 times, k3; rep from * to last st, k1.

Row 14 P1, * p2, k1, p3, k1, (p1, k1) 9 times, p3, k1, p3; rep from * to end.

Row 15 * K2, p1, k5, p1, (k1, p1) 8 times, k5, p1, k1; rep from * to last st, k1.

Row 16 P1, * k1, p7, k1, (p1, k1) 7 times, p7, k1, p1; rep from * to end.

Row 17 * P1, k9, p1, (k1, p1) 6 times, k9; rep from * to last st, p1.

Row 18 As row 16.

Row 19 As row 15.

Rows 20 to 32 Work from row 14 back to row 2.

Repeat these 32 rows.

Block Quilting

Multiple of 14 sts.

Row 1 (RS) * K4, p6, k4; rep from * to end.

Row 2 Purl.

Rows 3 and 4 Repeat rows 1 and 2 once more.

Row 5 As row 1.

Row 6 * P3, k2, p4, k2, p3; rep from * to end.

Row 7 * K2, p2, k6, p2, k2; rep from * to end.

Row 8 * P1, k2, p8, k2, p1; rep from * to end.

Row 9 * P2, k10, p2; rep from * to end.

Row 10 As row 8.

Row 11 As row 7.

Row 12 As row 6.

Repeat these 12 rows.

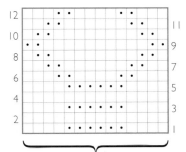

14 stitches

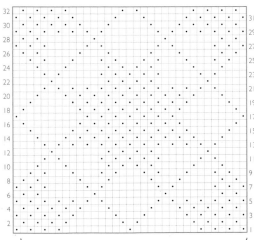

32 stitches

KEY

•   p on RS rows, k on WS rows

☐   k on RS rows, p on WS rows

GANSEY PATTERNS

Moss Stitch Ladder

Panel of 5 sts.
Row 1 (RS) P1, (k1, p1) twice.
Row 2 K5.
Repeat these 2 rows.

Two Stitch Ladder

Panel of 8 sts.
Row 1 (RS) P1, k1, p1, k2, p1, k1, p1.
Row 2 K1, p1, k1, p2, k1, p1, k1.
Row 3 P1, k1, p4, k1, p1.
Row 4 K1, p1, k4, p1, k1.
Repeat these 4 rows.

Ladder Stitch

Panel of 10 sts.
Row 1 (RS) P1, k8, p1.
Row 2 K1, p8, k1.
Row 3 P10.
Row 4 As row 2.
Repeat these 4 rows.

Panel of 5 stitches

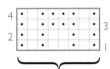

Panel of 8 stitches

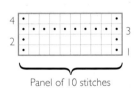

Panel of 10 stitches

Using gansey patterns

Gansey, Guernsey and Jersey are all names for the traditional sweater of fishermen of the British Isles. The stitches are worked in panels, either beginning above the rib or halfway up the body to form a yoke.

Simple ganseys have a repeat pattern of one wide panel, such as Inverness Diamond (page 100), and one narrow panel, such as Two Stitch Ladder (above).

More complicated patterns can be made by adding more narrow and wide panels to the repeat. Often ganseys will have a panel of a single four stitch cable to add more texture.

Patterns like Anchor (page 98), Tree (page 99) and Humber Star (page 100) can be separated by ridges of reverse stockinette (stocking) stitch to form squares.

KEY

⋅ p on RS rows, k on WS rows
☐ k on RS rows, p on WS rows

GANSEY PATTERNS

Anchor

Panel of 17 sts.
Row 1 (RS) K8, p1, k8.
Row 2 P7, k1, p1, k1, p7.
Row 3 K6, (p1, k1) twice, p1, k6.
Row 4 (P5, k1) twice, p5.
Row 5 K4, (p1, k3) twice, p1, k4.
Row 6 P3, k1, p9, k1, p3.
Row 7 K2, (p1, k5) twice, p1, k2.
Row 8 (P1, k1) twice, p9, (k1, p1) twice.
Row 9 K2, (p1, k5) twice, p1, k2.
Row 10 P1, k1, p13, k1, p1.
Row 11 K8, p1, k8.
Row 12 Purl.
Rows 13 and 14 Repeat rows 11 and 12 once more.
Row 15 K4, (p1, k1) 4 times, p1, k4.
Row 16 Purl.
Row 17 As row 1.
Row 18 As row 2.
Row 19 As row 1.
Row 20 Purl.
Row 21 Knit.
Row 22 Purl.
Repeat these 22 rows or work rows 1 to 20 for single motif.

Flags

Panel of 7 sts.
Row 1 (RS) K5, p1, k1.
Row 2 P1, k2, p4.
Row 3 K3, p3, k1.
Row 4 P1, k4, p2.
Row 5 K1, p5, k1.
Row 6 As row 4.
Row 7 As row 3.
Row 8 As row 2.
Repeat these 8 rows.

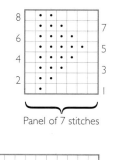

Panel of 7 stitches

Lightning

Panel of 8 sts.
Row 1 (RS) K1, p2, k5.
Row 2 P4, k2, p2.
Row 3 K3, p2, k3.
Row 4 P2, k2, p4.
Row 5 K5, p2, k1.
Row 6 As row 4.
Row 7 As row 3.
Row 8 As row 2.
Repeat these 8 rows.

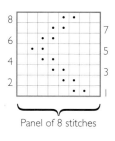

Panel of 8 stitches

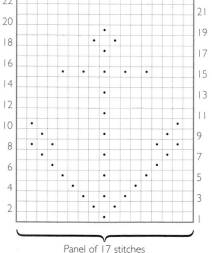

Panel of 17 stitches

KEY

 p on RS rows, k on WS rows
☐ k on RS rows, p on WS rows

GANSEY PATTERNS

Marriage Lines

Panel of 11 sts.
Row 1 (RS) (K1, p1) twice, k7.
Row 2 P6, k1, p1, k1, p2.
Row 3 K3, p1, k1, p1, k5.
Row 4 P4, k1, p1, k1, p4.
Row 5 K5, p1, k1, p1, k3.
Row 6 P2, k1, p1, k1, p6.
Row 7 K7, (p1, k1) twice.
Row 8 As row 6.
Row 9 As row 5.
Row 10 As row 4.
Row 11 As row 3.
Row 12 As row 2.
Repeat these 12 rows.

Full Diamonds

Panel of 15 sts.
Row 1 (RS) K6, p3, k6.
Row 2 P5, k5, p5.
Row 3 K4, p7, k4.
Row 4 P3, k9, p3.
Row 5 K2, p11, k2.
Row 6 P1, k13, p1.
Row 7 As row 5.
Row 8 As row 4.
Row 9 As row 3.
Row 10 As row 2.
Repeat these 10 rows.

Tree

Panel of 13 sts.
Row 1 (RS) K6, p1, k6.
Row 2 P5, k1, p1, k1, p5.
Row 3 K4, p1, k3, p1, k4.
Row 4 P3, (k1, p2) twice, k1, p3.
Row 5 (K2, p1) twice, k1, (p1, k2) twice.
Row 6 P1, k1, p2, k1, p3, k1, p2, k1, p1.
Row 7 K3, (p1, k2) twice, p1, k3.
Row 8 (P2, k1) twice, p1, (k1, p2) twice.
Row 9 As row 3.
Row 10 As row 4.
Row 11 K5, p1, k1, p1, k5.
Row 12 P4, k1, p3, k1, p4.
Row 13 As row 1.
Row 14 As row 2.
Row 15 As row 1.
Row 16 Purl.
Row 17 Knit.
Row 18 Purl.
Repeat these 18 rows or work rows 1 to 16 for single motif.

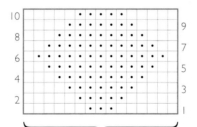

Panel of 15 stitches

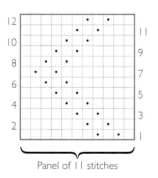

Panel of 11 stitches

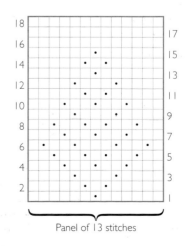

Panel of 13 stitches

KEY

• p on RS rows, k on WS rows
☐ k on RS rows, p on WS rows

GANSEY PATTERNS

Inverness Diamonds

Panel of 17 sts.
Row 1 (RS) K7, p3, k7.
Row 2 P6, k5, p6.
Row 3 K5, p3, k1, p3, k5.
Row 4 P4, k3, p3, k3, p4.
Row 5 K3, p3, k5, p3, k3.
Row 6 P2, k3, p7, k3, p2.
Row 7 K1, p3, k9, p3, k1.
Rows 8 to 12 Work from row 6
back to row 2.
Repeat these 12 rows.

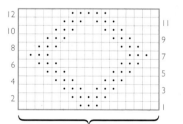

Panel of 17 stitches

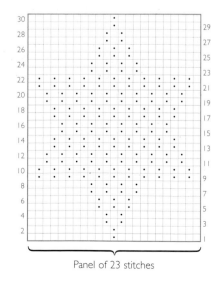

Panel of 23 stitches

Humber Star

Panel of 23 sts.
Row 1 (RS) K11, p1, k11.
Row 2 P11, k1, p11.
Row 3 K10, p1, k1, p1, k10.
Row 4 P10, k1, k1, k1, p10.
Row 5 K9, p1, (k1, p1) twice, k9.
Row 6 P9, k1, (p1, k1) twice, p9.
Row 7 K8, p1, (k1, p1) 3 times, k8.
Row 8 P8, k1, (p1, k1) 3 times, p8.
Row 9 K1, (p1, k1) 11 times.
Row 10 P1, (k1, p1) 11 times.
Row 11 K2, p1, (k1, p1) 9 times, k2.
Row 12 P2, k1, (p1, k1) 9 times, p2.
Row 13 K3, p1, (k1, p1) 8 times, k3.
Row 14 P3, k1, (p1, k1) 8 times, p3.
Row 15 K4, p1, (k1, p1) 7 times, k4.
Row 16 P4, k1, (p1, k1) 7 times, p4.
Row 17 As row 13.
Row 18 As row 14.
Row 19 As row 11.
Row 20 As row 12.
Row 21 As row 9.
Row 22 As row 10.
Row 23 As row 7.
Row 24 As row 8.
Row 25 As row 5.
Row 26 As row 6.
Row 27 As row 3.
Row 28 As row 4.
Row 29 As row 1.
Row 30 As row 2.
Repeat these 30 rows.

KEY

- • p on RS rows, k on WS rows
- ☐ k on RS rows, p on WS rows

Double Moss Stitch Diamond

Panel of 13 sts.
Row 1 (RS) K6, p1, k6.
Row 2 P6, k1, p6.
Row 3 K5, p1, k1, p1, k5.
Row 4 P5, k1, p1, k1, p5.
Row 5 K4, p1, (k1, p1) twice, k4.
Row 6 P4, k1, (p1, k1) twice, p4.
Row 7 K3, p1, (k1, p1) 3 times, k3.
Row 8 P3, k1, (p1, k1) 3 times, p3.
Row 9 K2, p1, k1, p1, k3, p1, k1, p1, k2.
Row 10 P2, k1, p1, k1, p3, k1, p1, k1, p2.
Row 11 (K1, p1) twice, k5, (p1, k1) twice.
Row 12 (P1, k1) twice, p5, (k1, p1) twice.
Row 13 As row 9.
Row 14 As row 10.
Row 15 As row 7.
Row 16 As row 8.
Row 17 As row 5.
Row 18 As row 6.
Row 19 As row 3.
Row 20 As row 4.
Repeat these 20 rows.

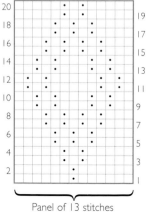

Panel of 13 stitches

TEXTURE STITCHES

Ruching

On an odd number of stitches.
Row 1 (RS) Knit.
Row 2 Purl.
Rows 3 and 4 Repeat rows 1 and 2 once more.
Row 5 K1, * k into front and back of next st, k1; rep from * to end.
Row 6 Knit.
Row 7 Purl.
Rows 8 to 12 Repeat rows 6 and 7 twice more, then row 6 again.
Row 13 P1, * p2tog, p1; rep from * to end.
Row 14 Knit.
Repeat these 14 rows.

Bubble Pattern

Multiple of 10 sts plus 2.
Row 1 (RS) Knit.
Row 2 Purl.
Row 3 K1, * (k5, turn, p5, turn) 3 times, k10; rep from * to end, ending last rep with k1.
Row 4 Purl.
Row 5 Knit.
Row 6 Purl.
Row 7 K6, * (k5, turn, p5, turn) 3 times, k10; rep from * to last st, k1.
Row 8 Purl.
Repeat these 8 rows.

Textured Picot Stripe

Abbreviation:
M7 – (k1, yfwd, k1, yfwd, k1, yfwd, k1) all into next st.

Multiple of 8 sts plus 5 (stitch count varies).
Row 1 (RS) K2, * M7, k7; rep from * to last 3 sts, M7, k2.
Row 2 Knit.
Row 3 K1, * k2tog, k5, ssk, k5; rep from * to last 10 sts, k2tog, k5, ssk, k1.
Row 4 P1, * ssp, p1, sl 1 wyif, p1, p2tog, p5; rep from * to last 8 sts, ssp, p1, sl 1 wyif, p1, p2tog, p1.
Row 5 K1, * k2tog, sl 1 wyib, ssk, k5; rep from * to last 6 sts, k2tog, sl 1 wyib, ssk, k1.
Row 6 Purl.
Row 7 K2, * k4, M7, k3; rep from * to last 3 sts, k3.
Row 8 Knit.
Row 9 K2, * k3, k2tog, k5, ssk, k2; rep from * to last 3 sts, k3.
Row 10 P3, * p2, ssp, p1, sl 1 wyif, p1, p2tog, p3; rep from * to last 2 sts, p2.
Row 11 K2, * k3, k2tog, sl 1 wyib, ssk, k2; rep from * to last 3 sts, k3.
Row 12 Purl.
Repeat these 12 rows.

TEXTURE STITCHES

Popcorn Pattern

Abbreviations:

MK – purl next 3 sts then pass 2nd and 3rd sts over first st.

MS – (k1, p1, k1) all into next st.

Multiple of 4 sts plus 3 (stitch count varies).
Row 1 (RS) Knit.
Row 2 P1, MS, p1, * p2, MS, p1; rep from * to end.
Row 3 * K1, MK, k2; rep from * to last 5 sts, k1, MK, k1.
Row 4 Purl.
Row 5 Knit.
Row 6 P3, * MS, p3; rep from * to end.
Row 7 * K3, MK; rep from * to last 3 sts, k3.
Row 8 Purl.
Repeat these 8 rows.

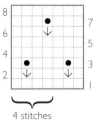

4 stitches

Bramble Stitch

Abbreviation:

MS – (k1, p1, k1) all into next st.

Multiple of 4 sts plus 2.
Row 1 (RS) Purl.
Row 2 K1, * MS, p3tog; rep from * to last st, k1.
Row 3 Purl.
Row 4 K1, * p3tog, MS; rep from * to last st, k1.
Repeat these 4 rows.

4 stitches

Smocking

Abbreviation:

smocking st – insert RH needle from front between 6th and 7th sts, wrap yarn around needle and draw through a loop, sl this loop on to LH needle and k tog with first st on LH needle.

Multiple of 16 sts plus 2.
Row 1 (RS) P2, * k2, p2; rep from * to end.
Row 2 * K2, p2; rep from * to last 2 sts, k2.
Row 3 P2, * smocking st, k1, p2, k2, p2; rep from * to end.
Rows 4 and 6 As row 2.
Row 5 As row 1.
Row 7 P2, k2, p2, * smocking st, k1, p2, k2, p2; rep from * to last 4 sts, k2, p2.
Row 8 As row 2.
Repeat these 8 rows.

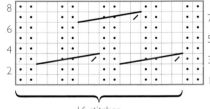

16 stitches

KEY

● MK
↓ MS
□ k on RS rows, p on WS rows

KEY

↑ p3tog
↓ MS
· p on RS rows, k on WS rows

KEY

· p on RS rows, k on WS rows
□ k on RS rows, p on WS rows
 k2tog
 smocking stitch

TEXTURE STITCHES

Smocked Honeycomb

Abbreviation:

tie st – sl next 5 sts on to cable needle, wrap yarn around these 5 sts twice, then k1, p3, k1 from cable needle.

Multiple of 16 sts plus 3.
Row 1 (RS) P3, * k1, p3; rep from * to end.
Row 2 * K3, p1; rep from * to last 3 sts, k3.
Row 3 P3, * tie st, p3; rep from * to end.
Rows 4 and 6 As row 2.
Row 5 As row 1.
Row 7 P3, k1, * p3, tie st; rep from * to end, ending last rep with k1, p3.
Row 8 As row 2.
Repeat these 8 rows.

Boxed Bobble

Abbreviation:

MB – k into front, back and front of next st and turn, k3 and turn, p3 and pass 2nd and 3rd sts over first st.

Multiple of 6 sts plus 1.
Row 1 (RS) Purl.
Row 2 and every foll alt row Purl.
Row 3 P1, * k5, p1; rep from * to end.
Row 5 P1, * k2, MB, k2, p1; rep from * to end.
Row 7 As row 3.
Row 8 Purl.
Repeat these 8 rows.

Gooseberry Stitch

Abbreviation:

M5 – (p1, yo, p1, yo, p1) all into next st.

Multiple of 4 sts plus 1.
Row 1 (RS) Knit.
Row 2 K1, * M5, k1; rep from * to end.
Row 3 Purl.
Row 4 K1, * sl 2 wyif, p3tog, psso, k1; rep from * to end.
Row 5 Knit.
Row 6 K1, * k1, M5, k1; rep from * to last st, k1.
Row 7 Purl.
Row 8 K1, * k1, sl 2 wyif, p3tog, psso, k1; rep from * to last st, k1.
Repeat these 8 rows.

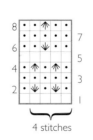

16 stitches

6 stitches

4 stitches

KEY

- • p on RS rows, k on WS rows
- ☐ k on RS rows, p on WS rows
- — tie stitch

KEY

- ■ MB
- • p on RS rows, k on WS rows
- ☐ k on RS rows, p on WS rows

KEY

- ⬆ sl 2 wyif, p3tog, psso
- ⬇ M5
- • p on RS rows, k on WS rows
- ☐ k on RS rows, p on WS rows

TEXTURE STITCHES

Dimple Stitch

Abbreviation:
gathering st – take yarn to back of work as though to knit, insert needle from below under 3 strands, k the next st, bring the st out under the strands.

Multiple of 6 sts plus 5.
Row 1 (RS) Knit.
Row 2 P1, * sl 3 wyif, p3; rep from * to end, ending last rep with p1.
Row 3 K1, * sl 3 wyib, k3; rep from * to end, ending last rep with k1.

Row 4 As row 2.
Rows 5 and 7 Knit.
Row 6 Purl.
Row 8 P2, * gathering st, p5; rep from * to end, ending last rep with p2.
Row 9 Knit.
Row 10 P1, * p3, sl 3 wyif; rep from * to last 4 sts, p4.
Row 11 K4, * sl 3 wyif, k3; rep from * to last st, k1.
Row 12 As row 10.
Rows 13 and 15 Knit.
Row 14 Purl.
Row 16 P5, * gathering st, p5; rep from * to end.
Repeat these 16 rows.

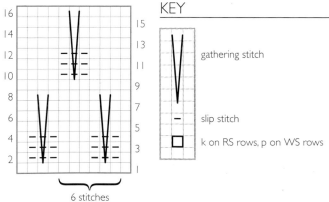

6 stitches

KEY

gathering stitch

slip stitch

k on RS rows, p on WS rows

Bobble Circle Pattern

Abbreviation:
MS – (k1, p1, k1) all into next st.

Multiple of 12 sts plus 3.
Row 1 (RS) Knit.
Row 2 * P6, MS, p1, MS, p3; rep from * to last 3 sts, p3.
Row 3 K3, * k3, p3, k1, p3, k6; rep from * to end.
Row 4 * P4, MS, (p1, p3tog) twice, p1, MS, p1; rep from * to last 3 sts, p3.
Row 5 K3, * k1, p3, k5, p3, k4; rep from * to end.
Row 6 * P3, MS, p3tog, p5, p3tog, MS; rep from * to last 3 sts, p3.

Row 7 K3, * p3, k7, p3, k3; rep from * to end.
Row 8 * P3, p3tog, p7, p3tog; rep from * to last 3 sts, p3.
Row 9 Knit.
Row 10 * P3, MS, p7, MS; rep from * to last 3 sts, p3.
Row 11 As row 7.
Row 12 * P3, p3tog, MS, p5, MS, p3tog; rep from * to last 3 sts, p3.
Row 13 As row 5.
Row 14 * P4, p3tog, (p1, MS) twice, p1, p3tog, p1; rep from * to last 3 sts, p3.
Row 15 As row 3.
Row 16 * P6, p3tog, p1, p3tog, p3; rep from * to last 3 sts, p3.
Row 17 Knit.
Row 18 Purl.
Repeat these 18 rows.

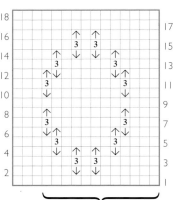

12 stitches

KEY

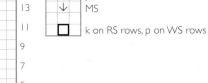

↑ p3tog
3 p3
↓ MS

☐ k on RS rows, p on WS rows

TEXTURE STITCHES

Cocoon Stitch

Abbreviation:
M5 – (p1, yo, p1, yo, p1) all into next st.

Multiple of 8 sts plus 7.
Row 1 (RS) * K1, p5, k1, p1; rep from *
to last 7 sts, k1, p5, k1.
Row 2 P1, sl 2 wyif, p3tog, psso, p1, *
M5, p1, sl 2 wyif, p3tog, psso, p1; rep
from * to end.
Rows 3, 5 and 7 * K1, p1, k1, p5; rep
from * to last 3 sts, k1, p1, k1.
Rows 4 and 6 P1, k1, p1, * k5, p1, k1,
p1; rep from * to end.
Row 8 P1, M5, p1, * sl 2 wyif, p3tog,
psso, p1, M5, p1; rep from * to end.
Row 9 As row 1.
Row 10 P1, k5, p1, * k1, p1, k5, p1; rep
from * to end.
Row 11 As row 1.
Row 12 As row 10.
Repeat these 12 rows.

Blind Buttonhole Stitch

Multiple of 8 sts plus 6.
Row 1 (WS) Knit.
Row 2 Purl.
Rep these 2 rows once more then row 1
again.
Row 6 K1, * sl 4 wyib, k4; rep from * to
last 5 sts, sl 4 wyib, k1.
Row 7 P1, sl 4 wyif, * p4, sl 4 wyif; rep
from * to last st, p1.
Rep these 2 rows once more then row 6
again.
Row 11 Knit.
Row 12 Purl.
Rep these 2 rows once more then row 11
again.
Row 16 K5, * sl 4 wyib, k4; rep from * to
last st, k1.
Row 17 P5, * sl 4 wyif, p4; rep from * to
last st, p1.
Rep these 2 rows once more.
Row 20 As row 16.
Repeat these 20 rows.

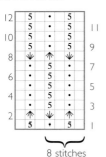

KEY

8 stitches

5	p5 on RS rows, k5 on WS rows
	sl 2 wyif, p3tog, psso
	M5
·	p on RS rows, k on WS rows
□	k on RS rows, p on WS rows

RIB STITCHES

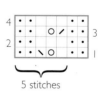

Mistake Rib

Multiple of 4 sts plus 3.
Row 1 * K2, p2; rep from * to last 3 sts, k2, p1.
Repeat this row.

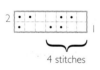

4 stitches

KEY

- • p on RS rows, k on WS rows
- ☐ k on RS rows, p on WS rows

Rick Rack Rib

Abbreviations:
twist k – take RH needle behind first st and k into back of second st, k first st, slip both sts off LH needle.
twist p – with yarn in front, miss first st and p into second st, p first st, sl both sts off LH needle together.

Multiple of 5 sts plus 1.
Row 1 (RS) K1, * p1, twist k, p1, k1; rep from * to end.
Row 2 * P1, k1, twist p, k1; rep from * to last st, p1.
Repeat these 2 rows.

5 stitches

KEY

⋈	twist k
⋎	twist p
•	p on RS rows, k on WS rows
☐	k on RS rows, p on WS rows

Openwork Rib

Multiple of 5 sts plus 2.
Row 1 (RS) P2, * k1, yo, ssk, p2; rep from * to end.
Row 2 * K2, p3; rep from * to last 2 sts, k2.
Row 3 P2, * k2tog, yo, k1, p2; rep from * to end.
Row 4 As row 2.
Repeat these 4 rows.

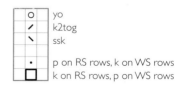

5 stitches

KEY

O	yo
╱	k2tog
╲	ssk
•	p on RS rows, k on WS rows
☐	k on RS rows, p on WS rows

RIB STITCHES

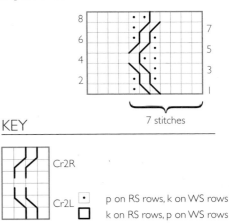

Brioche Stitch

Even number of sts.
Foundation row * Yo, sl 1 wyib, k1; rep from * to end.
Row 1 * Yo, sl 1 wyib, k2tog (sl st and yo of previous row); rep from * to end.
Repeat row 1.

Aran Rib 1

Abbreviation:
Cr3L – slip 1 st on to cable needle at front, k1 tbl, p1, then k1 tbl from cable needle.

Multiple of 8 sts plus 3.
Row 1 (RS) * K3, (p1, k1 tbl) twice, p1; rep from * to last 3 sts, k3.
Row 2 P3, * (k1, p1 tbl) twice, k1; rep from * to end.
Row 3 * K3, p1, Cr3L, p1; rep from * to last 3 sts, k3.
Row 5 As row 1.
Row 6 As row 2.
Repeat these 6 rows.

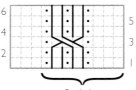

KEY

Cr3L

· p on RS rows, k on WS rows
□ k on RS rows, p on WS rows

Aran Rib 2

Abbreviations:
Cr2L – slip 1 st on to cable needle at front, p1, k1 tbl from cable needle.
Cr2R – slip 1 st on to cable needle at back, k1 tbl, p1 from cable needle.

Multiple of 7 sts plus 4.
Row 1 (RS) * K4, Cr2L, p1; rep from * to last 4 sts, k4.
Row 2 P4, * k1, p1 tbl, k1, p4; rep from * to end.
Row 3 * K4, p1, Cr2L; rep from * to last 4 sts, k4.
Row 4 P4, * p1 tbl, k2, p4; rep from * to end.
Row 5 * K4, p1, Cr2R; rep from * to last 4 sts, k4.
Row 6 As row 2.
Row 7 * K4, Cr2R, p1; rep from * to last 4 sts, k4.
Row 8 P4, * k2, p1 tbl, p4; rep from * to end.
Repeat these 8 rows.

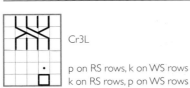

KEY

Cr2R

Cr2L

· p on RS rows, k on WS rows
□ k on RS rows, p on WS rows

CABLE STITCHES

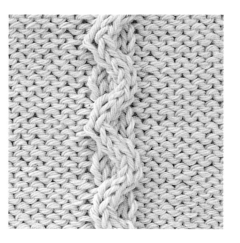

Four Stitch Cable

(crossed every 4th row)

Abbreviation:

C4F – sl 2 sts on to cable needle at front, k2, k2 from cable needle.

Panel of 4 sts on rev st st.
Row 1 (RS) K4.
Row 2 P4.
Row 3 C4F.
Row 4 P4.
Repeat these 4 rows.

Four Stitch Cable

(crossed every 6th row)

Abbreviation: C4F – sl 2 sts on to cable needle at front, k2, k2 from cable needle.

Panel of 4 sts on rev st st.
Rows 1 and 3 (RS) K4.
Rows 2 and 4 P4.
Row 5 C4F.
Row 6 P4.
Repeat these 6 rows.

To cross the cable to the right work C4B instead of C4F.

Abbreviation:

C4B – sl 2 sts on to cable needle at back, k2, k2 from cable needle.

Six Stitch Cable

(crossed every 6th row)

Abbreviation:

C6F – sl 3 sts on to cable needle at front, k3, k3 from cable needle.

Panel of 6 sts on rev st st.
Rows 1 and 3 (RS) K6.
Row 2 and every foll WS row P6.
Row 5 C6F.
Row 6 P6.
Repeat these 6 rows.

Six Stitch Cable

(crossed every 8th row)

Abbreviation:

C6F – sl 3 sts on to cable needle at front, k3, k3 from cable needle.

Panel of 6 sts on rev st st.
Rows 1, 3 and 5 (RS) K6.
Row 2 and every foll WS row P6.
Row 7 C6F.
Row 8 P6.
Repeat these 8 rows.

To cross the cable to the right work C6B instead of C6F.

Abbreviation:

C6B – sl 3 sts on to cable needle at back, k3, k3 from cable needle.

Four Stitch Wave Cable

Abbreviations:

C4F – sl 2 sts on to cable needle at front, k2, k2 from cable needle.
C4B – sl 2 sts on to cable needle at back, k2, k2 from cable needle.

Panel of 4 sts on rev st st.
Rows 1 and 5 (RS) K4.
Row 2 and every foll WS row P4.
Row 3 C4F.
Row 7 C4B.
Row 8 P4.
Repeat these 8 rows.

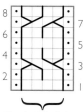

Panel of 4 stitches

KEY

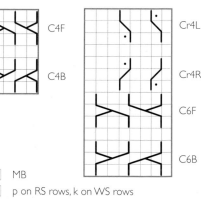

■ MB

• p on RS rows, k on WS rows

☐ k on RS rows, p on WS rows

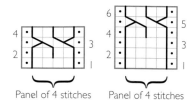

Panel of 4 stitches   Panel of 4 stitches

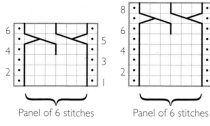

Panel of 6 stitches   Panel of 6 stitches

CABLE STITCHES

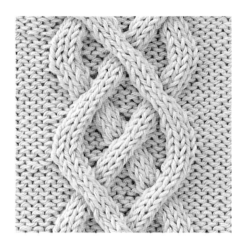

Ensign's Braid

Abbreviations:

Cr4L – sl 3 sts on to cable needle at front, p1, k3 from cable needle.
Cr4R – sl 1 st on to cable needle at back, k3, p1 from cable needle.
C6F – sl 3 sts on to cable needle at front, k3, k3 from cable needle.
C6B – sl 3 sts on to cable needle at back, k3, k3 from cable needle.

Panel of 20 sts on rev st st.
Row 1 (RS) K3, p4, C6B, p4, k3.
Row 2 and every foll WS row K all k sts and p all p sts.
Row 3 (Cr4L, p2, Cr4R) twice.
Row 5 (P1, Cr4L, Cr4R, p1) twice.
Row 7 P2, C6F, p4, C6B, p2.
Row 9 (P1, Cr4R, Cr4L, p1) twice.
Row 11 (Cr4R, p2, Cr4L) twice.
Row 13 K3, p4, C6F, p4, k3.
Row 15 As row 3.
Row 17 As row 5.
Row 19 P2, C6B, p4, C6F, p2.
Row 21 As row 9.
Row 23 As row 11.
Row 24 (P3, k4, p3) twice.
Repeat these 24 rows.

Oxo Cable

Abbreviations:

C4F – sl 2 sts on to cable needle at front, k2, k2 from cable needle.
C4B – sl 2 sts on to cable needle at back, k2, k2 from cable needle.

Panel of 8 sts on rev st st.
Row 1 (RS) K8.
Row 2 P8.
Row 3 C4B, C4F.
Row 4 P8.
Rows 5 to 8 As rows 1 to 4.
Row 9 K8.
Row 10 P8.
Row 11 C4F, C4B.
Row 12 P8.
Rows 13 to 16 As rows 9 to 12.
Repeat these 16 rows.

Medallion Bobble Cable

Abbreviation:

MB – (k1, p1) twice into next st and turn, p4 and turn, k4 and turn, (p2tog) twice and turn, k2tog.
C6F – sl 3 sts on to cable needle at front, k3, k3 from cable needle.
C6B – sl 3 sts on to cable needle at back, k3, k3 from cable needle.

Panel of 15 sts.
Rows 1, 3, 7, 11 and 15 (RS) P1, k13, p1.
Row 2 and every foll WS row K1, p13, k1.
Row 5 P1, C6B, k1, C6F, p1.
Row 9 P1, k6, MB, k6, p1.
Row 13 P1, C6F, k1, C6B, p1.
Row 16 As row 2.
Repeat these 16 rows.

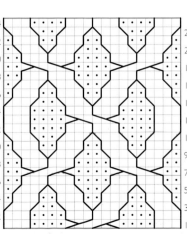

Panel of 20 stitches

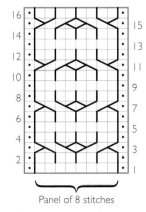

Panel of 8 stitches

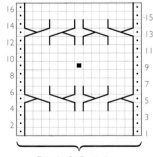

Panel of 15 stitches

109

CABLE STITCHES

Five Rib Braid

Abbreviations:

C5F – sl 3 sts on to cable needle at front, k2, sl p st back on to LH needle and p it, k2 from cable needle.

C5B – sl 3 sts on to cable needle at back, k2, sl p st back on to LH needle and p it, k2 from cable needle.

Panel of 18 sts on rev st st.
Row 1 (RS) P2, (k2, p1) 5 times, p1.
Row 2 and every foll WS row K2, (p2, k1) 5 times, k1.
Row 3 P2, k2, (p1, C5F) twice, p2.
Row 5 As row 1.
Row 7 P2, (C5B, p1) twice, k2, p2.
Row 8 As row 2.
Repeat these 8 rows.

Celtic Cable

Abbreviations:

Cr3L – sl 2 sts on to cable needle at front, p1, k2 from cable needle.

Cr3R – sl 1 st on to cable needle at back, k2, p1 from cable needle.

Cr4L – sl 2 sts on to cable needle at front, p2, k2 from cable needle.

Cr4R – sl 2 sts on to cable needle at back, k2, p2 from cable needle.

C4F – sl 2 sts on to cable needle at front, k2, k2 from cable needle.

C4B – sl 2 sts on to cable needle at back, k2, k2 from cable needle.

Panel of 24 sts on rev st st.
Row 1 (RS) (P2, C4B, p2) 3 times.
Row 2 and every foll WS row K all k sts and p all p sts.
Row 3 P1, Cr3R, (Cr4L, Cr4R) twice, Cr3L, p1.
Row 5 Cr3R, p1, (p2, C4F, p2) twice, p1, Cr3L.
Row 7 K2, p2, (Cr4R, Cr4L) twice, p2, k2.
Row 9 (K2, p2) twice, p2, C4B, p2, (p2, k2) twice.
Row 11 K2, p2, (Cr4L, Cr4R) twice, p2, k2.
Row 13 Cr3L, p1, (p2, C4F, p2) twice, p1, Cr3R.
Row 15 P1, Cr3L, (Cr4R, Cr4L) twice, Cr3R, p1.
Row 16 (K2, p4, k2) 3 times.
Repeat these 16 rows.

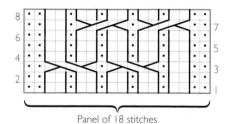

Panel of 18 stitches

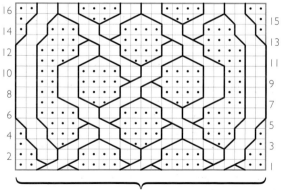

Panel of 24 stitches

CABLE STITCHES

Triple Twist Cable

Abbreviations:

Cr4L – sl 2 sts on to cable needle at front, p2, k2 from cable needle.
Cr4R – sl 2 sts on to cable needle at back, k2, p2 from cable needle.
C4F – sl 2 sts on to cable needle at front, k2, k2 from cable needle.
C4B – sl 2 sts on to cable needle at back, k2, k2 from cable needle.

Panel of 24 sts on rev st st.
Row 1 (RS) (P2, C4B, p2) 3 times.
Row 2 and every foll WS row K all k sts and p all p sts.
Row 3 Cr4R, Cr4L, p2, k4, p2, Cr4R, Cr4L.
Row 5 K2, p4, k2, p2, C4B, p2, k2, p4, k2.
Row 7 Cr4L, Cr4R, p2, k4, p2, Cr4L, Cr4R.
Row 9 As row 1.
Row 11 (Cr4R, Cr4L) 3 times.
Row 13 K2, (p4, C4F) twice, p4, k2.
Row 15 (Cr4L, Cr4R) 3 times.
Row 16 (K2, p4, k2) 3 times.
Repeat these 16 rows.

Hollow Oak

Abbreviations:

MB – (k1, k1 tbl, k1, k1 tbl, k1) all into next st, pass 2nd, 3rd, 4th and 5th sts over first.
Cr3L – sl 2 sts on to cable needle at front, p1, k2 from cable needle.
Cr3R – sl 1 st on to cable needle at back, k2, p1 from cable needle.
C3F – sl 2 sts on to cable needle at front, k1, k2 from cable needle.
C3B – sl 1 st on to cable needle at back, k2, k1 from cable needle.

Panel of 11 sts on rev st st.
Row 1 (RS) P3, k2, MB, k2, p3.
Rows 2, 4 and 6 K3, p5, k3.
Row 3 P3, MB, k3, MB, p3.
Row 5 As row 1.
Row 7 P2, C3B, p1, C3F, p2.
Row 8 K2, p2, k1, p1, k1, p2, k2.
Row 9 P1, Cr3R, k1, p1, k1, Cr3L, p1.
Row 10 K1, p3, k1, p1, k1, p3, k1.
Row 11 C3B, (p1, k1) twice, p1, C3F.
Row 12 P2, (k1, p1) 4 times, p1.
Row 13 K3, (p1, k1) 3 times, k2.
Row 14 As row 12.
Row 15 Cr3L, (p1, k1) twice, p1, Cr3R.
Row 16 As row 10.
Row 17 P1, Cr3L, k1, p1, k1, Cr3R, p1.
Row 18 As row 8.
Row 19 P2, Cr3L, p1, Cr3R, p2.
Row 20 As row 2.
Repeat these 20 rows.

KEY

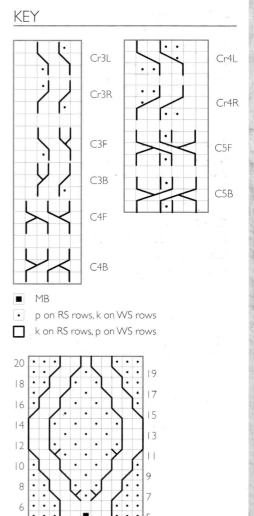

Cr3L
Cr3R
C3F
C3B
C4F
C4B

Cr4L
Cr4R
C5F
C5B

■ MB

• p on RS rows, k on WS rows

☐ k on RS rows, p on WS rows

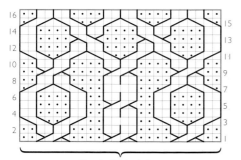

Panel of 24 stitches

Panel of 11 stitches

CABLE STITCHES

Circle Cable

Abbreviations:

Cr4L – sl 3 sts on to cable needle at front, p1, k3 from cable needle.
Cr4R – sl 1 st on to cable needle at back, k3, p1 from cable needle.
Cr5L – sl 3 sts on to cable needle at front, p2, k3 from cable needle.
Cr5R – sl 2 sts on to cable needle at back, k3, p2 from cable needle.
C6F – sl 3 sts on to cable needle at front, k3, k3 from cable needle.

Panel of 12 sts on rev st st.
Row 1 (RS) P1, Cr5R, Cr5L, p1.
Row 2 and every foll WS row K all k sts and p all p sts.
Row 3 Cr4R, p4, Cr4L.
Row 5 K3, p6, k3.
Row 7 Cr4L, p4, Cr4R.
Row 9 P1, Cr5L, Cr5R, p1.
Row 11 P3, C6F, p3.
Row 12 K3, p6, k3.
Repeat these 12 rows.

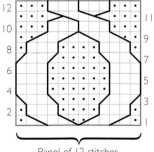

Panel of 12 stitches

Ripple and Rock

Abbreviations:

MB – (k1, yfwd, k1, yfwd, k1) all into next st, turn and p5, turn and k5, turn and p2tog, p1, p2tog, turn and k3tog.
Cr3L – sl 2 sts on to cable needle at front, p1, k2 from cable needle.
Cr3R – sl 1 st on to cable needle at back, k2, p1 from cable needle.

Panel of 13 sts on rev st st.
Row 1 (RS) P3, Cr3R, p1, Cr3L, p3.
Row 2 and every foll WS row K all k sts and p all p sts.
Row 3 P2, Cr3R, p3, Cr3L, p2.
Row 5 P1, Cr3R, p5, Cr3L, p1.
Row 7 Cr3R, p7, Cr3L.
Row 9 Cr3L, p7, Cr3R.
Row 11 P1, Cr3L, p5, Cr3R, p1.
Row 13 P2, Cr3L, p3, Cr3R, p2.
Row 15 P3, Cr3L, p1, Cr3R, p3.
Row 17 As row 1.
Row 19 As row 3.
Row 21 P2, k2, p2, MB, p2, k2, p2.
Row 23 As row 13.
Row 25 As row 15.
Row 26 K4, p2, k1, p2, k4.
Repeat these 26 rows.

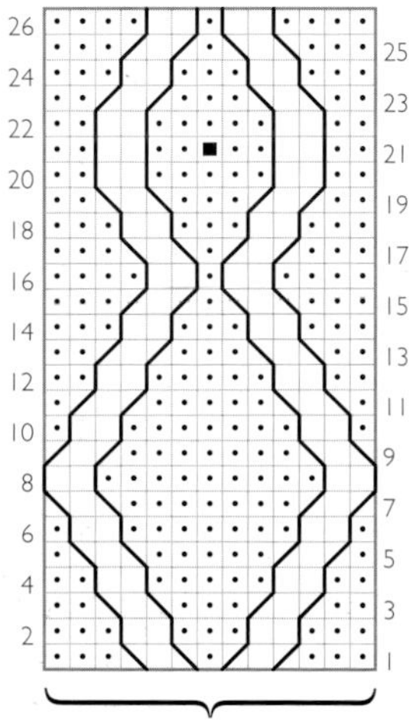

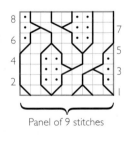

Panel of 13 stitches

Braid Cable

Abbreviations:

Cr3L – sl 2 sts on to cable needle at front, p1, k2 from cable needle.
Cr3R – sl 1 st on to cable needle at back, k2, p1 from cable needle.
C4F – sl 2 sts on to cable needle at front, k2, k2 from cable needle.
C4B – sl 2 sts on to cable needle at back, k2, k2 from cable needle.

Panel of 9 sts on rev st st.
Row 1 (RS) Cr3L, Cr3R, Cr3L.
Row 2 and every foll WS row K all k sts and p all p sts.
Row 3 P1, C4B, p2, k2.
Row 5 Cr3R, Cr3L, Cr3R.
Row 7 K2, p2, C4F, p1.
Row 8 K1, p4, k2, p2.
Repeat these 8 rows.

Panel of 9 stitches

CABLE STITCHES

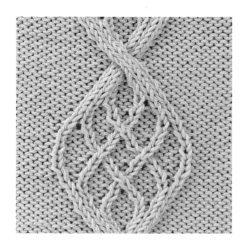

Trellis Diamond

Abbreviations:

Cr2L – sl 1 st on to cable needle at front, p1, k1 from cable needle.

Cr2R – sl 1 st on to cable needle at back, k1, p1 from cable needle.

Cr3L – sl 2 sts on to cable needle at front, p1, k2 from cable needle.

Cr3R – sl 1 st on to cable needle at back, k2, p1 from cable needle.

Cr4L – sl 3 sts on to cable needle at front, p1, k3 from cable needle.

Cr4R – sl 1 st on to cable needle at back, k3, p1 from cable needle.

C2FP – sl 1 st on to cable needle at WS, p1, p1 from cable needle.

C2BP – sl 1 st on to cable needle at RS, p1, p1 from cable needle.

C6F – sl 3 sts on to cable needle at front, k3, k3 from cable needle.

Panel of 18 sts on rev st st.

Row 1 (RS) P5, Cr4R, Cr4L, p5.

Row 2 and every foll WS row except rows 10, 14 and 18 K all k sts and p all p sts.

Row 3 P4, Cr4R, p2, Cr4L, p4.

Row 5 P3, Cr3R, k1, p4, k1, Cr3L, p3.

Row 7 P2, Cr3R, p1, Cr2L, p2, Cr2R, p1, Cr3L, p2.

Row 9 P1, Cr2R, k1, p3, Cr2L, Cr2R, p3, k1, Cr2L, p1.

Row 10 (K1, p1) twice, k4, C2FP, k4, (p1, k1) twice.

Row 11 Cr2R, p1, (Cr2L, p2, Cr2R) twice, p1, Cr2L.

Row 13 K1, p3, (Cr2L, Cr2R, p2) twice, p1, k1.

Row 14 P1, (k4, C2BP) twice, k4, p1.

Row 15 K1, p3, (Cr2R, Cr2L, p2) twice, p1, k1.

Row 17 Cr2L, p1, (Cr2R, p2, Cr2L) twice, p1, Cr2R.

Row 18 As row 10.

Row 19 P1, Cr2L, k1, p3, Cr2R, Cr2L, p3, k1, Cr2R, p1.

Row 21 P2, Cr3L, p1, Cr2R, p2, Cr2L, p1, Cr3R, p2.

Row 23 P3, Cr3L, k1, p4, k1, Cr3R, p3.

Row 25 P4, Cr4L, p2, Cr4R, p4.

Row 27 P5, Cr4L, Cr4R, p5.

Row 29 P6, C6F, p6.

Row 30 K6, p6, k6.

Repeat these 30 rows.

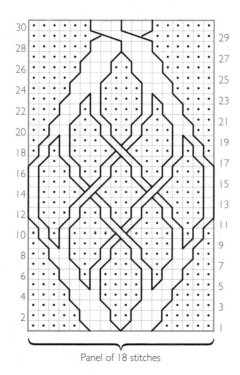

Panel of 18 stitches

KEY

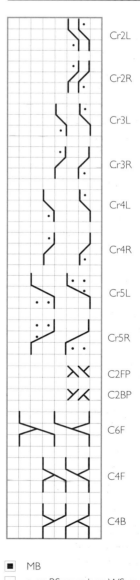

Cr2L

Cr2R

Cr3L

Cr3R

Cr4L

Cr4R

Cr5L

Cr5R

C2FP

C2BP

C6F

C4F

C4B

■ MB

· p on RS rows, k on WS rows

☐ k on RS rows, p on WS rows

CABLE STITCHES

Grapes on the Vine

Abbreviations:

MS – (k1, p1, k1) all into next st.
Cr2L – sl 1 st on to cable needle at front, p1, k1 from cable needle.
Cr2R – sl 1 st on to cable needle at back, k1, p1 from cable needle.
Cr3L – sl 2 sts on to cable needle at front, p1, k2 from cable needle.
Cr3R – sl 1 st on to cable needle at back, k2, p1 from cable needle.
Cr4L – sl 2 sts on to cable needle at front, p2, k2 from cable needle.
Cr4R – sl 2 sts on to cable needle at back, k2, p2 from cable needle.

Panel of 14 sts on rev st st (stitch count varies on some rows).
Row 1 (RS) P3, Cr3L, p4, k1, p3.
Rows 2, 4, 16 and 18 K all k sts and p all p sts.
Row 3 P4, Cr4L, p1, Cr2R, p3.
Row 5 P3, k1, p2, Cr4L, p4.
Row 6 K4, p2, k4, MS, k3. 16 sts.
Row 7 P2, (k1, p3) twice, Cr3L, p3.
Row 8 K3, p2, k4, MS, p3tog, MS, k2. 18 sts.
Row 9 P1, (k1, p3) 3 times, Cr3L, p2.
Row 10 K2, p2, k4, MS, (p3tog, MS) twice, k1. 20 sts.
Row 11 (K1, p3) 4 times, k2, p2.
Row 12 K2, p2, k4, p3tog, (MS, p3tog) twice, k1. 18 sts.
Row 13 P1, (k1, p3) 3 times, Cr3R, p2.
Row 14 K3, p2, k4, p3tog, p1, p3tog, k2. 14 sts.
Row 15 P3, k1, p4, Cr3R, p3.
Row 17 P3, Cr2L, p1, Cr4R, p4.

Row 19 P4, Cr4R, p2, k1, p3.
Row 20 K3, MS, k4, p2, k4. 16 sts.
Row 21 P3, Cr3R, (p3, k1) twice, p2.
Row 22 K2, MS, p3tog, MS, k4, p2, k3. 18 sts.
Row 23 P2, Cr3R, (p3, k1) 3 times, p1.
Row 24 K1, MS, (p3tog, MS) twice, k4, p2, k2. 20 sts.
Row 25 P2, k2, (p3, k1) 4 times.
Row 26 K1, p3tog, (MS, p3tog) twice, k4, p2, k2. 18 sts.
Row 27 P2, Cr3L, (p3, k1) 3 times, p1.
Row 28 K2, p3tog, p1, p3tog, k4, p2, k3. 14 sts.
Repeat these 28 rows.

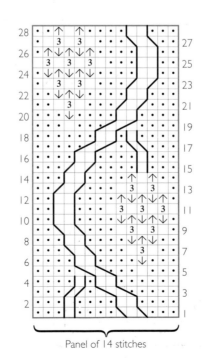

Panel of 14 stitches

KEY

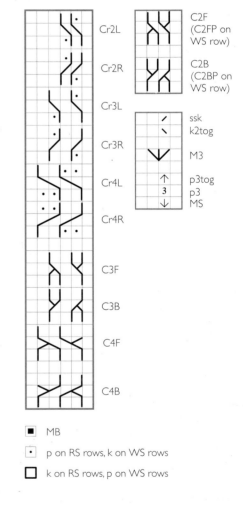

Cr2L	C2F (C2FP on WS row)
Cr2R	C2B (C2BP on WS row)
Cr3L	ssk
Cr3R	k2tog
Cr4L	M3
Cr4R	p3tog
C3F	p3
C3B	MS
C4F	
C4B	

■ MB

· p on RS rows, k on WS rows

□ k on RS rows, p on WS rows

CABLE STITCHES

Heart Cable

Abbreviations:

M3 – (k1 tbl, k1) into next st, pick up vertical strand between these 2 sts and k into back of it.

Cr3L – sl 2 sts on to cable needle at front, p1, k2 from cable needle.

Cr3R – sl 1 st on to cable needle at back, k2, p1 from cable needle.

Cr4L – sl 2 sts on to cable needle at front, p2, k2 from cable needle.

Cr4R – sl 2 sts on to cable needle at back, k2, p2 from cable needle.

C3F – sl 2 sts on to cable needle at front, k1, k2 from cable needle.

C3B – sl 1 st on to cable needle at back, k2, k1 from cable needle.

C4F – sl 2 sts on to cable needle at front, k2, k2 from cable needle.

C4B – sl 2 sts on to cable needle at back, k2, k2 from cable needle.

Panel of 21 sts.

Row 1 (RS) P1, k3, (p1, k1) twice, ssk, M3, k2tog, (k1, p1) twice, k3, p1.

Row 2 K1, p2, (k1, p1) 3 times, p3, (p1, k1) 3 times, p2, k1.

Row 3 P1, Cr3L, p1, k1, p1, ssk, k1, M3, k1, k2tog, p1, k1, p1, Cr3R, p1.

Row 4 K2, p3, k1, p1, k1, p5, k1, p1, k1, p3, k2.

Row 5 P2, Cr4L, C4B, p1, C4F, Cr4R, p2.

Row 6 K4, p5, k1, p1, k1, p5, k4.

Row 7 P4, C4B, (p1, k1) twice, p1, C4F, p4.

Row 8 K4, p3, (k1, p1) 4 times, p2, k4.

Row 9 P2, C4B, (p1, k1) 4 times, p1, C4F, p2.

Row 10 K2, p3, (k1, p1) 6 times, p2, k2.

Row 11 P1, C3B, (p1, k1) 6 times, p1, C3F, p1.

Row 12 K1, p2, (k1, p1) 7 times, k1, p2, k1.

Repeat these 12 rows.

Nosegay Pattern

Abbreviations:

MB – (k1, p1) twice into next st and turn, p4 and turn, k4 and turn, (p2tog) twice and turn, k2tog.

Cr2L – sl 1 st on to cable needle at front, p1, k1 from cable needle.

Cr2R – sl 1 st on to cable needle at back, k1, p1 from cable needle.

C2F – sl 1 st on to cable needle at front, k1, k1 from cable needle.

C2B – sl 1 st on to cable needle at back, k1, k1 from cable needle.

C2FP – sl 1 st on to cable needle at WS, p1, p1 from cable needle.

C2BP – sl 1 st on to cable needle at RS, p1, p1 from cable needle.

Panel of 16 sts on rev st st.

Row 1 (RS) P6, C2B, C2F, p6.

Row 2 K5, C2FP, p2, C2BP, k5.

Row 3 P4, Cr2R, C2B, C2F, Cr2L, p4.

Row 4 K3, Cr2L, k1, p4, k1, Cr2R, k3.

Row 5 P2, Cr2R, p1, Cr2R, k2, Cr2L, p1, Cr2L, p2.

Row 6 (K2, p1) twice, k1, p2, k1, (p1, k2) twice.

Row 7 P2, MB, p1, Cr2R, p1, k2, p1, Cr2L, p1, MB, p2.

Row 8 K4, p1, k2, p2, k2, p1, k4.

Row 9 P4, MB, p2, k2, p2, MB, p4.

Row 10 K7, p2, k7

Repeat these 10 rows.

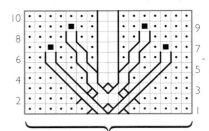

Panel of 16 stitches

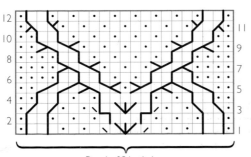

Panel of 21 stitches

CABLE STITCHES

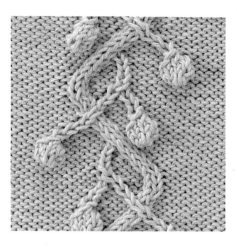

Twisted Vine

Abbreviations:

MB – (k1, p1, k1, p1, k1) all into next st and turn, p5 and turn, k5 and turn, p2tog, p1, p2tog and turn, k3tog. P st above bobble on next row.

Cr2L – sl 1 st on to cable needle at front, p1, k1 from cable needle.

Cr2R – sl 1 st on to cable needle at back, k1, p1 from cable needle.

Cr3L – sl 1 st on to cable needle at front, p2, k1 from cable needle.

Cr3R – sl 2 sts on to cable needle at back, k1, p2 from cable needle.

Cr4L – sl 2 sts on to cable needle at front, p2, k2 from cable needle.

Cr4R – sl 2 sts on to cable needle at back, k2, p2 from cable needle.

C3F – sl 1 st on to cable needle at front, k2, k1 from cable needle.

C3B – sl 2 sts on to cable needle at back, k1, k2 from cable needle.

Panel of 17 sts on rev st st.
Row 1 (RS) P6, k1, p4, Cr4R, p2.
Row 2 and every foll WS row K all k sts and p all p sts.
Row 3 MB, p5, Cr2L, p1, Cr4R, p4.
Row 5 Cr3L, p4, Cr4R, p6.
Row 7 P2, Cr3L, Cr4R, p3, MB, p4.
Row 9 P4, C3F, p4, Cr2R, p4.
Row 11 P2, Cr4R, Cr3L, p1, Cr2R, p5.
Row 13 P2, k2, p4, Cr3L, p6.
Row 15 P2, Cr4L, p4, k1, p6.
Row 17 P4, Cr4L, p1, Cr2R, p5, MB.
Row 19 P6, Cr4L, p4, Cr3R.
Row 21 P4, MB, p3, Cr4L, Cr3R, p2.
Row 23 P4, Cr2L, p4, C3B, p4.
Row 25 P5, Cr2L, p1, Cr3R, Cr4L, p2.
Row 27 P6, Cr3R, p4, k2, p2.
Row 28 K2, p2, k6, p1, k6.
Repeat these 28 rows.

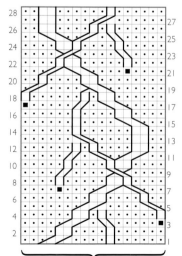

Panel of 14 stitches

KEY

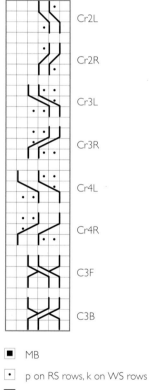

Cr2L
Cr2R
Cr3L
Cr3R
Cr4L
Cr4R
C3F
C3B

■ MB

· p on RS rows, k on WS rows

□ k on RS rows, p on WS rows

LACE STITCHES

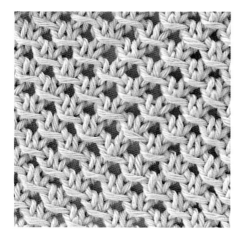

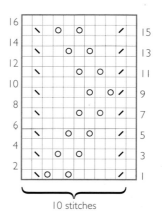

Lace Mesh

Multiple of 3 sts (cast on a minimum of 6 sts).
Row I K2, * yo, sl 1, k2, psso the 2 k sts; rep from * to last st, k1.
Row 2 Purl.
Row 3 K1, * sl 1, k2, psso the 2 k sts, yo; rep from * to last 2 sts, k2.
Row 4 Purl.
Repeat these 4 rows.

Zig Zag Lace

Multiple of 10 sts.
Row I (RS) * K2, p3, k2tog, yo, k3; rep from * to end.
Row 2 and every WS row Purl.
Row 3 * K1, p3, k2tog, yo, k4; rep from * to end.
Row 5 * P3, k2tog, yo, k5; rep from * to end.
Row 7 * K3, yo, ssk, p3, k2; rep from * to end.
Row 9 * K4, yo, ssk, p3, k1; rep from * to end.
Row II * K5, yo, ssk, p3; rep from * to end.
Row 12 Purl.
Repeat these 12 rows.

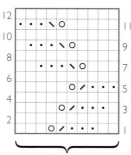

10 stitches

Vine Lace Zig Zag

Multiple of 10 sts plus 1.
Row I (RS) K1, * k2tog, k4, yo, k1, yo, ssk, k1; rep from * to end.
Row 2 and every foll WS row Purl.
Row 3 K1, * k2tog, k3, (yo, k1) twice, ssk, k1; rep from * to end.
Row 5 K1, * k2tog, k2, yo, k1, yo, k2, ssk, k1; rep from * to end.
Row 7 K1, * k2tog, (k1, yo) twice, k3, ssk, k1; rep from * to end.
Row 9 K1, * k2tog, yo, k1, yo, k4, ssk, k1; rep from * to end.
Row II K1, * k2tog, (k1, yo) twice, k3, ssk, k1; rep from * to end.
Row 13 K1, * k2tog, k2, yo, k1, yo, k2, ssk, k1; rep from * to end.
Row 15 K1, * k2tog, k3, (yo, k1) twice, ssk, k1; rep from * to end.
Row 16 Purl.
Repeat these 16 rows.

10 stitches

KEY

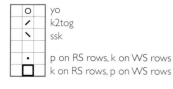

o		yo
╱		k2tog
╲		ssk
•		p on RS rows, k on WS rows
□		k on RS rows, p on WS rows

LACE STITCHES

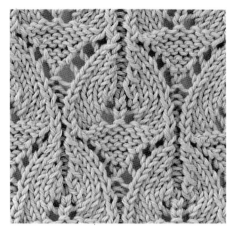

Crest of the Wave

Multiple of 12 sts plus 1.
Rows 1 to 4 Knit.
Rows 5, 7, 9 and 11 K1, * (k2tog) twice, (yo, k1) 3 times, yo, (ssk) twice, k1; rep from * to end.
Rows 6, 8, 10 and 12 Purl.
Repeat these 12 rows.

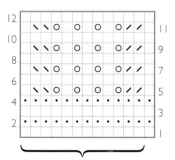

12 stitches

Gothic Window

Multiple of 12 sts plus 1.
Row 1 (RS) P1, * ssk, k3, yo, k1, yo, k3, k2tog, p1; rep from * to end.
Row 2 * K1, p11; rep from * to last st, k1.
Rows 3 to 6 Rep rows 1 and 2 twice more.
Row 7 P1, * yo, k3, ssk, p1, k2tog, k3, yo, p1; rep from * to end.
Row 8 * K1, p5; rep from * to last st, k1.
Row 9 P1, * p1, yo, k2, ssk, p1, k2tog, k2, yo, p2; rep from * to end.
Row 10 * K2, (p4, k1) twice; rep from * to last st, k1.
Row 11 P1, * p2, yo, k1, ssk, p1, k2tog, k1, yo, p3; rep from * to end.
Row 12 * K3, p3, k1, p3, k2; rep from * to last st, k1.
Row 13 P1, * p3, yo, ssk, p1, k2tog, yo, p4; rep from * to end.
Row 14 * K4, p2, k1, p2, k3; rep from * to last st, k1.
Row 15 K1, * yo, k3, k2tog, p1, ssk, k3, yo, k1; rep from * to end.
Row 16 * P6, k1, p5; rep from * to last st, p1.
Rows 17 to 20 Repeat rows 15 and 16 twice more.
Row 21 P1, * k2tog, k3, yo, p1, yo, k3, ssk, p1; rep from * to end.
Row 22 As row 8.
Row 23 P1, * k2tog, k2, yo, p3, yo, k2, ssk, p1; rep from * to end.

Row 24 * K1, p4, k3, p4; rep from * to last st, k1.
Row 25 P1, * k2tog, k1, yo, p5, yo, k1, ssk, p1; rep from * to end.
Row 26 * K1, p3, k5, p3; rep from * to last st, k1.
Row 27 P1, * k2tog, yo, p7, yo, ssk, p1; rep from * to end.
Row 28 * K1, p2, k7, p2; rep from * to last st, k1.
Repeat these 28 rows.

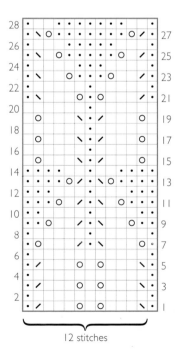

12 stitches

KEY

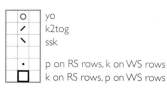

o	yo
/	k2tog
\	ssk
•	p on RS rows, k on WS rows
□	k on RS rows, p on WS rows

LACE STITCHES

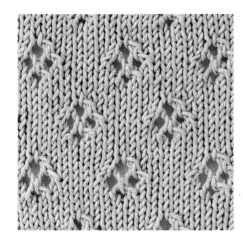

Quatrefoil Eyelets

Multiple of 8 sts plus 7.
Row 1 (RS) K2, * k1, yo, ssk, k5; rep from * to last 5 sts, k1, yo, ssk, k2.
Row 2 and every foll WS row Purl.
Row 3 K1, k2tog, * yo, k1, yo, ssk, k3, k2tog; rep from * to last 5 sts, yo, k1, yo, ssk, k1.
Row 5 As row 1.
Row 7 Knit.
Row 9 K2, * k5, yo, ssk, k1; rep from * to last 5 sts, k5.
Row 11 K2, * k3, k2tog, yo, k1, yo, ssk; rep from * to last 5 sts, k5.
Row 13 As row 9.
Row 15 Knit.
Row 16 Purl.
Repeat these 16 rows.

Quatrefoil Eyelets in Diamonds

Multiple of 12 sts plus 3.
Row 1 (RS) K1, * k1, yo, ssk, k3, p1, k3, k2tog, yo; rep from * to last 2 sts, k2.
Row 2 P2, * p4, k1, p1, k1, p5; rep from * to last st, p1.
Row 3 K1, * yo, ssk, k2, p1, k3 (twice); rep from * to last 2 sts, yo, ssk.
Row 4 P2, * p2, k1, p5, k1, p3; rep from * to last st, p1.
Row 5 K1, * k2, p1, k2, k2tog, yo, k3, p1, k1; rep from * to last 2 sts, k2.
Row 6 P2, * k1, p9, k1, p1; rep from * to last st, p1.
Row 7 K1, * p1, k3, k2tog, yo, k1, yo, ssk, k3; rep from * to last 2 sts, p1, k1.
Row 8 As row 6.
Row 9 K1, * k2, p1, k3, yo, ssk, k2, p1, k1; rep from * to last 2 sts, k2.
Row 10 As row 4.
Row 11 K2tog, * yo, (k3, p1) twice, k2, k2tog; rep from * to last st, yo, k1.
Row 12 As row 2.
Repeat these 12 rows.

Lace Rib

Multiple of 4 sts plus 1.
Row 1 (RS) * P1, k3; rep from * to last st, p1.
Row 2 K1, * p1, yo, p2tog, k1; rep from * to end.
Row 3 As row 1.
Row 4 Knit.
Repeat these 4 rows.

4 stitches

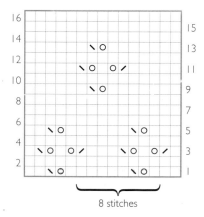

8 stitches

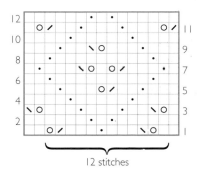

12 stitches

KEY

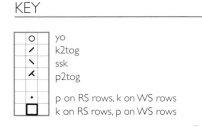

O	yo
╱	k2tog
╲	ssk
⋏	p2tog
•	p on RS rows, k on WS rows
☐	k on RS rows, p on WS rows

LACE STITCHES

Ridged Feather Stitch

Multiple of 11 sts.
Row 1 (RS) Knit.
Row 2 Purl.
Row 3 (P2tog) twice, (yo, k1) 3 times, yo, (p2tog) twice.
Row 4 Purl.
Repeat these 4 rows.

Norwegian Fir

Multiple of 12 sts plus 1.
Row 1 (RS) P1, * p3, k5, p4; rep from * to end.
Row 2 and every foll WS row Purl.
Row 3 P2tog, * p2, k2, yo, k1, yo, k2, p2, p3tog; rep from * to end, ending last rep with p2tog.
Row 5 P2tog, * p1, k2, yo, k3, yo, k2, p1, p3tog; rep from * to end, ending last rep with p2tog.
Row 7 P2tog, * k2, yo, k5, yo, k2, p3tog; rep from * to end, ending last rep with p2tog.
Row 8 Purl.
Repeat these 8 rows.

Dainty Chevron

Multiple of 8 sts plus 1.
Row 1 (RS) K1, * ssk, (k1, yo) twice, k1, k2tog, k1; rep from * to end.
Row 2 and every foll WS row Purl.
Row 3 As row 1.
Row 5 K1, * yo, ssk, k3, k2tog, yo, k1; rep from * end.
Row 7 K1, * k1, yo, ssk, k1, k2tog, yo, k2; rep from * to end.
Row 9 K1, * k2, yo, sl2tog-k1-psso, yo, k3; rep from * to end.
Row 10 Purl.
Repeat these 10 rows.

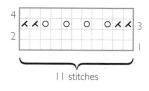

11 stitches

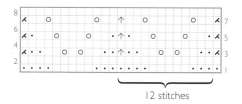

12 stitches

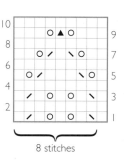

8 stitches

KEY

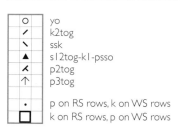

o	yo
╱	k2tog
╲	ssk
▲	sl2tog-k1-psso
⋌	p2tog
↑	p3tog
·	p on RS rows, k on WS rows
☐	k on RS rows, p on WS rows

LACE STITCHES

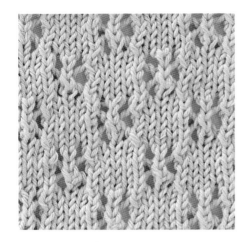

Snowflake Eyelets

Multiple of 8 sts plus 5.
Row 1 (RS) K1, * k3, ssk, yo, k1, yo, k2tog; rep from * to last 4 sts, k4.
Row 2 and every foll WS row Purl.
Row 3 K1, * k4, yo, sl2tog-k1-psso, yo, k1; rep from * to last 4 sts, k4.
Row 5 As row 1.
Row 7 Ssk, * yo, k1, yo, k2tog, k3, ssk; rep from * to last 3 sts, yo, k1, yo, k2tog.
Row 9 K1, * yo, sl2tog-k1-psso, yo, k5; rep from * to last 4 sts, yo, sl2tog-k1-p2sso, yo, k1.
Row 11 As row 7.
Row 12 Purl.
Repeat these 12 rows.

Mini Horseshoe Lace

Multiple of 6 sts plus 1.
Row 1 (RS) K1, * yo, k1, sk2po, k1, yo, k1; rep from * to end.
Row 2 Purl.
Row 3 K1, * k1, yo, sk2po, yo, k2; rep from * to end.
Row 4 Purl.
Repeat these 4 rows.

Horseshoe Lace

Multiple of 10 sts plus 1.
Row 1 (RS) K1, * yo, k3, sk2po, k3, yo, k1; rep from * to end.
Row 2 Purl.
Row 3 P1, * k1, yo, k2, sk2po, k2, yo, k1, p1; rep from * to end.
Row 4 K1, * p9, k1; rep from * to end.
Row 5 P1, * k2, yo, k1, sk2po, k1, yo, k2, p1; rep from * to end.
Row 6 As row 4.
Row 7 P1, * k3, yo, sk2po, yo, k3, p1; rep from * to end.
Row 8 Purl.
Repeat these 8 rows.

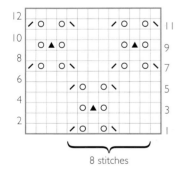

8 stitches

6 stitches

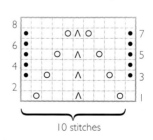

10 stitches

KEY

O	yo
╱	k2tog
╲	ssk
∧	sk2po
•	p on RS rows, k on WS rows
☐	k on RS rows, p on WS rows

LACE STITCHES

Diamonds

Multiple of 8 sts plus 1.

Row 1 (RS) K1, * k1, k2tog, yo, k1, yo, ssk, k2; rep from * to end.

Row 2 and every foll WS row Purl.

Row 3 K1, * k2tog, yo, k3, yo, ssk, k1; rep from * to end.

Row 5 K2tog, * yo, k5, yo, sk2po; rep from * to end, ending last rep with ssk.

Row 7 K1, * yo, ssk, k3, k2tog, yo, k1; rep from * to end.

Row 9 K1, * k1, yo, ssk, k1, k2tog, yo, k2; rep from * to end.

Row 11 K1, * k2, yo, sk2po, yo, k3; rep from * to end.

Row 12 Purl.

Repeat these 12 rows.

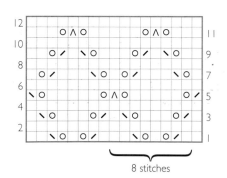

8 stitches

Leaf Patterned Lace

Multiple of 10 sts plus 1.

Row 1 (RS) K1, * k2, k2tog, yo, k1, yo, ssk, k3; rep from * to end.

Row 2 and every foll WS row Purl.

Row 3 K1, * k1, k2tog, (k1, yo) twice, k1, ssk, k2; rep from * to end.

Row 5 K1, * k2tog, k2, yo, k1, yo, k2, ssk, k1; rep from * to end.

Row 7 K2tog, * k3, yo, k1, yo, k3, sk2po; rep from * to end, ending last rep with ssk.

Row 9 K1, * yo, ssk, k5, k2tog, yo, k1; rep from * to end.

Row 11 K1, * yo, k1, ssk, k3, k2tog, k1, yo, k1; rep from * to end.

Row 13 K1, * yo, k2, ssk, k1, k2tog, k2, yo, k1; rep from * to end.

Row 15 K1, * yo, k3, sk2po, k3, yo, k1; rep from * to end.

Row 16 Purl.

Repeat these 16 rows.

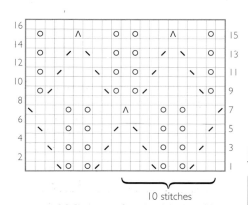

10 stitches

Ladder Lace

Multiple of 14 sts plus 11.

Row 1 (RS) K2tog, k3, yo, * k1, yo, k3, ssk, yo, sk2po, yo, k2tog, k3, yo; rep from * to last 6 sts, k1, yo, k3, ssk.

Row 2 Purl.

Repeat these 2 rows.

14 stitches

KEY

O	yo
∕	k2tog
＼	ssk
∧	sk2po
·	p on RS rows, k on WS rows
□	k on RS rows, p on WS rows

LACE STITCHES

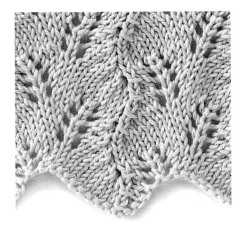

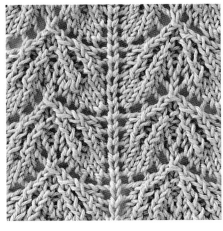

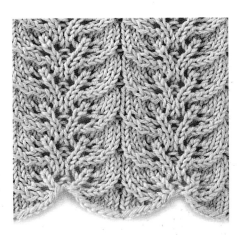

Fern Lace

Multiple of 16 sts.
Row 1 (RS) * K9, yo, k1, yo, k3, sk2po; rep from * to end.
Row 2 and every foll WS row Purl.
Row 3 * K10, yo, k1, yo, k2, sk2po; rep from * to end.
Row 5 * K3tog, k4, yo, k1, yo, k3, (yo, k1) twice, sk2po; rep from * to end.
Row 7 * K3tog, k3, yo, k1, yo, k9; rep from * to end.
Row 9 * K3tog, k2, yo, k1, yo, k10; rep from * to end.
Row 11 * K3tog, (k1, yo) twice, k3, yo, k1, yo, k4, sk2po; rep from * to end.
Row 12 Purl.
Repeat these 12 rows.

Beech Leaf Lace

Multiple of 14 sts plus 1 (stitch count varies).
Row 1 (RS) K1, * yo, k5, yo, sk2po, yo, k5, yo, k1; rep from * to end. 16 sts.
Row 2 Purl.
Row 3 K1, * yo, k1, k2tog, p1, ssk, k1, yo, p1, yo, k1, k2tog, p1, ssk, k1, yo, k1; rep from * to end.
Row 4 * P4, (k1, p3) 3 times; rep from * to last st, p1.
Row 5 K1, * yo, k1, k2tog, p1, ssk, k1, p1, k1, k2tog, p1, ssk, k1, yo, k1; rep from * to end. 14 sts.
Row 6 * P4, k1, p2, k1, p2, k1, p3; rep from * to last st, p1.
Row 7 K1, * yo, k1, yo, k2tog, p1, ssk, p1, k2tog, p1, ssk, (yo, k1) twice; rep from * to end.
Row 8 * P5, (k1, p1) twice, k1, p4; rep from * to last st, p1.
Row 9 K1, * yo, k3, yo, sk2po, k1, k3tog, yo, k3, yo, k1; rep from * to end.
Row 10 Purl.
Repeat these 10 rows.

Twin Leaf Lace

Multiple of 18 sts plus 1.
Row 1 (RS) P1, * k4, k3tog, yo, k1, yo, p1, yo, k1, yo, sk2po, k4, p1; rep from * to end.
Row 2 and every foll WS row * K1, p8; rep from * to last st, k1.
Row 3 P1, * k2, k3tog, (k1, yo) twice, k1, p1, k1, (yo, k1) twice, sk2po, k2, p1; rep from * to end.
Row 5 P1, * k3tog, k2, yo, k1, yo, k2, p1, k2, yo, k1, yo, k2, sk2po, p1; rep from * to end.
Row 6 As row 2.
Repeat these 6 rows.

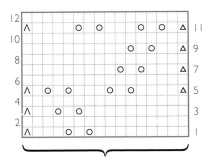

16 stitches

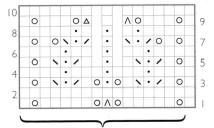

14 stitches

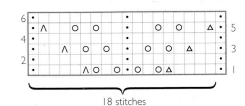

18 stitches

KEY

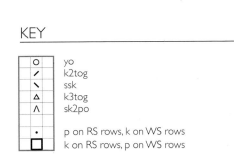

O	yo
/	k2tog
\	ssk
△	k3tog
Λ	sk2po
•	p on RS rows, k on WS rows
□	k on RS rows, p on WS rows

LACE STITCHES

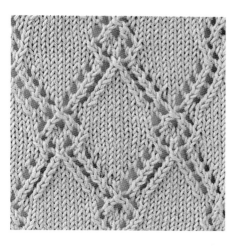

Diamond Lace with Rosettes

Multiple of 14 sts plus 3.

Row 1 (RS) K1, yo, * k3tog, yo, k9, yo, ssk, yo; rep from * to last 2 sts, k2tog.

Row 2 and every foll WS row Purl.

Row 3 K1, k2tog, * yo, k11, yo, sk2po; rep from * to end, ending last rep with ssk, k1.

Row 5 K2, * (yo, ssk) twice, k5, (k2tog, yo) twice, k1; rep from * to last st, k1.

Row 7 K2, * k1, (yo, ssk) twice, k3, (k2tog, yo) twice, k2; rep from * to last st, k1.

Row 9 K2, * k2, (yo, ssk) twice, k1, (k2tog, yo) twice, k3; rep from * to last st, k1.

Row 11 K2, * k3, yo, ssk, yo, sk2po, yo, k2tog, yo, k4; rep from * to last st, k1.

Row 13 K2, * k4, k2tog, yo, k1, yo, ssk, k5; rep from * to last st, k1.

Row 15 K2, * k3, k2tog, yo, k3, yo, ssk, k4; rep from * to last st, k1.

Row 17 K2, * k4, yo, ssk, yo, k3tog, yo, k5; rep from * to last st, k1.

Row 19 K2, * k5, yo, sk2po, yo, k6; rep from * to last st, k1.

Row 21 K2, * k2, (k2tog, yo) twice, k1, (yo, ssk) twice, k3; rep from * to last st, k1.

Row 23 K2, * k1, (k2tog, yo) twice, k3, (yo, ssk) twice, k2; rep from * to last st, k1.

Row 25 K2, * (k2tog, yo) twice, k5, (yo, ssk) twice, k1; rep from * to last st, k1.

Row 27 K1, k2tog, * yo, k2tog, yo, k7, yo, ssk, yo, sk2po; rep from * to end, ending last rep with ssk, k1.

Row 29 K2, * yo, ssk, k9, k2tog, yo, k1; rep from * to last st, k1.

Row 31 K2, * k1, yo, ssk, k7, k2tog, yo, k2; rep from * to last st, k1.

Row 32 Purl.

Repeat these 32 rows.

14 stitches

KEY

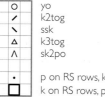

o	yo
⟋	k2tog
⟍	ssk
△	k3tog
⋀	sk2po
•	p on RS rows, k on WS rows
▢	k on RS rows, p on WS rows

EDGINGS

Loop Edging

Cast on 6 sts.
Row 1 (RS) K1, k2tog, yo, k2, (yo) twice, k1.
Row 2 K1, (k1, p1) into double yo, k3.
Row 3 K1, k2tog, yo, k5.
Row 4 Bind (cast) off 2 sts, p2tog, yo, k3.
Repeat these 4 rows.

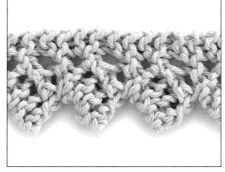

Openwork Garter Stitch

Cast on 4 sts.
Row 1 (RS) K2, yfwd, k2.
Row 2 and every foll WS row Knit.
Row 3 K3, yfwd, k2.
Row 5 K2, yfwd, k2tog, yfwd, k2.
Row 7 K3, yfwd, k2tog, yfwd, k2.
Row 8 Bind (cast) off 4 sts, k to end.
Repeat these 8 rows.

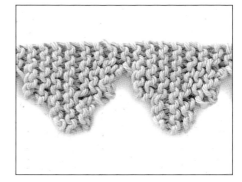

Turret Edging

Cast on 3 sts.
Rows 1 to 3 Knit.
Row 4 Cast on 3 sts, k to end.
Rows 5 to 7 Knit.
Row 8 Cast on 3 sts, k to end.
Rows 9 to 11 Knit.
Row 12 Bind (cast) off 3 sts, k to end.
Rows 13 to 15 Knit.
Row 16 Bind (cast) off 3 sts, k to end.
Repeat these 16 rows.

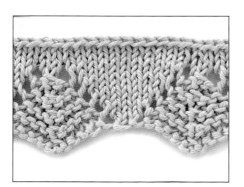

Scallop Border

Multiple of 13 sts.
Row 1 (RS) * K1, yo, k4, sk2po, k4, yo, k1; rep from * to end.
Row 2 * P2, k9, p2; rep from * to end.
Row 3 * K2, yo, k3, sk2po, k3, yo, k2; rep from * to end.
Row 4 * P3, k7, p3; rep from * to end.
Row 5 * K3, yo, k2, sk2po, k2, yo, k3; rep from * to end.
Row 6 * P4, k5, p4; rep from * to end.
Row 7 * K4, yo, k1, sk2po, k1, yo, k4; rep from * to end.
Row 8 * P5, k3, p5; rep from * to end.
Row 9 * K5, yo, sk2po, yo, k5; rep from * to end.
Row 10 Purl. Repeat these 10 rows.

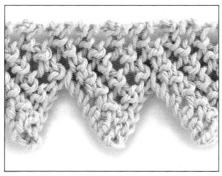

Openwork Edging

Cast on 5 sts.
Row 1 (RS) Sl 1, yo, k2tog, yo, k2.
Row 2 and every foll WS row Knit.
Row 3 Sl 1, (yo, k2tog) twice, yo, k1.
Row 5 Sl 1, (yo, k2tog) twice, yo, k2.
Row 7 Sl 1, (yo, k2tog) 3 times, yo, k1.
Row 9 Sl 1, (yo, k2tog) 3 times, yo, k2.
Row 11 Bind (cast) off 6 sts, yo, k2tog, k1.
Row 12 Knit.
Repeat these 12 rows.

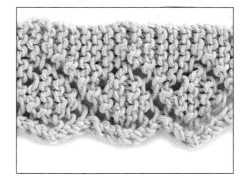

Garter Stitch Diamond

Cast on 10 sts.
Row 1 (RS) K5, k2tog, yo, k3tog.
Row 2 and every foll WS row Yo, k to end.
Row 3 K4, k2tog, yo, k1, yo, k2tog.
Row 5 K3, k2tog, yo, k3, yo, k2tog.
Row 7 K2, k2tog, yo, k5, yo, k2tog.
Row 9 K4, yo, k2tog, k1, k2tog, yo, k3tog.
Row 11 K5, yo, k3tog, yo, k3tog.
Row 12 Yo, k to end.
Repeat these 12 rows.

EDGINGS

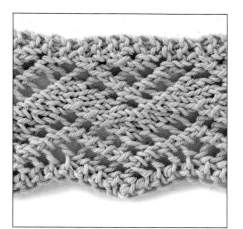

Zig Zag Edging

Cast on 11 sts.
Row 1 (RS) K3, yo, k2tog, k2, yo, k2tog, yo, k2.
Row 2 Yo, k2tog, p8, k2.
Row 3 K2, (yo, k2tog) twice, k2, yo, k2tog, yo, k2.
Row 4 Yo, k2tog, p9, k2.
Row 5 K3, (yo, k2tog) twice, k2, yo, k2tog, yo, k2.
Row 6 Yo, k2tog, p10, k2.
Row 7 K2, (yo, k2tog) 3 times, k2, yo, k2tog, yo, k2.
Row 8 Yo, k2tog, p11, k2.
Row 9 K2, (ssk, yo) twice, k2, (ssk, yo) twice, k2tog, k1.
Row 10 Yo, k2tog, p10, k2.
Row 11 K1, (ssk, yo) twice, k2, (ssk, yo) twice, k2tog, k1.
Row 12 Yo, k2tog, p9, k2.
Row 13 K2, ssk, yo, k2, (ssk, yo) twice, k2tog, k1.
Row 14 Yo, k2tog, p8, k2.
Row 15 K1, ssk, yo, k2, (ssk, yo) twice, k2tog, k1.
Row 16 Yo, k2tog, p7, k2.
Repeat these 16 rows.

Leaf Edging

Abbreviation:
k-fb – knit into front and back of next st.

Cast on 6 sts.
Row 1 (RS) K3, yfwd, k1, yfwd, k2.
Row 2 P6, k-fb, k1.
Row 3 K2, p1, k2, yfwd, k1, yfwd, k3.
Row 4 P8, k-fb, k2.
Row 5 K2, p2, k3, yfwd, k1, yfwd, k4.
Row 6 P10, k-fb, k3.
Row 7 K2, p3, ssk, k5, k2tog, k1.
Row 8 P8, k-fb, p1, k3.
Row 9 K2, p1, k1, p2, ssk, k3, k2tog, k1.
Row 10 P6, k-fb, k1, p1, k3.
Row 11 K2, p1, k1, p3, ssk, k1, k2tog, k1.
Row 12 P4, k-fb, k2, p1, k3.
Row 13 K2, p1, k1, p4, sk2po, k1.
Row 14 P2tog, bind (cast) off 3 sts, k1, p1, k3.
Repeat these 14 rows.

Tassel Border

Multiple of 13 sts.
Row 1 (RS) * P2, (k1, p1) 4 times, k1, p2; rep from * to end.
Row 2 * K2, (p1, k1) 4 times, p1, k2; rep from * to end.
Rows 3 and 4 Repeat rows 1 and 2 once more.
Row 5 * P2, k1, p1, ssk, k1, k2tog, p1, k1, p2; rep from * to end.
Row 6 * K2, p1, k1, p3, k1, p1, k2; rep from * to end.
Row 7 * P2, k1, p1, sl2tog-k1-psso, p1, k1, p2; rep from * to end.
Row 8 * K2, (p1, k1) twice, p1, k2; rep from * to end.
Row 9 * P2, ssk, k1, k2tog, p2; rep from * to end.
Row 10 * K2, p3, k2; rep from * to end.
Row 11 * P2, sl next 3 sts on to cable needle, wrap yarn around them twice, k3 from cable needle, p2; rep from * to end.
Row 12 * K2, p3, k2; rep from * to end.
Row 13 * P1, sl2tog-k1-psso, p2; rep from * to end.
Row 14 Purl.
Repeat these 14 rows.

EDGINGS

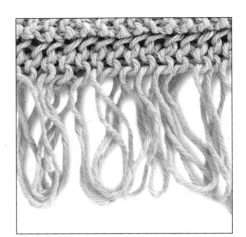

Welted Ruffle

Cast on 9 sts.
Row 1 Knit.
Row 2 P6 and turn, k6.
Row 3 P6, k3.
Row 4 K3, p6.
Row 5 K6 and turn, p6.
Row 6 Knit.
Repeat these 6 rows.

Cobweb Frill

Multiple of 3 sts plus 1.
Row 1 (RS) K1 tbl, * p1, p1 tbl, k1 tbl;
rep from * to end.
Row 2 P1 tbl, * k1 tbl, k1, p1 tbl; rep
from * to end.
Rows 3 to 8 Repeat rows 1 and 2 three
times more.
Row 9 K1 tbl, * drop next st off needle,
p1 tbl, k1 tbl; rep from * to end.
Row 10 P1 tbl, * k1 tbl, p1 tbl; rep from
* to end.
Row 11 K1 tbl, * p1 tbl, k1 tbl; rep from
* to end.
Rows 12 and 13 Repeat rows 10 and 11
once more.
Unravel dropped sts down to cast on edge.

Fringe

Cast on 8 sts.
Row 1 (RS) K2, yo, k2tog, k4.
Row 2 P3, k2, yo, k2tog, k1.
Repeat these 2 rows for required length,
ending with a WS row.
Last row Bind (cast) off 4 sts, draw yarn
through next st and fasten off.
Slip rem 3 sts off needle and unravel.

Projects

The projects given in this book use the techniques described in the earlier sections. Full instructions are given to create each item and the introduction to each project refers you back to any specific techniques used to create it. If a stitch pattern or motif forms part of the design you will find references to the Stitch library or the Motif section and suggestions are given for when you can substitute an alternative pattern or design to the one used.

The yarns specified are widely available in yarn shops, by mail order or from the internet. If the recommended yarn is unavailable then a substitute yarn of the same thickness or weight can be used. The replacement yarn must knit up to the same gauge (tension) and this information can be found on the ball band.

Substituting yarns

All the information you need to calculate yarn amounts is on the yarn's ball band. To work out how much replacement yarn you need follow these simple steps.

1 Take the number of balls of the recommended yarn from the Materials section of the pattern and multiply them by the number of yards/metres per ball. For example, 10 × 1¾oz (50g) balls of worsted (DK) 100% cotton yarn – 125yd/115m per ball would give a total length of 10 × 125yd = 1250yd (10 × 115m = 1150m).

2 Look at the ball band of the replacement yarn to find the number of yards/metres per 1¾oz (50g). For example, 154yd/140m.

3 Divide the total length required by the length of the replacement ball to give the number of balls of replacement yarn needed. For example 1250yd ÷ 154 = 8.1 (1150m ÷ 140 = 8.2) rounded up to 9 balls.

If the project uses more than one colour yarn, repeat these steps for each colour.

◄ KNIT SOMETHING NOW!

This Shaker-style sampler hangs on a wire quilt hanger and is embroidered in swiss darning with details added in backstitch.

The **house sampler** is knitted in a sport (4ply) weight tweed yarn using size 6 (4mm/UK8) needles and embroidered in tapestry wool. See page 153 for pattern.

GARTER STITCH SCARF

This cosy scarf is easy to knit using only three simple techniques, casting on, garter stitch and binding (casting) off (see pages 17–20). Use the recommended yarns, and follow the basic instructions, to knit either a plain or striped version. To substitute the yarns see Substituting yarns left and below. If you want to add a tasselled fringe (see page 76), you will need extra yarn.

■ Scarf measures 6in (15cm) wide by 62in (158cm) long

Choosing a different yarn

If you want to use a different yarn than those given choose a thick one like aran, bulky (chunky) or thicker. The scarf will grow quickly and you may even finish it in a day.

All the information you need to knit the scarf is on the yarn's ball band. The number of stitches to cast on is determined by the gauge (tension), which is given to 4in (10cm). For a scarf 6in (15cm) wide you will need to cast on 1½ times the number of stitches to 4in (10cm).

For example, a worsted (DK) weight yarn has a gauge (tension) of 22 sts to 4in (10cm) using size 6 (4mm/UK8) needles. You would cast on 33 sts and use size 6 (4mm/UK8) needles. For a bulky weight yarn with a gauge (tension) of 14 sts to 4in (10cm) on size 8 (5mm/UK6) needles you would cast on 21 sts and use size 8 (5mm/UK6) needles. To calculate how many balls you will need see page 128.

STRIPED SCARF

you will need

MATERIALS
Aran merino wool yarn –
90yd/82m per ball
1 × 1¾oz/50g ball each in colours:
A purple
B dark lilac
C lilac
D cream

NEEDLES
Size 7 (4.5mm/UK7) needles

■ **Gauge (Tension)**
19 sts to 4in (10cm) measured over garter stitch on size 7 (4.5mm/UK7) needles

Using size 7 (4.5mm/UK7) needles and A, cast on 28 sts. Working in g st (k every row), work in stripe patt of 10 rows A, 10 rows B, 10 rows C, 10 rows D, until scarf measures 62in (158cm) or length required. Bind (cast) off. Sew in yarn ends (see page 32).

PLAIN SCARF

you will need

MATERIALS
Chunky wool yarn (wool/alpaca mix) – 109yd/100m per ball
2 × 3½oz/100g balls in lilac

If you want a scarf longer than 62in (158cm) add another ball of yarn.

NEEDLES
Size 11 (8mm/UK0) needles

■ **Gauge (Tension)**
12 sts to 4in (10cm) measured over garter stitch on size 11 (8mm/UK0) needles

Using size 11 (8mm/UK0) needles, cast on 18 sts and work as given for striped version using one colour throughout.

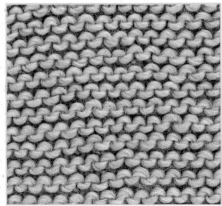

FLOWER TOP

This simple T-shaped top has a pretty frilled bottom edge made by decreasing stitches (see page 28). The simple three colour motif is knitted from the chart on page 156 and outlined in chain stitch (see page 83). It fastens at the back of the neck.

To fit age 6–12 [12-18] months
Actual chest measurement 18 [21] in (46 [54] cm)

you will need

MATERIALS
Worsted (DK) yarn (wool/cotton mix) – 123yd/113m per ball
1 × 1¾oz (50g) each in colour:
A green
B aqua blue
C pale lilac

2 buttons

NEEDLES
Size 3 (3.25mm/UK10) needles
Size 6 (4mm/UK8) needles

3 stitch holders

Gauge (Tension)
22 sts and 28 rows to 4in (10cm) measured over stockinette (stocking) stitch on size 6 (4mm/UK8) needles

FRONT
Using size 6 (4mm/UK8) needles and B, cast on 123[143] sts.
Row 1 (RS) P3, * k7, p3; rep from * to end.
Row 2 K3, * p7, k3; rep from * to end.
Row 3 P3, * skpo, k3, k2tog, p3; rep from * to end.
Row 4 K3, * p5, k3; rep from * to end.
Row 5 P3, * skpo, k1, k2tog, p3; rep from * to end.
Row 6 K3, * p3, k3; rep from * to end.
Row 7 P3, *sk2po, p3; rep from * to end. 51[59] sts.
Change to A.
Work 3[4]in (9[10] cm) in st st, beginning and ending with a p row.
Start colour pattern.
Next row K17[21]A, work first row of chart, k17[21]A.
Next row P17[21]A, work 2nd row of chart, p17[21]A.
Cont in this way until 18th row of chart has been completed.
Using A only, work 2 rows in st st.
SHAPE NECK
Next row K22[25] and turn, leaving rem sts on a stitch holder.
Dec 1 st at neck edge on next and every foll row to 17[19] sts.
Work straight until front measures 8[9]in (20.5[23]cm) from beg, ending with a p row.
Bind (cast) off.
With RS of work facing, slip centre 7[9] sts on to a stitch holder, rejoin A and k to end.
Dec 1 st at neck edge on next and every foll row to 17[19] sts.
Work straight until work measures same as other side of neck, ending with a p row.
Bind (cast) off.

BACK
Work as given for Front (omitting chart) until back measures 5[6]in (12.5[15cm), ending with a p row.
BACK NECK OPENING
Next row K25[29] and turn, leaving rem sts on a stitch holder.
Work straight on these 25[29] sts until back measures same as front, ending with a p row.
Bind (cast) off 17[19] sts, leave rem 8[10] sts on a stitch holder.
With RS of work facing, rejoin yarn to rem 26[30] sts and bind (cast) off 1 st, k to end. 25[29] sts.
Work straight to match first side, ending with a p row.
Next row K8[10], bind (cast) off 17[19] sts.
Slip these 8[10] sts on to a stitch holder.

SLEEVES (BOTH ALIKE)
Using size 6 (4mm/UK8) needles and B, cast on 29[35] sts.
Knit 3 rows.
Change to C and cont in st st, starting with a k row. Inc 1 st at each end of 3rd and every foll 4th row to 41[55] sts.
Work straight until sleeve measures 5[7]in (12.5[18]cm), ending with a p row.
Bind (cast) off.

FINISHING
NECKBAND
Join shoulder seams. With RS facing, using size 3(3.25mm/UK10) needles and B, k across 8[10] sts at left back neck, pick up and k 9[11] sts down left side of front neck, k across 7[9] sts at centre front, pick

up and k 9[11] sts up right side of neck, k across 8[10] sts at right back neck. 41[51] sts.
Knit 2 rows. Bind (cast) off.

BUTTON BAND
With RS of work facing, using size 3 (3.25mm/UK10) needles and B, pick up and k 20 sts up left side of back neck opening.
Knit 1 row.
Buttonhole row (K8, yo, k2tog) twice.
Knit 1 row.
Bind (cast) off.

BUTTONHOLE BAND
With RS of work facing, using size 3 (3.25mm/ UK10) needles and B, pick up and k 20 sts down right side of back neck opening.
Knit 2 rows.
Bind (cast) off.

CHAIN STITCH
Using A, work chain stitch (page 83) around the flower. Outline the centre with B.

FINISHING
Place markers 4[5]in (10[12.5]cm) from shoulder seam on armhole edges.
Sew in sleeves between markers.
Join side and sleeve seams.
Sew on buttons.

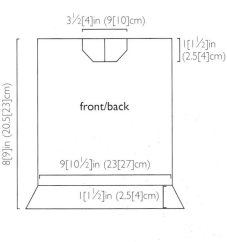

3½[4]in (9[10]cm)
1[1½]in (2.5[4]cm)
8[9]in (20.5[23]cm)
front/back
9[10½]in (23[27]cm)
1[1½]in (2.5[4]cm)

8[10]in (20.3[25.5]cm)
5[7]in (12.5[18]cm)
sleeve
5[6]in (12.5[15]cm)

STRIPED BAG

The back and front of this simple yet eye-catching bag are knitted in one piece in stockinette (stocking) stitch (see page 23). It is then sewn up and the handles and lining attached.

■ Bag measures 6¾in (17cm) wide by 7in (18cm) long, excluding handles

you will need

MATERIALS
Mercerized sport weight (4ply) cotton yarn – 125yd/115m per ball
1 x 1¾oz (50g) each in colour:
A wine
B pale pink
C rose pink
D white
E leaf green

15in (37cm) x 8in (19.5cm) calico or closely woven cotton fabric for lining

Sewing thread to match lining

NEEDLES
Size 3 (3.25mm/UK10) needles

■ Gauge (Tension)
23 sts and 32 rows to 4in (10cm) measured over st st on size 3 (3.25mm/UK10) needles

BACK AND FRONT
Using size 3 (3.25mm/UK10) needles and A, cast on 80 sts.
Working in st st, work in stripe patt of
* 6 rows A, 2 rows B, 4 rows C, 2 rows B, 2 rows D, 2 rows A, 2 rows C, 4 rows E, 6 rows B *, 2 rows D, 2 rows C, 2 rows E.
Work another 30 rows in stripe patt from * to *.
Using B, bind (cast) off.

HANDLES (MAKE 2 ALIKE)
Using size 3 (3.25mm/UK10) needles and A, cast on 60 sts.
Working in st st, work in stripe patt of 2 rows A, 2 rows C, 2 rows E, 6 rows B.
Using B, bind (cast) off.

FINISHING
Block the piece to measurements.
Fold front and back in half with RS together and sew side and bottom seams. Fold the 6 rows of B to the inside to form a facing and sew into place. Fold handles along their length and slipstitch cast on edge to bound (cast) off edge. Place markers for handles 1½in (4cm) from the sides along the top edge. Sew handles to bag, through facing only.

LINING
Neaten the edges of the fabric. Fold in half and sew side seams, using a seam allowance of ⅝in (1.5cm). Fold over the seam allowance along top edge and press. Push lining into bag with wrong sides together and sew along the facing.

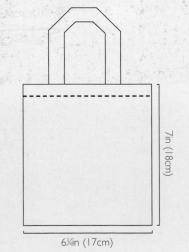

7in (18cm)
6¾in (17cm)

CABLE THROW

Each cable panel is knitted separately so this throw is quick and easy to knit (see page 40). All the cable designs used are included in the Stitch library (see pages 108–16) so simply follow the instructions for each one to make the panels. There are additional cable patterns in the library so you could substitute your own choice of pattern but make sure you choose a mix of large and small cables. The throw can be knitted in stripes as shown or all in one colour.

Throw measures approx 46in (117cm) wide by 50in (127cm) long

you will need

MATERIALS
Chunky tweed-effect wool yarn – 142yd/130m per ball as follows:
3 x 3½oz/100g hanks each in colours:
A oatmeal
B blue green
C moss green

2 x 3½oz/100g hanks in colour:
D grey

To make the throw in one colour you will need 11 hanks

NEEDLES
Size 10½ (7mm/UK2) needles
Cable needle

Gauge (Tension)
12 sts and 17 rows to 4in (10cm) measured over stockinette (stocking) stitch on size 10½ (7mm/UK2) needles

BASIC CABLE PANEL
Using size 10½ (7mm/UK2) needles cast on number of stitches required for cable pattern plus 3 sts of rev st st and 3 sts of st st each side (cable pattern sts plus 12 sts).
Knit 3 rows.
Row 1 (RS) K3, p3, work first row of cable pattern, p3, k3.
Row 2 P3, k3, work 2nd row of cable pattern, k3, p3.
Cont in patt as set until cable panel measures 50in (127cm) from beg, ending with a RS row.
Knit 3 rows.
Bind (cast) off.

Celtic cable, panel 3

Triple twist cable, panel 5

Use these instructions to work the following cable panels.
PANEL 1
Ripple and rock (see page 112) using C.
PANEL 2
Oxo cable (see page 109) using B.
PANEL 3
Celtic cable (see page 110) using A.
PANEL 4
Four stitch wave cable (see page 108) using D.
PANEL 5
Triple twist cable (see page 111) using B.
PANEL 6
Six stitch cable – crosses every eighth row (see page 108) using C.
PANEL 7
Hollow oak cable (see page 111) using D.
PANEL 8
Braid cable (see page 112) using A.

FINISHING
Work as many panels as required. Block the pieces to length measurement. Lay the pieces out side by side and sew together (see page 70).

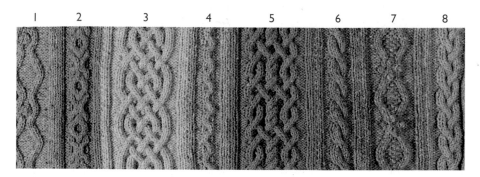

1 2 3 4 5 6 7 8

PLACE MAT AND COASTER

The place mat is made up of panels of stitches twisted symmetrically to the left and right forming heart-shaped outlines in the stocking stitch (see page 46). The panels are separated by columns of moss stitch, which is also used to give a firm edge round the mats. A single heart-shaped panel is used on the moss stitch coaster. A final touch is a handy pocket at the side to hold cutlery.

Mat measures 13in (33cm) wide by 10in (25.5cm) side
Coaster measures 4in (10cm) square

you will need

MATERIALS
Worsted (DK) weight cotton (92yd/84m per ball) as follows:
3 x 1¾oz/50g balls in bright green

NEEDLES
Size 6 (4mm/UK8) needles
Spare needle

Gauge (Tension)
22 sts and 29 rows to 4in (10cm) measured over stockinette (stocking) stitch on size 6 (4mm/UK8) needles

PLACE MAT

POCKET LINING
Using size 6 (4mm/UK8) needles cast on 12 sts.
Row 1 P1, k3, RT, LT, k3, p1,
Row 2 P to end.
Row 3 P1, LT, RT, k2, LT, RT, p1.
Row 4 P1, k1, p8, k1, p1.
Row 5 P1, k1, RT, k4, LT, k1, p1.
Row 6 As row 4.
Row 7 P1, RT, k6, LT, p1.
Row 8 P to end.
Rep these 8 rows twice more, then rows 1 and 2 again.
Leave these 12 sts on a spare needle.
MAT
Using 6 (4mm/UK8) needles cast on 63 sts.
Row 1 P1, * k1, p1; rep from * to end.
This row forms moss st. Rep this row twice more.
Inc row Moss st 7 sts, M1 knitwise, (moss st 12 sts, M1 knitwise) 4 times, moss st to end. 68 sts.
Start patt.
Row 1 P1, k1, p1, * k3, RT, LT, k3, p1, k1, p1; rep from * to end.
Row 2 P1, k1, * p12, k1; rep from * to last st, p1.
Row 3 P1, k1, p1, * LT, RT, k2, LT, RT, p1, k1, p1; rep from * to end.
Row 4 (P1, k1) twice, * p8, (k1, p1) twice, k1; rep from * to last 12 sts, p8, (k1, p1) twice.
Row 5 (P1, k1) twice, * RT, k4, LT, (k1, p1) twice, k1; rep from * to last 12 sts, RT, k4, LT, (k1, p1) twice.
Row 6 As row 4.
Row 7 P1, k1, p1, * RT, k6, LT, p1, k1, p1; rep from * to end.
Row 8 As row 2.
Rep these 8 rows twice more, then rows 1 to 5 again.
POCKET BORDER
Next row (WS) Patt to last 17 sts, (k1, p1) twice, k1, p2tog, (k1, p1) 5 times.

Next row (P1, k1) 7 times, p1, patt to end.
Next row Patt to last 15 sts, (p1, k1) 7 times, p1.
Next row (P1, k1) 7 times, p1, patt to end.
Next row Patt to last 13 sts, cast off 11 sts in patt, patt to end.
JOIN IN POCKET LINING
Next row P1, k1, patt across 12 sts of pocket lining, patt to end.
Cont in patt until piece measures approx 10in (25cm) from beg, ending with row 5.
Dec row (P1, k1) twice, p2tog, * (k1, p1) 5 times, k1, p2tog; rep from * 4 times, (k1, p1) 5 times.
Moss st 3 rows.
Bind (cast) off in patt.

COASTER

Using size 6 (4mm/UK8) needles cast on 19 sts and work 3 rows in moss st as given for mat.
Inc row Moss st 9 sts, M1 knitwise, moss st to end. 20 sts.
Row 1 (P1, k1) twice, p1, k3, RT, LT, k3, (p1, k1) twice, p1.
Row 2 (P1, k1) twice, p12, (k1, p1) twice.
Row 3 (P1, k1) twice, p1, LT, RT, k2, RT, LT, (p1, k1) twice, p1.
Row 4 (P1, k1) 3 times, p8, (k1, p1) 3 times.
Row 5 (P1, k1) 3 times, RT, k4, LT, (k1, p1) 3 times.
Row 6 As row 4.
Row 7 (P1, k1) twice, p1, RT, k6, LT, (p1, k1) twice, p1.
Row 8 (P1, k1) twice, p12, (k1, p1) twice.
Rep these 8 rows once more, then rows 1 to 5 again.
Dec row (P1, k1) 3 times, p2tog, (k1, p1) 6 times.
Moss st 3 rows.
Bind (cast) off in patt.

FINISHING
Block pieces to measurements. Sew pocket lining to mat.

FUN CHILDREN'S MITTENS

Bear   Tiger

These brightly coloured mittens with their animal faces are fun to knit and introduce the technique of circular knitting using a set of double-pointed needles (see page 50). The faces are knitted and embroidered separately and stitched on to the backs of the mittens in pairs (see page 85).

Mittens measure 3½ [4]in (9 [10]cm) across palm and are 5 [5½]in (12.5 [14]cm) long

you will need

MATERIALS
Worsted (DK) weight wool yarn (131yd/120m per ball)
1 x 1¾oz/50g ball each in colours:

Tiger

MC orange
A black
B cream
oddment of pink for nose

Bear

MC dark brown
A light brown
oddment of black for face

Dog

MC light brown
A beige
oddment of black for face

Cat

MC ginger
A cream
oddments of pink for nose and black for face

Note: oddments mean that only a small amount is needed;, use tapestry wool with an equivalent thickness to a worsted (DK) or leftover yarn

NEEDLES
Set of 4 size 3 (3.25mm/UK10) double-pointed needles
Set of 4 size 6 (4mm/UK8) double-pointed needles

Stitch holder

Gauge (Tension)
22 sts and 28 rows to 4in (10cm) measured over stockinette (stocking) stitch on size 6 (4mm/UK8) needles

TIGER MITTENS
(make 2)
Using size 3 (3.25mm/UK10) needles and MC, cast on 30[36] sts and divide between 3 needles.
Round 1 K1, * p1, k1; rep from * to end. Rep this round 12 times more.
Change to size 6 (4mm/UK8) needles and, working in st st and stripe pattern of 4 rows MC and 2 rows A, knit 2[4] rows.
START THUMB GUSSET
Round 1 K14[17], M1, k2, M1, k14[17]. Knit 2 rounds straight.
Round 4 K14[17], M1, k4, M1, k14[17]. Knit 2 rounds straight.
Round 7 K14[17], M1, k6, M1, k14[17]. Knit 2 rounds straight.
Round 10 K14[17], M1, k8, M1, k14[17]. Knit 2 rounds straight.
Round 13 K14[17], slip next 10 sts on to st holder, cast on 2 sts, k to end. 30[36] sts. Knit 8[12] rows straight.
SHAPE TOP
Dec round (K4, k2tog) 5[6] times. Knit 2 rounds straight.
Dec round (K3, k2tog) 5[6] times. Knit 2 rounds straight.
Dec round (K2, k2tog) 5[6] times. Bind (cast) off rem 15[18] sts.
THUMB
Slip 10 sts from stitch holder on to 3 needles, rejoin yarn and k10 then pick up and k 2 sts from those bound (cast) off previously. 12 sts.
Knit 7[9] rounds straight.
Dec round (K1, k2tog) 4 times.
Dec round (K2tog) 4 times.
Cut yarn, thread through rem 4 sts and pull up.
FACE (MAKE 1 FOR EACH MITTEN)
Using 2 size 3 (3.25mm/UK10) needles and B, cast on 9[11] sts. Turn the work at the end of each row for flat knitting. Working in st st, starting with a k row, inc 1 st at each end of 2nd and foll 2 rows. 15[17] sts.
Work 4[6] rows without shaping.
Dec 1 st at each end of next 3 rows.
Bind (cast) off.

EYES (MAKE 2 FOR EACH MITTEN)
Using 2 size 3 (3.25mm/UK10) needles and A, cast on 2 sts.
P 1 row.
Cont in st st, starting with a k row, inc 1 st at each end of next row.
Work 2 rows.
Dec 1 st at each end of next row.
Bind (cast) off.
NOSE (MAKE 1 FOR EACH MITTEN)
Using 2 size 3 (3.25mm/UK10) needles and pink, cast on 3 sts.
P 1 row.
Cont in st st, starting with a k row, inc 1 st at each end of next and foll alt row.
P 1 row.
Bind (cast) off.
OUTER EARS (MAKE 2 FOR EACH MITTEN)
Using 2 size 3 (3.25mm/UK10) needles and MC, cast on 10 sts.
Knit 2 rows.
Cont in g st, dec 1 st at each end of next and every foll alt row to 2 sts.
K2tog, cut yarn and pull through rem st.
INNER EARS (MAKE 2 FOR EACH MITTEN)
Using 2 size 3 (3.25mm/UK10) needles and B, cast on 6 sts.
P 1 row.
Cont in st st, starting with a k row, dec 1 st at each end of next and foll alt row.
Work 1 row.
K2tog, cut yarn and pull through rem st.

FINISHING
Sew nose on face, matching bind (cast) off edges. Using black, and referring to the picture, backstitch the mouth and use long straight stitches for the whiskers. Sew the face on to the mitten. Sew the eyes on to the mitten above the face. Sew the inner ear to the outer ear, matching cast on edges and points. Sew the ears either side of the mitten at the top.

BEAR MITTENS

Using MC only, work two mittens as given for Tiger.

FACE, NOSE AND EYES

Work as given for Tiger, using A for the face and black for the nose and eyes.

OUTER EARS (MAKE 2 FOR EACH MITTEN)

Using 2 size 3 (3.25mm/UK10) needles and A, cast on 12 sts.
Knit 4 rows.
Cont in g st, dec 1 st at each end of every row to 4 sts.
Bind (cast) off.

INNER EARS (MAKE 2 FOR EACH MITTEN)

Using 2 size 3 (3.25mm/UK10) needles and MC, cast on 6 sts.
Work 3 rows in st st, starting with a k row.
Dec 1 st at each end of next row.
Bind (cast) off.

FINISHING

Finish as given for Tiger (omit whiskers).

CAT MITTENS

Using MC only, work two mittens as given for Tiger.

FACE, NOSE, EYES AND EARS

Work as given for Tiger, using A for the face, pink for the nose, black for the eyes, MC for the outer ear and A for the inner ear. Finish as given for Tiger.

DOG MITTENS

Using MC only, work two mittens as given for Tiger.

FACE, NOSE, EYES AND OUTER EARS

Work as given for Tiger, using A for the face and outer ears, and black for the nose, mouth and eyes. Finish as given for Tiger (omitting inner ears and whiskers).

Cat

Dog

RIB STITCH SCARF

This warm sampler scarf is worked in blocks of six different rib patterns and is ideal for practising knitting ribs (see page 30). The first stitch of every row is slipped to give a neat edge (see page 32).

Scarf measures approx 6in (15cm) wide by 64in (162cm) long

you will need

MATERIALS
Chunky tweed-effect wool yarn (142yd/130m per ball):
2 x 3½oz/100g balls in colour dark red

NEEDLES
Size 10½ (6.5mm/UK3)

Gauge (Tension)
18 sts and 18 rows to 4in (10cm) measured over k2, p2 rib (slightly stretched) on size 10½ (6.5mm/UK3) needles

SCARF

Using size $10^{1}/_{2}$ (6.5mm/UK3) needles cast on 27 sts.
Row 1 (RS) Sl 1, k1, (p3, k2) 5 times.
Row 2 Sl 1, p1, (k3, p2) 5 times.
Rep these 2 rows 8 times more.
Row 19 Sl 1, k1, (p2, k1) 8 times, k1.
Row 20 Sl 1, p1, (k2, p1) 8 times, p1.
Rep these 2 rows 8 times more.
Row 37 Sl 1, k1, (p2, k3) 5 times.
Row 38 Sl 1, p2, k2, (p3, k2) 4 times, p2.
Rep these 2 rows 8 times more.
Row 55 Sl 1, k1, (p2, k2) 6 times, k1.
Row 56 Sl 1, p2, (k2, p2) 6 times.
Rep these 2 rows 8 times more.
Row 73 Sl 1, k1, (p3, k1) 6 times, k1.
Row 74 Sl 1, p1, (k3, p1) 6 times, p1.
Rep these 2 rows 8 times more.
Row 91 Sl 1, k2, (p4, k4) 3 times.
Row 92 Sl 1, p3, (k4, p4) twice, k4, p3.
Rep these 2 rows 8 times more.
These 108 rows form the patt.
Cont in patt, beg with row 1, until scarf measures 64in (162cm) or length required, ending with the last row of a rib stripe.
Bind (cast) off in patt.

FINISHING

Block scarf to measurements, without overstretching the ribs.

SHORT ROW CUSHION

Knitted in a luxurious multicoloured silk yarn this elegant cushion has V-shaped points which are worked individually along one row of knitting. Each point is finished with a pair of beads and the rows are set alternately to give a tiled effect. The finished cushion is unusual and gives practise in the technique of knitting short rows (see page 44).

■ Cushion measures 15in (38cm) square

you will need

MATERIALS
Sport (4ply) weight silk yarn:
2 × 1¾oz/50g skeins in shades of blue

Fabric for back of cushion

15in (38cm) square cushion pad

36 large beads and 72 small beads in shades of blue and green

NEEDLES
Size 3 (3.25mm/UK10) needles

Gauge (Tension)
26 sts and 32 rows to 4in (10cm) measured over stockinette (stocking) stitch on size 3 (3.25mm/UK10) needles

Special Abbreviation
MAKE A POINT
Row 1 P14 and turn.
Row 2 K13 and turn.
Row 3 P12 and turn.
Row 4 K11 and turn.
Row 5 P10 and turn.
Row 6 K9 and turn.
Row 7 P8 and turn.
Row 8 K7 and turn.
Row 9 P6 and turn.
Row 10 K5 and turn.
Row 11 P4 and turn.
Row 12 K3 and turn.
Row 13 P4 and turn.
Row 14 K5 and turn.
Row 15 P6 and turn.
Row 16 K7 and turn.
Row 17 P8 and turn.
Row 18 K9 and turn.
Row 19 P10 and turn.
Row 20 K11 and turn.
Row 21 P12 and turn.
Row 22 K13 and turn.
Row 23 P14 and turn.

FRONT
Using size 3 (3.25mm/UK10) needles, cast on 97 sts and work 16 rows in st st, beg with a k row.
** Work a row of 5 points as follows:
K20 and turn, make a point, (k33 and turn, make a point) 4 times, k20 (end of row).
Working across all sts, work 13 rows in st st, beg with a p row.
Work a row of 4 points as follows:
K29 and turn, make a point, (k33 and turn, make a point) 3 times, k29 (end of row). **
Working across all sts, work 13 rows in st st, beg with a p row. ***
Work from ** to *** 3 times more, ending with 5 rows of st st, instead of 13 rows. Bind (cast) off.

FINISHING
Sew all the points closed at the top by joining the first and last rows. Block the front to 15in (38cm) square, pulling the points into shape. To sew on the beads, secure strong thread behind the point, put one large bead and then two small beads on to the needle, pull the thread through. Take the thread back through the small bead next to the large bead and through the large bead. Secure the thread behind the point. Cut a 17in (43cm) square from fabric and neaten the edges to prevent fraying. With RS together, pin the knitting to the fabric, taking care not to stretch the knitting. Sew around three sides, leaving the bottom edge open. Turn right side out and insert cushion pad. Sew the bottom seam closed.

BERET

This pretty beret is knitted in three sizes to fit a child and a small and average size for a woman. Knit it in an attractive tweedy wool for winter or make a fun striped version. All the shaping is done by increasing and decreasing stitches (see page 26–9).

■ To fit head circumference 18 [20:22]in (45.5 [51:56]cm)

STRIPED BERET

you will need

MATERIALS
Worsted (DK) weight wool yarn (131yd/120m per ball):
1 x 1¾oz/50g balls each in colour:
A pale rose
B purple

NEEDLES
Size 3 (3.25mm/UK10) needles
Size 6 (4mm/UK8) needles

Gauge (Tension)
22 sts and 28 rows to 4in (10cm) measured over stockinette (stocking) stitch on size 6 (4mm/UK8) needles

Using size 3 (3.25mm/UK10) needles and A, cast on 91[101:111] sts.
Row 1 (RS) K1, * p1, k1; rep from * to end.
Row 2 P1, * k1, p1; rep from * to end.
Rep these 2 rows twice more.
Change to size 6 (4mm/UK8) needles and B. Work in stripe patt of 4 rows B, 4 rows A throughout.
Inc row (K5[5:6], M1, k4[5:5], M1) 10 times, k1. 111[121:131] sts.
Work 11 rows in st st, beg with a p row.
Inc row (K6[6:7], M1, k5[6:6], M1) 10 times, k1. 131[141:151] sts.
Work 9[11:13] rows in st st.
3rd size only
Dec row (K13, k2tog) 10 times, k1. 141 sts.
Work 3 rows in st st.
2nd and 3rd sizes only
Dec row (K12, k2tog) 10 times, k1. 131 sts.
Work 3 rows in st st.
All sizes
Dec row (K11, k2tog) 10 times, k1. 121 sts.
Work 3[3:1] rows.
Dec row (K10, k2tog) 10 times, k1. 111 sts.
Work 3[1:1] rows.
Dec row (K9, k2tog) 10 times, k1. 101 sts.
P 1 row.
Dec row (K8, k2tog) 10 times, k1. 91 sts.
P 1 row.
Dec row (K7, k2tog) 10 times, k1. 81 sts.
P 1 row.
Dec row (K6, k2tog) 10 times, k1. 71 sts.
P 1 row.
Dec row (K5, k2tog) 10 times, k1. 61 sts.
P 1 row.
Dec row (K4, k2tog) 10 times, k1. 51 sts.
P 1 row.
Dec row (K3, k2tog) 10 times, k1. 41 sts.
Dec row P1, (p2tog, p2) 10 times. 31 sts.
Dec row (K1, k2tog) 10 times, k1. 21 sts.
Dec row P1, (p2tog) 9 times, p2. 12 sts.
Cut yarn and draw through rem 12 sts.

FINISHING
Sew up seam (see page 70).

PLAIN BERET

you will need

MATERIALS
Sport (4ply) weight tweed wool yarn (123yd/113m per ball)

1[2:2] x 1¾oz/50g balls in colour green

NEEDLES
Size 3 (3.25mm/UK10) needles
Size 6 (4mm/UK8) needles

Gauge (Tension)
22 sts and 28 rows to 4in (10cm) measured over stockinette (stocking) stitch on size 6 (4mm/UK8) needles

Work as given for striped beret using one colour throughout.

GARDEN PLOT SQUARES THROW

The medallion square used here is adapted from a traditional pattern called the Garden plot square or great-grandmother's bedspread. The square is knitted from corner to corner (see page 53) with a single leaf at the beginning and a line of smaller leaves across the middle at the widest point (see page 43). They are joined with the four single leaves placed together. Because it is knitted in squares, the work can be any size required, either to be used as a throw or made to fit a bed.

Throw measures 56in (142cm) square. A quarter of the throw is shown left
Each square measures approximately 8½in (21.5cm)
Border measures 2½in (6.5cm) wide

you will need

MATERIALS
Worsted (DK) weight cotton yarn (93yd/85m per ball):
34 x 1¾oz/50g balls in colour pale grey

NEEDLES
Size 6 (4mm/UK8) needles

Gauge (Tension)
19 sts and 28 rows to 4in (10cm) measured over stockinette (stocking) stitch on size 6 (4mm/UK8) needles

Special Abbreviation
MB (make a bobble) – (k1, k1tbl) twice, k1 all into next st, pass 2nd, 3rd, 4th and 5th sts over first st (see page 42)

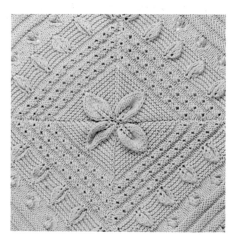

SQUARE (MAKE 36)
Using size 6 (4mm/UK8) needles cast on 3 sts.
Row 1 Yo, k3.
Row 2 Yo, k4.
Row 3 Yo, k2, yo, k1, yo, k2.
Row 4 Yo, k2, p3, k3.
Row 5 Yo, k4, yo, k1, yo, k4.
Row 6 Yo, k3, p5, k4.
Row 7 Yo, k6, yo, k1, yo, k6.
Row 8 Yo, k4, p7, k5.
Row 9 Yo, k8, yo, k1, yo, k8.
Row 10 Yo, k5, p9, k6.
Row 11 Yo, k10, yo, k1, yo, k10.
Row 12 Yo, k6, p11, k7.
Row 13 Yo, k7, ssk, k7, k2tog, k7.
Row 14 Yo, k7, p9, k8.
Row 15 Yo, k8, ssk, k5, k2tog, k8.
Row 16 Yo, k8, p7, k9.
Row 17 Yo, k9, ssk, k3, k2tog, k9.
Row 18 Yo, k9, p5, k10.
Row 19 Yo, k10, ssk, k1, k2tog, k10.
Row 20 Yo, k10, p3, k11.
Row 21 Yo, k11, sl2tog-k1-psso, k11. 24 sts.
Rows 22 and 23 Yo, k to end.
Row 24 Yo, p to end.
Rows 25 and 26 Yo, k to end.
Row 27 Yo, p2, * yo, p2tog, p1; rep from * to end.
Rep rows 22 to 27 twice more, then rows 22 to 26 once more. 47 sts.
Row 45 Yo, k3, yo, k1, yo, (k7, yo, k1, yo) 5 times, k3.
Row 46 Yo, k3, p3, (k7, p3) 5 times, k4.
Row 47 Yo, k5, yo, k1, yo, (k9, yo, k1, yo) 5 times, k5.
Row 48 Yo, k4, p5, (k7, p5) 5 times, k5.
Row 49 Yo, k7, yo, k1, yo, (k11, yo, k1, yo) 5 times, k7.
Row 50 Yo, k5, p7, (k7, p7) 5 times, k6. (Place a marker here for corner of square. The square now begins to decrease.)

Row 51 Ssk, k4, ssk, k3, k2tog, (k7, ssk, k3, k2tog) 5 times, k4, k2tog.
Row 52 K5, p5, (k7, p5) 5 times, k5.
Row 53 Ssk, k3, ssk, k1, k2tog, (k7, ssk, k1, k2tog) 5 times, k3, k2tog.
Row 54 K4, p3, (k7, p3) 5 times, k4.
Row 55 Ssk, k2, sl2tog-k1-psso, (k7, sl2tog-k1-psso) 5 times, k2, k2tog. 47 sts.
Row 56 K to end.
Row 57 Ssk, k43, k2tog.
Row 58 P to end.
Row 59 Ssk, k4, yo, ssk, (k6, yo, ssk) 4 times, k3, k2tog.
Row 60 P to end.
Row 61 Ssk, k1, k2tog, yo, k1, yo, ssk, (k3, k2tog, yo, k1, yo, ssk) 4 times, k1, k2tog.
Row 62 P to end.
Row 63 Ssk, k2, MB, (k7, MB) 4 times, k2, k2tog.
Row 64 P to end. 39 sts.
Row 65 Ssk, k to last 2 sts, k2tog.
Row 66 K to end.
Row 67 P2tog, p to last 2 sts, ssp.
Row 68 K to end.
Row 69 Ssk, k to last 2 sts, k2tog.
Row 70 P to end.
Rep rows 65 to 70 twice more. 21 sts.
Row 83 Ssk, k8, yo, ssk, k7, k2tog.
Row 84 P to end.
Row 85 Ssk, k5, k2tog, yo, k1, yo, ssk, k5, k2tog.
Row 86 P to end.
Row 87 Ssk, k6, MB, k6, k2tog.
Row 88 P to end. 15 sts.
Row 89 Ssk, k to last 2 sts, k2tog.
Row 90 K to end.
Rep rows 89 and 90 until 3 sts remain.
Row 99 Sk2po.
Cut yarn and draw through rem st.

FINISHING

Block each medallion square to 8$\frac{1}{2}$in (21.5cm), making sure the corners are square. Join together with single leaves meeting in the middle.

BORDER

The number of sts increases by one on every RS row until row 14 where the extra sts are bound (cast) off.
Using size 6 (4mm/UK8) needles cast on 7 sts.
Row 1 (RS) K3, yfwd, k2tog, yfwd, k2.
Rows 2, 4, 6, 8, 10 and 12 K to end.
Row 3 K4, yfwd, k2tog, yfwd, k2.
Row 5 K5, yfwd, k2tog, yfwd, k2.
Row 7 K6, yfwd, k2tog, yfwd, k2.
Row 9 K7, yfwd, k2tog, yfwd, k2.
Row 11 K8, yfwd, k2tog, yfwd, k2.
Row 13 K9, yfwd, k2tog, yfwd, k2.
Row 14 Bind (cast) off 7 sts, k to end.
7 sts.
Rep these 14 rows until border is long enough to fit around throw.
Sew on border, easing it around corners.

MAKING A LARGER BEDSPREAD

You can knit more squares to make a larger throw or a bedspread. For a bedspread, measure the width and length of the bed or an existing bedspread of the required size. Your bedspread will look best if it is an even number of squares wide and long. Each square is 8$\frac{1}{2}$in (21.5cm). Divide the width and length by 8$\frac{1}{2}$in (21.5cm) and round the results up or down to an even number and then add 5in (13cm) for the border.

For example, to make a single bedspread measuring 83in (211cm) x 100in (254cm):
The width 83in (211cm) is divided by 8$\frac{1}{2}$in (21.5cm) = 9.8 squares.
Round up to 10.
The length 100in (254cm) is divided by 8$\frac{1}{2}$in (21.5cm) = 11.8 squares. Round up to 12. A total of 120 squares.

Yarn Amounts

$\frac{4}{5}$ (0.8) of a ball will knit 1 square.
1 ball will knit approx 52in (132cm) of border.
For a bedspread of 120 squares multiply 120 by $\frac{4}{5}$ (0.8) = 96 balls.
Border measures 2 x 90in (228cm) + 2 x 107in (271cm) = 394in (998cm) divided by 52in (132cm) = 7.5 balls.
Total number of balls required = 103.5 rounded up to 104 balls.

BEADED BAG

This shimmering evening bag is knitted in lurex and for added glitz tiny bronze beads are set around the eyelet holes of the lace pattern. The beads are threaded on to the yarn before starting to knit and added in as instructed (see page 56).

Bag measures 6in (17cm) wide by 7in (18cm) long, excluding handles

you will need

MATERIALS

Sport (4ply) weight lurex yarn (80% viscose/20% polyester – 104 yd/95m)

2 x 1$\frac{3}{4}$oz/50g balls in colour gold

About 500 bronze beads

Fabric for handle and lining

NEEDLES
Size 3 (3.25mm/UK10) needles

Gauge (Tension)
29 sts and 41 rows to 4in (10cm) measured over lace pattern on size 3 (3.25mm/UK10) needles

Beads
Before beginning to knit, divide the beads in half and thread one half on to one ball and the rest of the beads on to the other ball.

BACK AND FRONT (MAKE 2)

Using size 3 (3.25mm/UK10) needles cast on 51 sts.
Start lace and bead patt.
Row 1 and every foll WS row P to end.
Row 2 (RS) K2, * yfwd, ssk, k5, PB, k5, k2tog, yfwd, k1; rep from * to last st, k1.
Row 4 K1, * yfwd, ssk, k4, PB, k3, PB, k5; rep from * to last 2 sts, yfwd, ssk.
Row 6 K5, PB, * k7, PB; rep from * to last 5 sts, k5.
Row 8 K3, * PB, k4, k2tog, yfwd, k5, PB, k3; rep from * to end.
Row 10 K1, PB, * k5, k2tog, yfwd, k1, yfwd, ssk, k5, PB; rep from * to last st, k1.
Row 12 K3, * PB, k5, yfwd, ssk, k4, PB, k3; rep from * to end.
Row 14 As row 6.
Row 16 * K2tog, yfwd, k5, PB, k3, PB, k4; rep from * to last 3 sts, k2tog, yfwd, k1.
Rep these 16 rows 4 times more, then rows 1 to 3 again.
Bind (cast) off loosely.

FINISHING

Block the back and front to 7in (18cm) wide by 8in (20.5cm) long. Join together along bottom and side edges. From the lining fabric, cut a piece 15$\frac{1}{4}$in (39cm) wide by 9$\frac{1}{4}$in (23.5cm) long. Neaten the edges to prevent fraying. With RS facing, fold in half and join the side seams with a $\frac{5}{8}$in (1.5cm) seam allowance. Fold $\frac{5}{8}$in (1.5cm) over at the top to the wrong side.

For the handle, cut two pieces of fabric 3in (7.5cm) wide and 13in (33cm) long. Fold in half and press, open out and then fold each edge into the middle and press. Fold in half again, along first fold line, to make a handle of four fabric thicknesses. Topstitch close to each edge.

Attach the handle firmly to the wrong side of the bag lining at the side seam and on the fold opposite. Push lining into bag with wrong sides together and sew into place around top edge.

SHEEP TOY

A great way to try the looped knitting technique (see page 55), this charming sheep has the fleece for its back and head knitted in one piece, with another piece for the underbelly. It isn't a suitable toy for babies and very young children to play with but will be treasured for future years.

■ Sheep's height is 5in (13cm)

you will need

MATERIALS
Worsted (DK) weight wool yarn (131yd/120m)
1 x 1¾oz/50g ball each in colours:
A white
B black

White toy stuffing

NEEDLES
Size 3 (3.25mm/UK10) needles

Gauge (Tension)
26 sts and 32 rows to 4in (10cm) measured over stockinette (stocking) stitch on size 3 (3.25mm/UK10) needles

BODY
Using size 3 (3.25mm/UK10) needles and A, cast on 42 sts, placing markers between sts 11 and 12 and between sts 30 and 31. Do not slip markers as you knit, leave them on the first row to use when sewing up.
** **Row 1** K1 tbl into each st to end.
Row 2 K1 tbl, loop st into each st to last st, k1 tbl.
Rep these 2 rows 4 times more.

SHAPE BACK LEGS
Next row Cast off 6 sts, k1 tbl into each st to end.
Next row Cast off 6 sts, loop st into each st to last st, k1 tbl.
Patt 8 rows.

SHAPE FRONT LEGS
Next row Cast on 6 sts, k1 tbl into each st to end.
Next row Cast on 6 sts, k1 tbl into first st, loop st into each st to last st, k1 tbl.
Patt 8 rows.
Next row Cast off 11 sts, k1 tbl into each st to end.
Next row Cast off 11 sts, loop st into each st to last st, k1 tbl. *** 20 sts.

SHAPE HEAD
Dec 1 st at each end of next and foll alt row. 16 sts.
Patt 12 rows.
Bind (cast) off loosely by k1 tbl into each st.

UNDERBELLY
Using size 3 (3.25mm/UK10) needles and A, cast on 22 sts and place a marker between sts 11 and 12.
Work as given for body from ** to ***.

HEAD
Using size 3 (3.25mm/UK10) needles and B, cast on 18 sts and work 2 rows in st st, starting with a k row.
Inc row K4, M1, (k1, M1) twice, k6, M1, (k1, M1) twice, k4. 24 sts.
P 1 row.
Inc row K5, M1, k3, M1, k8, M1, k3, M1, k5. 28 sts.
P 1 row.

Inc row K6, M1, k3, M1, k10, M1, k3, M1, k6. 32 sts.
P 1 row.
Inc row K7, M1, k3, M1, k12, M1, k3, M1, k7. 36 sts.
Work 11 rows in st st, starting with a p row.
Dec row K7, k2tog, k1, ssk, k12, k2tog, k1, ssk, k7. 32 sts.
Work 3 rows in st st.
Dec row K6, k2tog, k1, ssk, k10, k2tog, k1, ssk, k6. 28 sts.
P 1 row.
Dec row K5, k2tog, k1, ssk, k8, k2tog, k1, ssk, k5. 24 sts.
P 1 row.
Dec row K3, (k2tog, k2) 5 times, k1. 19 sts.
P1 row.
Bind (cast) off.

EARS (MAKE 2)
Using size 3 (3.25mm/UK10) needles and B, cast on 10 sts and work 2 rows in st st, starting with a k row.
Inc row K1, M1, k8, M1, k1. 12 sts.
P 1 row.
Inc row K1, M1, k10, M1, k1. 14 sts.
Work 3 rows in st st.
Dec 1 st at each end of next and every foll alt row to 8 sts.
P 1 row.
Cut yarn and thread through rem sts.

BACK LEGS (MAKE 2)
Join the body to the underbelly at back leg seams by matching markers. Join rem centre back seam.
With RS of work facing and using size 3 (3.25mm/UK10) needles and A, pick up and knit 20 sts evenly around back leg of body.
** **Dec row** K4, k2tog, k8, k2tog, k4. 18 sts.
Change to B and work 8 rows in st st, starting with a k row.
Dec row K1, (k2tog) 8 times, k1. 10 sts.
Dec row P1, (p2tog) 4 times, p1. 6 sts.
Cut yarn and thread through rem sts. ***
Join back leg seams. Join underbelly seam from top of back leg to bottom of front leg.

FAIR ISLE BABY BLANKET

For a first fair isle project this pretty patch is ideal. Knitted in the traditional way with only two colours used on each row it gives practise in holding the yarn in both hands and weaving the yarns in as you knit (see page 37-9). Colour charts for each of the pattern bands are given (see page 157) and the finished patch is sewn on to a piece of cosy fleece, edged in blanket stitch (see page 84). You can personalize the patch by inserting the baby's name using the alphabet given on page 156.

Patch measures 16in (40.5cm) wide by 23in (58.5cm) long
Blanket measures 26in (66cm) wide by 33in (84cm) long

FRONT LEGS (MAKE 2)

With RS of work facing and using A, pick up and knit 20 sts evenly around front leg of body.
Work as given for back legs from ** to ***.
Join front leg seams, leaving neck open.

FINISHING

Stuff the body making sure the legs are firm. Join centre back head seam. Join head at cast on edge, making sure the back seam is in the middle. Stuff the head firmly and join top seam. Fold the ears in half and join the seam. Attach to each side of the head at the beginning of the head decreases. Attach the loop stitch head piece to front of black head by sewing cast off edge between ears. Position the head into the neck opening and sew loop stitch fabric around head. Embroider two eyes using A.

you will need

MATERIALS

Worsted (DK) weight wool/cotton mix yarn (123yd/113m per ball):
1 x 1¾oz/50g ball each in colours:
MC cream
A light blue violet
B blue violet
C dark blue
D pale lilac
E mauve
F dark mauve
G light pink

26in (66cm) wide by 33in (84cm) long piece of fleece fabric in a complementary colour

NEEDLES
Size 6 (4mm/UK8) needles

Gauge (Tension)
24 sts and 24 rows to 4in (10cm) measured over fair isle pattern on size 6 (4mm/UK8) needles

FAIR ISLE PATCH

When working from the charts read RS rows (odd numbers) from right to left and WS rows (even numbers) from left to right.
Using size 6 (4mm/UK8) needles and D, cast on 97 sts and work 2 rows in st st, starting with a k row.
Work 10 rows from chart A.
Work 12 rows from chart B.
Work 14 rows from chart C.
Work 8 rows from chart D.
Work 10 rows from chart A.
Work 12 rows from chart B.
Work 18 rows from chart E.
Work 8 rows from chart D.
Work 10 rows from chart A. Insert baby's name if required on rows 2 to 8 using the alphabet given on page 156. Chart the name on to graph paper. If there is more than one name, use the small four-stitch motifs to separate them. Make sure the name is centred on the panel and that the fair isle pattern is the same each side. Use MC to work the name.
Work 12 rows from chart B.
Work 14 rows from chart F.
Work rows 1 to 4 from chart D.
Using G, bind (cast) off.

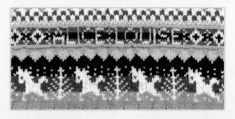

FINISHING

Block the knitted piece to 16in (40.5cm) wide by 23in (58.5cm) long. Sew it on to the centre of the fleece fabric. Using one of the yarn colours to contrast with the fleece, work blanket stitch around the edge of the fleece.

SCENTED SACHETS AND COVER

Fulling makes a denser knitted fabric (see page 60), which makes it ideal for these scented sachets and coat hanger cover. The attractive gingham pattern and the heart motif worked from a chart from the motif library (page 156) both use the fair isle method of stranding yarns (see page 38).

▌ Envelope sachet about 4in (10cm) square
▌ Heart sachet about 4in (10in) square
▌ Hanger cover 2in (5cm) wide by 14in (35.5cm) long

you will need

MATERIALS
Sport (4ply) weight shetland wool yarn (129yd/118m per ball)
1 x 1oz/25g ball each in colours:
A cream
B lilac
C purple

Lavender or similar to fill heart and envelope sachets

Envelope sachet: button, fabric for sachet 4in x 8in (10cm x 20cm)

Coat hanger cover: wadding

NEEDLES
Size 3 (3.25mm/UK10) needles

Gauge (Tension)
Before fulling: 30 sts and 30 rows to 4in (10cm) measured over gingham pattern on size 3 (3.25mm/UK10) needles
After fulling: 38 sts and 38 rows to 4in (10 cm) measured over gingham pattern

ENVELOPE SACHET

Using size 3 (3.25mm/UK10) needles and C, cast on 26 sts and work 4 rows in st st, beg with a k row.

START HEART MOTIF
Work from the chart given on page 156 of the Motif library.
Next row K5, work 16 sts of first row of chart from right to left, k to end.
Next row P5, work 16 sts of 2nd row of chart from left to right, p to end.
Cont as set until the 14th row of chart has been completed.
Work 80 rows in st st.
Bind (cast) off loosely.

FULLING
The piece is fulled until it measures approximately 4in (10cm) wide. Steam press flat.

FINISHING
Place markers to divide the length into three sections, making the heart motif end 1in (2.5cm) shorter than the other two sections. Fold the opposite end to the heart motif up at the marker and join the side seams to form an envelope. Fold the heart motif flap over. Make a 2in (5cm) twisted cord (see page 77) using two strands of purple wool. Sew on button. Make a small bag to contain the lavender by folding the fabric in half and joining the side seams. Fill with lavender and sew the top closed. Put lavender sachet into envelope.

HEART SACHET

(MAKE 2)
This is worked from the top down, the two top sections are worked separately, then joined to continue the heart shape. Carry yarn not in use loosely up the edge. Use the fair isle method of stranding.

FIRST SECTION
Using size 3 (3.25mm/UK10) needles and A, cast on 6 sts.
* **Row 1** (RS) K2B, k2A, k2B.
Row 2 Using A, cast on and p 2 sts, p2B, p2A, p2B. 8 sts.
Row 3 Using B, cast on and k 2 sts, k2C, k2B, k2C, k2B. 10 sts.
Row 4 Using B, p into front and back of first st, p1B, p2C, p2B, p2C, p1B, using B, p into front and back of last st. 12 sts.
Row 5 Using B, k into front and back of first st, (k2A, k2B) twice, k2A, using B, k into front and back of last st. 14 sts.
Row 6 Using B, p into front and back of first st, p1B, (p2A, p2B) twice, p2A, p1B, using B, p into front and back of last st. 16 sts. *
Cut yarns and push these 16 sts to the end of the needle.

SECOND SECTION
Using A, cast on 6 sts on to the same needle and work from * to *.
Row 7 K1B, (k2C, k2B) 7 times (working across first section as well), k2C, k1B. 32 sts.
Row 8 Using B, p into front and back of first st, (p2C, p2B) 7 times, p2C, using B, p into front and back of last st. 34 sts.
Row 9 K2A, * k2B, k2A; rep from * to end.
Row 10 P2A, * p2B, p2A; rep from * to end.
Row 11 K2B, * k2C, k2B; rep from * to end.
Row 12 P2B, * p2C, p2B; rep from * to end.
These 4 rows form the gingham check patt. Rep these 4 rows once more.
Keeping gingham patt correct as set, dec 1 st at each end of next and foll 2 alt rows, then at each end of every foll row to 2 sts. Bind (cast) off loosely.

LACE BAGS

Knitted in a 4ply mercerized cotton, these dainty lace bags can be filled with lavender, dried roses or pot pourri. The techniques required to create the lace pattern are yarn over (see page 35) and decreasing (see page 28).

Bag measures approximately 3in (7.5cm) wide by 4in (10cm) long

FULLING

The pieces are fulled until they measure approximately 4in (10cm) wide. Steam press each piece flat.

FINISHING

Join the two heart shapes together, leaving a gap at the top. Fill with lavender and sew gap closed. Make a twisted cord, 8in (20cm) long using two strands of purple yarn (see page 77) and sew to the top as a hanging loop.

COAT HANGER COVER

Using size 3 (3.25mm/UK10) needles and A, cast on 30 sts and work 142 rows in gingham check patt as given for heart sachet.
Bind (cast) off loosely.

FULLING

The piece is fulled until it measures approximately 4in (10cm) wide. Steam press flat.

FINISHING

Wrap wadding neatly around the hanger until it is covered. Fold the knitted cover in half along its length. Mark the centre of the long fold and push the hook of the coat hanger carefully through the fabric from the WS at this point. Pull the cover around the wadding and pin the ends together and the long seam at the bottom. Adjust the wadding if necessary. Sew the seams closed. Tie a piece of ribbon or twisted cord around the base of the hook and sew in place.

you will need

MATERIALS

Sport (4ply) weight mercerized cotton yarn (153yd/140m per ball)

Light Pink Bag

1 x 1¾oz/50g ball in light pink

Dark Pink Bag

1 x 1¾oz/50g ball in dark pink

Dark Purple Bag

1 x 1¾oz/50g ball in dark purple

20in (51cm) of ¼in (7mm) wide ribbon in a colour to match your chosen cotton yarn

White voile or organza for lining

Lavender, dried rose petals, pot pourri or similar

NEEDLES

Size 2 (3mm/UK11) needles

Gauge (Tension)

28 sts and 30 rows to 4in (10cm) measured over stockinette (stocking) stitch on size 2 (3mm/UK11) needles

LIGHT PINK BAG

Using size 2 (3mm/UK11) needles and A, cast on 41 sts and purl 1 row.
Work 40 rows in Dainty Chevron stitch (see Stitch library page 120), ending with a p row.

PICOT BIND (CAST) OFF

Next row Bind (cast) off 2 sts, * slip st back on to left-hand needle, cast on 2 sts using cable cast on method (see page 24), bind (cast) off 5 sts; rep from * to end. Cut yarn and draw through last st.

DARK PINK BAG

Using size 2 (3mm/UK11) needles and B, cast on 41 sts and purl 1 row.
Work 32 rows in Horseshoe Lace (see Stitch library page 121), ending with a p row.
Work the picot bind (cast) off as given for light pink bag.

DARK PURPLE BAG

Using size 2 (3mm/UK11) needles and C, cast on 45 sts and purl 1 row.
Work 36 rows in Snowflake Eyelets (see Stitch library page 121), ending with a p row.
Work the picot bind (cast) off as given for light pink bag.

FINISHING

Block bag to measurements, pinning each picot point separately. When dry remove pins and fold in half, wrong sides together, and join side and bottom seams. Cut a piece of lining fabric 7in (18cm) wide by 4in (10cm) long. Fold in half and join side and bottom seams. Finish the top edge to prevent fraying. Fill with lavender or chosen filling. Put filled lining into bag. Thread ribbon through holes in lace, approximately 1in (2.5cm) from top, beginning and ending at centre front. Pull up and tie securely with a bow.

FUNNEL NECK SWEATER

Knitted in stockinette (stocking) stitch, this sweater has square set in sleeves and a funnel neck. Because there's no neck shaping, a cable panel can easily be added to the front (see left). The instructions are for a plain sweater with suggestions on where to alter the length of the sleeves and body (see page 72). Separate instructions are given for the cable panel sweater (see page 73). Sizes are given for women, men and children.

ADULT'S PLAIN SWEATER

To fit bust/chest measurement 32/34[36/38:40/42:44/46]in (81.5/86.5[91.5/96.5:101.5/106.5:112/117]cm)

you will need

MATERIALS
Fisherman (aran) weight merino wool yarn (85yd/78m per ball): 15[16:17:18] x 1¾oz/50g balls in colour denim blue

NEEDLES
Size 6 (4mm/UK8) needles
Size 8 (5mm/UK6) needles

Gauge (Tension)
18 sts and 24 rows to 4in (10cm) measured over stockinette (stocking) stitch on size 8 (5mm/UK6) needles

Adult's sweater size diagram measurements

A 20 [22:24:26]in (51 [56:61:66]cm)

B 3in (7.5cm)

C 23½ [24½:25½:26]in (59.5 [62:65:66]cm)

D 2½in (6cm)

E 1in (2.5cm)

F 9 [10:10½:11]in (23 [25.5:26.5:28]cm)

G 13½ [13½:14:14]in (34.5 [34.5:35.5:35.5]cm)

H 8½ [9:9½:10]in (21.5 [23:24:25.5]cm)

I 5¾ [6½:7¼:8]in (14.5 [16.5:18.5:20.5]cm)

J 18 [20:21:22]in (46 [51:54:56]cm)

K 19 [21½:23:24]in (48.5 [54.5:58.5:61]cm)

L 11¾ [12½:13½:14½]in (30 [32:34.5:37]cm)

BACK AND FRONT (BOTH ALIKE)
Using size 6 (4mm/UK8) needles, cast on 91[99:109:117] sts.
Row 1 (RS) K1, * p1, k1; rep from * to end.
Row 2 P1, * k1, p1; rep from * to end.
Rep these 2 rows until rib measures 3in (7.5cm), ending with a WS row.
Change to size 8 (5mm/UK6) needles and work in st st (beg with a k row) until piece measures 13½[13½:14:14]in (34.5[34.5:35.5:35.5]cm) from beg, ending with a p row. (Alter this measurement to lengthen or shorten the sweater.)
SHAPE ARMHOLES
Cast off 5 sts at beg of next 2 rows. 81[89:99:107] sts.
Cont without shaping until armhole measures 9[10:10½:11]in (23[25.5:26.5:28]cm), ending with a p row.
SHAPE SHOULDERS
Cast off 7[8:9:0] sts at beg of next 4 rows then 5[6:8:9] sts at beg of next 2 rows. 43[45:47:49] sts.
SHAPE NECK
Dec 1 st at each end of next and foll alt row. Work straight on rem 39[41:43:45] sts until neck measures 2½in (6cm), ending with a k row. Knit 4 rows. Bind (cast) off loosely knitwise.

SLEEVES (BOTH ALIKE)
Using size 6 (4mm/UK8) needles, cast on 53[57:61:65] sts and work 3in (7.5cm) in rib as given for back, ending with a WS row. Change to size 8 (5mm/UK6) needles and work in st st (beg with a k row), inc 1 st at each end of 3rd[5th:5th:3rd] and every foll 6th[6th:6th:7th] row to 85[91:95:99] sts. Work straight until piece measures 19[21.5:23:24]in (48.5[54½:58.5:61]cm) from beg, ending with a p row. (Alter this measurement to lengthen or shorten sleeve; if making the sleeve shorter you will need to increase more frequently – see page 72.)
Bind (cast) off.

FINISHING
Block pieces to measurements. Join shoulder and neck seams. Place a marker at the centre of the sleeve top and match to shoulder seam. Using the square set in method (see page 71), sew in sleeve. Join side seams and underarm seams.

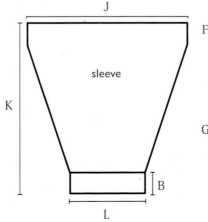

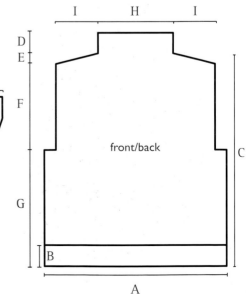

you will need

MATERIALS
Fisherman (aran) weight merino wool yarn (85yd/78m per ball): 12[12:13:13] × 1¾oz/50g balls in colour denim blue

NEEDLES
Size 6 (4mm/UK8) needles
Size 8 (5mm/UK6) needles

Gauge (Tension)
18 sts and 24 rows to 4in (10cm) measured over stockinette (stocking) stitch on size 8 (5mm/UK6) needles

Child's sweater
size diagram measurements

A 14 [15:16:17]in (36 [38:41:43]cm)

B 2in (5cm)

C 15 [16½:18:19½]in (37 [42:46:50]cm)

D 1¼in (3cm)

E 1in (2.5cm)

F 6 [6½:7:7½]in (15 [16.5:18:19]cm

G 8 [9:10:11]in (20.5 [23:25.5:28]cm)

H 6 [6:6½:7]in (15 [15:16.5:18]cm)

I 4 [4½:4¾:5]in (10 [11.5:12:12.5]cm)

J 12 [13:14:15]in (30.5 [33:35.5:38]cm)

K 13 [14:15:16]in (33 [35.5:38:40.5]cm)

L 6 [6½:6¾:7¾]in (15 [16.5:17:19.5]cm)

Back view of sweater

CHILD'S PLAIN SWEATER

Child's sweater for age 5-6[7-8:9-10:11-12] years
To fit chest measurement 24[26:28:30]in (61 [66:71:76]cm)

BACK AND FRONT (BOTH ALIKE)
Using size 6 (4mm/UK8) needles, cast on 63[67:73:77] sts.
Row 1 (RS) K1, * p1, k1; rep from * to end.
Row 2 P1, * k1, p1; rep from * to end.
Rep these 2 rows until rib measures 2in (5cm), ending with a WS row.
Change to size 8 (5mm/UK6) needles and work in st st (beg with a k row), until piece measures 8[9:10:11]in (20.5[23:25.5:28]cm) from beg, ending with a p row. (Alter this measurement to lengthen or shorten the sweater.)
SHAPE ARMHOLES
Cast off 5 sts at beg of next 2 rows. 53[57:63:67] sts.
Cont without shaping until armhole measures 6[6½:7:7.½]in (15[16.5:18:19]cm), ending with a p row.
SHAPE SHOULDERS
Cast off 4[5:5:6] sts at beg of next 4 rows then 3[3:5:4] sts at beg of next 2 rows. 31[31:33:35] sts.
SHAPE NECK
Dec 1 st at each end of next and foll alt row. Work straight on rem 27[27:29:31] sts until neck measures 1¼in (3cm),

ending with a k row. Knit 4 rows.
Bind (cast) off loosely knitwise.
SLEEVES (BOTH ALIKE)
Using size 6 (4mm/UK8) needles, cast on 27[29:31:35] sts and work 2in (5cm) in rib as given for back, ending with a WS row.
Change to size 8 (5mm/UK6) needles and work in st st (beg with a k row), inc 1 st at each end of 3rd and every foll 4th[4th:4th:5th] row to 55[59:63:67] sts.
Cont without shaping until piece measures 13[14:15:16]in (33[35.5:38:40.5]cm) from beg, ending with a p row. (Alter this measurement to lengthen or shorten sleeve; if making the sleeve shorter you will need to increase more frequently – see page 72.)
Bind (cast) off.

FINISHING
Block pieces to measurements given on size diagrams. Join shoulder and neck seams. Place a marker at the centre of the sleeve top and match to shoulder seam. Using the square set in method (see page 71), sew in sleeve. Join side seams and underarm seams.

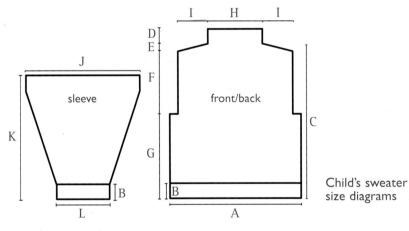

Child's sweater size diagrams

CABLE PANEL SWEATER (see main picture, facing page)

BACK
Work as given for back of plain sweater.

FRONT
Work 1 row less in rib as given for back.
Inc row Rib to end, including increases required for cable panel (see page 73).
Change to size 8 (5mm/UK6) needles.
START CABLE PANEL
Row 1 K to first stitch of cable panel, work first row of cable panel, k to end.

Row 2 P to cable panel, work second row of cable panel, p to end.
These 2 rows set st st panels and cable panel.
Complete front to match back.

SLEEVES (BOTH ALIKE)
Work as given for plain sweater.

FINISHING
Work as given for plain sweater.

LACE CARDIGAN

This pretty cardigan, knitted in a simple four row lace pattern, is ideal for learning how to shape knitting while keeping the pattern correct (see page 74). The neck edge has eyelet holes through which a ribbon is threaded and the moss stitch button and buttonhole bands use the technique of picking up stitches evenly down the fronts (see page 68) and making buttonholes (see page 69).

To fit bust/chest 30/32[34/36:38/40]in
(76/81.5[86.5/91.5:96.5/101.5]cm)

you will need

MATERIALS
Worsted (DK) weight merino wool yarn (109yd/100m per ball): 8[9:10] x 1¾oz/50g balls in colour lilac

8[8:9] buttons

34in (86cm) of ¼in (0.6cm) wide ribbon in colour to match

NEEDLES
Size 3 (3.25mm/UK10) needles
Size 6 (4mm/UK8) needles

Gauge (Tension)
22 sts and 28 rows to 4in (10cm) measured over lace pattern on size 6 (4mm/UK8) needles

Lace pattern for gauge (tension) square
Using size 6 (4mm/UK8) needles, cast on 31 sts.
Row 1 (RS) K1, * yfwd, k1, sk2po, k1, yfwd, k1; rep from * to end.
Row 2 P to end.
Row 3 K1, * k1, yfwd, sk2po, yfwd, k2; rep from * to end.
Row 4 P to end.
Rep these 4 rows for at least 6in (15cm).
Bind (cast) off.
Measure your gauge (tension) (see page 31).

BACK
Using size 3 (3.25mm/UK10) needles, cast on 85[97:109] sts.
Row 1 K1, * p1, k1; rep from * to end.
This forms moss st.
Rep this row 3 times more.
Change to size 6 (4mm/UK8) needles. Start lace patt.
Row 1 (RS) K1, * yfwd, k1, sk2po, k1, yfwd, k1; rep from * to end.
Row 2 P to end.
Row 3 K1, * k1, yfwd, sk2po, yfwd, k2; rep from * to end.
Row 4 P to end.
These 4 rows form the lace patt and are repeated.

SHAPE SIDE EDGES
Cont in lace patt as set, and working extra sts into patt, inc 1 st at each end of next and every foll 8th row to 97[109:121] sts. Cont without shaping until back measures 8[8½:9]in (20.5[21.5:23]cm) from beg, ending with a WS row.

SHAPE ARMHOLES
Keeping patt correct, bind (cast) off 5[7:9] sts at beg of next 2 rows.
Dec 1 st at each end of next 7[7:9] rows. 73[81:85] sts.
Cont in patt without shaping until armhole measures 8[8½:9]in (20.5[21.5:23]cm), ending with a WS row.

SHAPE SHOULDERS
Bind (cast) off 7[7:8] sts at beg of next 4 rows then cast off 5[7:7] sts at beg of next 2 rows.
Bind (cast) off rem 35[39:39] sts.

LEFT FRONT
Using size 3 (3.25mm/UK10) needles, cast on 43[49:55] sts and work 4 rows in moss st as given for back.
Change to size 6 (4mm/UK8) needles and work 4 rows in lace patt as given for back.

SHAPE SIDE EDGE
Cont in lace patt as set, and working extra sts into patt, inc 1 st at beg of next

and on same edge of every following 8th row to 49[55:61] sts.
Cont in patt without shaping until front measures same as back to armhole shaping, ending at side edge.

SHAPE ARMHOLE
Bind (cast) off 5[7:9] sts at beg of next row. Work 1 row.
Dec 1 st at armhole edge on foll 7[7:9] rows. 37[41:43] sts.
Cont in patt without shaping until armhole is 21 rows less than back to shoulder shaping, ending at front edge.

SHAPE NECK
Next row Bind (cast) off 7[8:8] sts, patt to end.
Patt 1 row.
Next row Bind (cast) off 4[5:5] sts, patt to end. 26[28:30] sts.
Dec 1 st at neck edge on foll 7 rows. 19[21:23] sts.
Cont in patt without shaping until front measures same as back to shoulder shaping, ending at armhole edge.

SHAPE SHOULDER
Bind (cast) off 7[7:8] sts at beg of next and foll alt row.
Patt 1 row.
Bind (cast) off rem 5[7:7] sts.

RIGHT FRONT
Work as given for left front reversing all shapings.

SLEEVES (BOTH ALIKE)
Using size 3 (3.25mm/UK10) needles, cast on 43[49:55] sts and work 4 rows in moss st.
Change to size 6 (4mm/UK8) needles and work 4 rows in lace patt as given for back.
Cont in patt as set, and working extra sts into patt, inc 1 st at each end of next and every foll 6th row to 67[69:71] sts, then at each end of every foll 8th row to 75[81:87] sts.
Cont in patt without shaping until sleeve measures 17[18:19]in (43[45.5:48.5]cm), ending with a WS row.

SHAPE TOP

Bind (cast) off 5[7:9] sts at beg of next 2 rows.

Dec 1 st at each end of foll 5 rows, then at each end of foll 2 alt rows. 51[53:55] sts.

Dec 1 st at each end of every foll 4th row to 43 sts, then at each end of every foll alt row to 35 sts, and then at each end of every foll row to 29 sts.

Bind (cast) off 4 sts at beg of next 2 rows.

Bind (cast) off rem 21 sts.

FINISHING

Block pieces to measurements given on size diagram. Join shoulder seams.

NECKBAND

With RS of work facing and using size 3 (3.25mm/UK10) needles, pick up and k 11 sts across bound (cast) off sts at right front neck, 22 sts up right side of neck, 35[39:39] sts at back neck, 22 sts down left side of neck, and 11 sts across bound (cast) off sts at left front neck. 101[105:105] sts.

Work 1 row in moss st.

Eyelet row K1, yfwd, k2tog, patt 2[4:4] sts, yfwd, k2tog, * patt 4 sts, yfwd, k2tog; rep from * to last 4[6:6] sts, patt 2[4:4] sts, yfwd, k2tog.

Work 2 rows in moss st.

Bind (cast) off in moss st.

BUTTON BAND

Using size 3 (3.25mm/UK10) needles, pick up and k 73[77:83] sts evenly down left front edge, and work 4 rows in moss st.

Bind (cast) off in moss st.

BUTTONHOLE BAND

Using size 3 (3.25mm/UK10) needles, pick up and k 73[77:83] sts evenly up right front edge, and work 1 row in moss st.

Buttonhole row K1[3:1], (yfwd, k2tog, patt 8 sts) 7[7:8] times, yfwd, k2tog, patt 0[2:0] sts.

Work 2 rows in moss st.

Bind (cast) off in moss st.

Join side and sleeve seams. Sew sleeves into armholes using set in sleeve method (see page 71). Sew on buttons. Thread ribbon through eyelets around neckband.

BABY BOOTEES

These delightful bootees with roll top edges will keep a baby's toes cosy and show how easy it is to knit three-dimensional shapes. The techniques used include M1 to make a stitch between stitches (see page 27) and decreasing stitches (see page 28).

To fit ages 0-3 months and 3-6 months
Foot length 3½in (9cm) and 4¼in (10.5cm)

you will need

MATERIALS

Worsted (DK) weight merino wool yarn (131yd/120m)
1 x 1¾oz/50g ball in colour lilac

NEEDLES

Size 6 (4mm/UK8) needles

Gauge (Tension)

22 sts and 30 rows to 4in (10cm) measured over stockinette (stocking) stitch on size 6 (4mm/UK8) needles

BOOTEE (MAKE 2)

Using size 6 (4mm/UK8) needles cast on 30[36] sts and purl 1 row.

Inc row K2, M1, k12[15], M1, k2, M1, k12[15], M1, k2. 34[40] sts.

Purl 1 row.

Inc row K2, M1, k14[17], M1, k2, M1, k14[17], M1, k2. 38[44] sts.

Purl 1 row.

Inc row K2, M1, k16[19], M1, k2, M1, k16[19], M1, k2. 42[48] sts.

Beg with p row, work 7 rows in st st.

Dec row K14[17], (k2tog) 3 times, k2, (skpo) 3 times, k14[17]. 36[42] sts.

SHAPE TOP

Next row P21[24], p2tog and turn work as though at the end of the row, leaving the unworked sts on the RH needle.

Next row K7, skpo and turn, leaving unworked sts on the RH needle.

Next row P7, p2tog and turn.

Rep the last 2 rows once more.

Next row K7, skpo and turn.

Next row P7, p2tog, p across all unworked sts on LH needle to end of row.

Next row K17, skpo, k across all unworked sts on LH needle to end of row. 28[34] sts.

Beg with a p row, work 7 rows in st st.

Bind (cast) off.

FINISHING

Join seam along sole and at back of bootee.

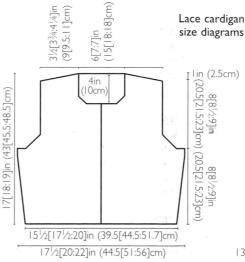

Lace cardigan size diagrams

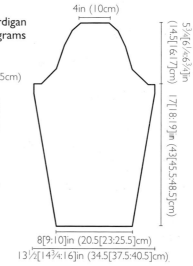

DAINTY KNITTED TRIMS

Use these trims to add a finishing touch to a piece of knitting, or decorate an item to make it special. The knitted rose brooch has been fulled to give it body (see page 60); a book is fastened by a button with an embroidered knitted cover and a matching twisted cord (see pages 80, 85 and 77); and a lacy leaf trim is the perfect edging to a scented sachet.

ROSE BROOCH

you will need

MATERIALS
Sport (4ply) weight shetland wool yarn (129yd/118m per ball):
1 x 1oz/25g ball each in colours:
A rose red
B green

Small amount of dark green embroidery thread

Brooch pin

NEEDLES
Size 3 (3.25mm/UK10) needles

Gauge (Tension)
28 sts and 36 rows to 4in (10cm) measured over stockinette (stocking) stitch on size 3 (3.25mm/UK10) needles

Using size 3 (3.25mm/UK10) needles and A, work a rose as given on page 82, bind (cast) off the stitches instead of threading the yarn through them.
Using B, work two leaves as given on page 82, working the increases as M1 instead of yarn over (see page 27).
The rose and leaves are fulled following the instructions on page 60.

FINISHING
Run a gathering thread through the base of the rose and pull up. Form the rose by twisting it round and round from the centre with right side of fabric facing outwards. Pull the rose into shape as you go. Work a few stitches through the base to secure it. Embroider veins on to the leaves. Sew the leaves either side of the rose. Sew the brooch pin on securely.

ROSE BUTTON FASTENING

you will need

MATERIALS
Sport (4ply) weight mercerized cotton yarn (53yd/140m per ball):
1 x 1¾oz/50g ball in dark purple

Stranded cotton embroidery threads:
1 hank in each of the colours dark rose, light pink and green

1in (2.5cm) button or button covering kit

Notebook

Ribbon the width to fit down spine of book and three times the length of the spine

NEEDLES
Size 2 (3mm/UK11) needles

Using size 2 (3mm/UK11) needles and 4ply yarn, work a covered button as given on page 80. Using embroidery threads, work a group of roses (rose stitch) and french knots. Work single chain stitches for the leaves. (See embroidery stitches, page 83–5.) Finish the button. Thread the ribbon through the spine of the book and tie the ends together and hide the knot in the spine. Make twisted cords in each of the light pink and dark rose embroidery threads, using two strands (see page 77). Sew one end of each on to the base of the button. Place the button on the front of the book, close to the edge. Wrap the twisted cords around the book, passing under the ribbon on the spine. Secure the cords to the ribbon with a few neat stitches. To close the book, tie the cords around the button in a bow.

LEAF EDGED SACHET

you will need

MATERIALS
Sport (4ply) weight mercerized cotton yarn (153yd/140m per ball):
1 x 1¾oz/50g ball in colour light pink

Fabric sachet with rose petal filling

Large bead

NEEDLES
Size 2 (3mm/UK11) needles

Measure the edge of the sachet where the edging will be stitched.
Using size 2 (3mm/UK11) needles and 4ply yarn, work this length of leaf edging as given on page 126. Sew on to the sachet. If required, make a fastening loop from a short twisted cord, using two strands of the yarn (see page 77) and sew behind the edging. Sew on the bead.

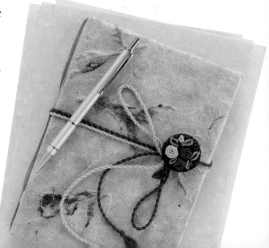

DRAWSTRING BAGS

These dainty drawstring bags have knitted background fabrics taken from patterns in the Stitch library. The ones chosen are particularly suitable for further embellishment with embroidery, whether you choose simple ribbon roses or cross stitch motifs. Add a swiss darned initial to make the bag truly personal (see page 83–85).

Bags measure 8in (20.5cm) wide by 9in (23cm) long

GINGHAM CHECK BAG

you will need

MATERIALS
Worsted (DK) weight cotton yarn (92yd/82m per ball):
2 x 1¾oz/50g balls in white

Oddments of blue yarn for embroidery

NEEDLES
Size 6 (4mm/UK8) needles

Gauge (Tension)
20 sts and 28 rows to 4in (10cm) measured over stockinette (stocking) stitch on size 6 (4mm/UK8) needles

BACK AND FRONT (MAKE 2 THE SAME)
Using size 6 (4mm/UK8) needles cast on 37 sts and work in gingham check pattern from Stitch library, page 94 until work measures approx 7½in (19cm), ending with row 5 of pattern.
** Work 5 rows in st st, beg with a p row.
Next row P to end. (Turning row for drawstring channel).
Work 5 rows in st st, beg with p row.
Bind (cast) off.

FINISHING
Block pieces to 8in (20.5cm) wide and 10in (25.5cm) long. Embroider bag with initial using duplicate stitch. Fill other squares with motifs worked in cross stitch (see page 156). Join back and front together along bottom seam. Join side seams, leaving a small gap for drawstring in first 5 rows of st st. Turn hem over to the inside and slipstitch in place. Make two twisted cords the same length and thread through gaps from each side.

ROSE BROCADE BAG

you will need

MATERIALS
Worsted (DK) weight cotton yarn (92yd/82m per ball):
2 x 1¾oz/50g balls in mauve

Embroidery threads for roses

NEEDLES
Size 6 (4mm/UK8) needles

Gauge (Tension)
20 sts and 28 rows to 4in (10cm) measured over stockinette (stocking) stitch on size 6 (4mm/UK8) needles

BACK AND FRONT (MAKE 2 THE SAME)
Using size 6 (4mm/UK8) needles cast on 37 sts and work in King Charles brocade from Stitch library, page 92, until work measures approx 8in (20cm) from beg, ending with row 7 of pattern.
Work as given for gingham check bag from **.

FINISHING
Block pieces to 8in (20.5cm) wide and 10in (25.5cm) long. Embroider bag with roses (see page 85). Finish as given for gingham check bag.

PATCHWORK CUSHION

This sampler cushion cover uses squares knitted in a range of stitch patterns taken from the Stitch library including cables, bobbles and twisted stitches (see pages 40, 42 and 46). They give it a rich texture, and dividing up some of the squares into smaller patches further enhances the visual interest.

■ Cushion measures approximately 16in (40.5cm) square

you will need

MATERIALS
Worsted (DK) weight cotton yarn (93yd/85m per ball):
1 x 1¾oz/50g ball in colour
A pale grey

Worsted (DK) weight wool/cotton mix yarn (123yd/113m per ball):
1 x 1¾oz/50g ball each in colours:
B light blue violet
C pale lilac
D light pink

Worsted (DK) weight cotton yarn (92yd/84m per ball)
2 x 1¾oz/50g balls in colour:
E bright green

Backing fabric

16in (40.5cm) square cushion pad

NEEDLES
Size 6 (4mm/UK8) needles

■ Gauge (Tension)
20 sts and 28 rows to 4in (10cm) measured over stockinette (stocking) stitch on size 6 (4mm/UK8) needles using A

			3a	3b
1		2	3c	3d
4a	4b			
4c	4d	5		6
7		8		9

SQUARE 1
Using size 6 (4mm/UK8) needles and D, cast on 27 sts and work 36 rows in Bobble circle pattern (see page 104). Bind (cast) off in patt.

SQUARE 2
Using size 6 (4mm/UK8) needles and E, cast on 30 sts and work 36 rows in Bramble stitch (see page 102). Bind (cast) off in patt.

SQUARE 3
This is made up of four smaller squares.
SQUARE 3A
Using size 6 (4mm/UK8) needles and A, cast on 15 sts and work 20 rows of Medallion bobble cable (see page 109). Bind (cast) off in patt.
SQUARE 3B
Using size 6 (4mm/UK8) needles and B, cast on 15 sts and work 20 rows in Moss stitch (see page 89). Bind (cast) off in patt.
SQUARE 3C
Using size 6 (4mm/UK8) needles and D, cast on 19 sts and work 20 rows in Boxed bobble pattern (see page 103). Bind (cast) off in patt.
SQUARE 3D
Using size 6 (4mm/UK8) needles and E, cast on 18 sts and work 20 rows in Five rib braid (see page 110). Bind (cast) off in patt.

SQUARE 4
This is made up of four smaller squares.
SQUARE 4A
Using size 6 (4mm/UK8) needles and E, cast on 16 sts and work 20 rows in Nosegay pattern (see page 115). Bind (cast) off in patt.
SQUARE 4B
Using size 6 (4mm/UK8) needles and B, cast on 18 sts and work 20 rows in Two stitch check (see page 90). Bind (cast) off in patt.

SQUARE 4C
Using size 6 (4mm/UK8) needles and C, cast on 15 sts and work 20 rows in Mistake rib (see page 106). Bind (cast) off in patt.
SQUARE 4D
Using size 6 (4mm/UK8) needles and A, cast on 21 sts and work 20 rows in Heart cable (see page 115). Bind (cast) off in patt.

SQUARE 5
Using size 6 (4mm/UK8) needles and C, cast on 26 sts and work 36 rows in Stepped diamonds pattern (see page 93). Bind (cast) off in patt.

SQUARE 6
Using size 6 (4mm/UK8) needles and A, cast on 31 sts and work 36 rows in Double moss stitch and Rib check (see page 89). Bind (cast) off in patt.

SQUARE 7
Using size 6 (4mm/UK8) needles and A, cast on 29 sts and work 36 rows in Basketweave stitch (see page 90). Bind (cast) off in patt.

SQUARE 8
Using size 6 (4mm/UK8) needles and D, cast on 30 sts and work 36 rows in Mock cable (see page 93). Bind (cast) off in patt.

GREETINGS CARDS

Knit these delightful patches in stocking stitch with a moss stitch frame. Then use embroidery silks to swiss darn an appropriate motif in the centre (see page 85). You can use the charts in this book or create your own on graph paper.

SQUARE 9

Using size 6 (4mm/UK8) needles and E, cast on 29 sts and work 36 rows in Heart squares pattern (see page 94). Bind (cast) off in patt.

FINISHING

Block the large squares to about 5½in (14cm) square and the smaller ones to about 3in (7.5cm). These measures are a guide only; some of the smaller squares are slightly longer or narrower. The squares are sewn together using E with the seam on the outside; use a small neat running stitch.

SQUARE 3

With WS together, sew 3A to 3C, and 3B to 3D. Sew the two strips together.

SQUARE 4

With WS together, sew 4A to 4C, and 4B to 4D. Sew the two strips together.
Sew squares 1, 4 and 7 together, 2, 5 and 8 together, and then 3, 6 and 9 together. Sew the three strips together. Block the whole piece to about 16in (40.5cm) square. Cut a piece of backing fabric to 17¼in (43.5cm) square. Neaten the edges and press a seam allowance of ⅝in (1.5cm) to the wrong side on all edges. With WS facing, place the front and back together and sew around three sides using a small neat running stitch. Insert the cushion pad and sew the remaining side closed.

you will need

MATERIALS

Sport (4ply) weight mercerized cotton yarn (153yd/140m per ball):

1 x 1¾oz/50g ball in colour light pink

1 skein of 12ply silk embroidery thread in shades of pinks and reds

Card blank 4in (10cm) square

NEEDLES

Size 2 (3mm/UK11) needles

Gauge (Tension)

28 sts and 38 rows to 4in (10cm) measured over stockinette (stocking) stitch on size 2 (3mm/UK11) needles

you will need

MATERIALS

Sport (4ply) weight mercerized cotton yarn (153yd/140m per ball):

1 x 1¾oz/50g ball in colour dark purple

1 skein of 12ply silk embroidery thread in shades of green

Card blank 4in (10cm) square

VALENTINE CARD

Using size 2 (3mm/UK11) needles and 4ply yarn, cast on 20 sts.
Row 1 * K1, p1; rep from * to end.
Row 2 * P1, k1; rep from * to end. (These 2 rows form moss st).
Row 3 K1, p1, k to last st, p1.
Row 4 P1, k1, p to last st, k1.
Rep rows 3 and 4, six times more.
Work 2 rows in moss st.
Bind (cast) off.

FINISHING

Block the piece. Using all the strands of the 12ply embroidery thread, swiss darn the heart from the chart on page 156 on to the st st in the centre of the patch. Using double-sided tape, stick patch on to card.

CHRISTMAS TREE CARD

Using size 2 (3mm/UK11) needles and 4ply yarn, cast on 17 sts.
Row 1 K1, * p1, k1; rep from * to end. (This row forms moss st).
Rep this row once more.
Row 3 K1, p1, k to last 2 sts, p1, k1.
Row 4 K1, p to last st, k1.
Rep rows 3 and 4, six times more.
Work 2 rows in moss st.
Bind (cast) off.

FINISHING

Block the piece. Using all the strands of the 12ply embroidery thread, swiss darn the tree from the chart on page 156 on to the st st in the centre of the patch. Using double-sided tape, stick patch on to card.

GIFT BAGS

These small bags are a great way to practise the basic knitting techniques of casting on, stockinette (stocking) stitch, binding (casting) off, blocking and making up (see pages 17–23, 66, 70). And if you are using a novelty yarn they give an idea of how it will look knitted up. Measuring 4in (10cm) square, they can be decorated with ribbons, trims, buttons, beads, flowers or jewels. Make them for presenting small gifts at Christmas, birthdays or just as a thank-you gift. The bags are also shown on pages 12–13.

you will need

MATERIALS
1 x ball of a novelty yarn such as fun fur, metallic, fleece, mohair, ribbon, boucle or chenille. Yarns with a gauge (tension) of less than 15 stitches to 4in (10cm) will be too bulky and are unsuitable. Check the ball band first.
The yarns used to knit the bags illustrated are given with each pattern.

NEEDLES
The ball band gives the needle size that you will need.

BALL BAND
All the information you need to knit a bag is on the yarn's ball band. The number of stitches to cast on is determined by the gauge (tension) information.

For example, a worsted (DK) yarn has a gauge (tension) of 22 sts and 28 rows to 4in (10cm) using size 6 (4mm/UK8) needles. You would cast on 22 sts using this size needles.

A metallic yarn may have a gauge (tension) of 29 sts and 41 rows to 4in (10cm) on size 3 (3.25mm/UK10) needles. You would cast on 29 sts using these needles.

BASIC BAG PATTERN (MAKE 2)
Using the recommended size of needles, cast on number of stitches to 4in (10cm). Beginning with a knit row, work in stockinette (stocking) stitch until piece measures 4in (10cm) from beg, ending with a knit row.
Knit 2 rows.
Bind (cast) off knitwise.

OPTIONAL KNITTED HANDLES
Cast on 1¹/₂ times the number of stitches cast on for the bag and knit four rows. Bind (cast) off knitwise.

FINISHING
Block the pieces to measure 4in (10cm) square, according to the information on the ball band. Some novelty yarns require careful pressing. Place the two bag pieces together with wrong sides facing. Work a neat running stitch around three sides, leaving top edge open. If the bag is knitted in fun fur or brushed yarn, use a smooth yarn or thread in a close colour match. Attach knitted handles (if made) to the inside on the side seams. Alternatively, use ribbon or felt cut to length. Add trims as required.

GOLD STAR RIBBON BAG
Yarn Jaeger Albany (cotton ribbon) in colour 270.
Trimming 29in (74cm) length of ¹/₂in (1.5cm) wide gold ribbon.
Using size 8 (5mm/UK6) needles cast on 22 sts and knit two squares.
Cut a 7in (18cm) length of the ribbon for the handle. Divide the remaining ribbon into five equal lengths with a tape measure, marking with

pins. Fold the ribbon into points, one by one, bringing the pins and the ribbon ends into the centre. Secure with a few stitches in the centre through all thicknesses. Attach to one square of the bag. Sew bag together and attach a ribbon handle to the inside of the side seams.

ROSEBUD BAG
Yarn Rowan Kidsilk Haze in colour 597 used double.
Trimming 10 ready-made ¹/₂in (1.5cm) roses, 7in (18cm) of ¹/₂in (7mm) wide ribbon to match roses.
Using size 5 (3.75mm/UK9) needles cast on 23 sts and knit two squares.
Sew on the roses in alternating lines of 3, 2, 3 and 2, on one square. Sew bag together and attach the ribbon handle to the inside of the side seams.

HEART AND BIRD BAG
(this page, top left)
Yarn Sirdar Snowflake Chunky (fleece effect) in colour 376.
Trimming felt, wooden bird button or similar and embroidery thread.
Using size 9 (5.5mm/UK5) needles cast on 14 sts and knit two squares.
Draw a heart shape on a 2¹/₂in (6cm) square of felt and cut it out. Cut a 7in (18cm) long by ³/₄in (2cm) wide handle from the felt. Using embroidery thread, work blanket stitch around the edges of the heart and handle (see page 84). Sew the heart on to one of the bag pieces and sew the button in the centre. Sew the bag together and attach the handle to the inside of the side seams.

HOUSE SAMPLER

Knit this sampler for someone who has moved into a new home. The house is swiss darned once the knitting is complete (see page 85).

■ Sampler measures 7in (18cm) square

DENIM HEART BAG

Yarn Rowan All Seasons Cotton in colour 160.
Trimming ready-made denim heart-shaped patch or similar.
Using size 7 (4.5mm/UK7) needles, cast on 18 sts and knit two squares. Knit a handle on 27 sts.

HOLOGRAM DAISY BAG

(opposite page, top right)
Yarn Rowan Lurex Shimmer in colour 336.
Trimming three ready-made hologram effect daisy patches or similar.
Using size 3 (3.25mm/UK10) needles cast on 29 sts and knit two squares. Knit a handle on 43 sts.

FLUFFY PINK RIBBON BAG

Yarn Sirdar Funky Fur in colour 536.
Trimming 24in (61cm) length of ¹⁄₂in (1.5cm) wide pink ribbon.
Using size 6 (4mm/UK8) needles cast on 20 sts and knit two squares.
Cut a 7in (18cm) length of ribbon for the handle. Tie the remaining ribbon into a bow and attach to one bag piece.
Sew the bag together and attach the handle to the inside of the side seams.

SNOWFLAKE BAG

Yarn Patons Tapestry (boucle) in colour 5000.
Trimming ready-made star, snowflake or similar.
Using size 6 (4mm/UK8) needles cast on 22 sts and knit two squares. Knit a handle on 33 sts.

you will need

MATERIALS

Sport (4ply) weight tweed wool yarn (120yd/110m per ball): 2 x 25g balls of colour oatmeal

Tapestry Wool (100% wool – 8.7yd/8m per skein):
1 skein each of:
dark red
red
light red
dark blue
blue
gold
dark green
green

Stranded cotton
1 x dark brown

Wire hanger

NEEDLES
Size 6 (4mm/UK8) needles

Gauge (Tension)
20 sts and 28 rows to 4in (10cm) over stockinette (stocking) stitch using 2 strands of sport (4ply) together and size 6 (4mm/UK8) needles

SAMPLER

Using size 6 (4mm/UK8) needles and 2 strands of sport (4ply) together, cast on 35 sts.
Row 1 P1, * k1, p1; rep from * to end. This row forms moss st.
Rep this row 3 times more.
Row 5 P1, k1, p1, k29, p1, k1, p1.
Row 6 P1, k1, p31, k1, p1.
Rep these 2 rows 20 times more, then row 5 again.
Work 4 rows in moss st.
Next row Bind (cast) off 5 sts in patt, patt 7 sts (including last st used in binding (casting) off), bind (cast) off 11 sts in patt, patt 7 sts (including last st used in binding (casting) off), bind (cast) off rem 5 sts in patt.

TABS (MAKE 2)
With RS of work facing, rejoin yarn to first set of 7 sts and work 12 rows in moss st. Bind (cast) off in patt.

FINISHING
Block the piece to 7in (18cm) square. Use 1 strand of tapestry wool to swiss darn the design on to the knitted piece, following the chart on page 156.
Use 6 strands of the stranded cotton to backstitch the smoke and use 2 long straight stitches for each window.
Sew the tabs over the wire hanger to the wrong side of the knitted piece.

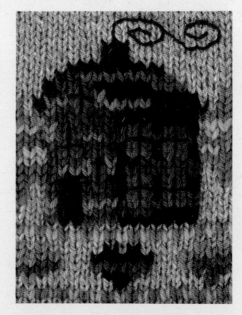

INTARSIA CUSHION

This cushion was inspired by the colours and forms of Jacobean crewel work and uses the intarsia method (see page 47). The back is worked in two halves to insert the cushion pad. It is fastened with buttonholes and four buttons covered with knitted fabric (see page 69 and 80). The contrast trim round the edge is a simple cord, knitted with double-pointed needles (see page 77).

■ Cushion front measures 15in (38cm) square

you will need

MATERIALS

Worsted (DK) weight wool yarn (131yd/120m):
3 x 1¾oz/50g balls in colour
MC natural:
1 x 1¾oz/50g ball each in colours:
A dark green
B green
C red
D light red
E purple
F pink
G light pink

4 self-cover buttons

15in (38cm) square cushion pad

NEEDLES

Size 6 (4mm/UK8) needles
2 size 6 (4mm/UK8) double-pointed needles

Gauge (Tension)

22 sts and 30 rows to 4in (10cm) measured over stockinette (stocking) stitch on size 6 (4mm/UK8) needles

FRONT

Using size 6 (4mm/UK8) needles and MC, cast on 83 sts.
Work 4 rows in st st, beg with a k row.

START CHART

Using the intarsia method work from the chart on page 155, starting at the bottom right-hand corner and reading the odd rows (k rows) from right to left and the even rows (p rows) from left to right. Cont until all 104 rows of chart have been completed.
Using MC only, work 4 rows in st st, beg with a k row.
Bind (cast) off.

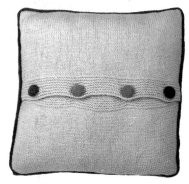

BACK (IN TWO SECTIONS)

BUTTON SECTION

Using size 6 (4mm/UK8) needles and MC, cast on 83 sts.
Work 51 rows in st st, ending with a k row. **
Knit 14 rows.
Bind (cast) off.

BUTTONHOLE SECTION

Work as given for button section to **.
Knit 7 rows.
Buttonhole row 1 K11, * bind (cast) off 2 sts, k18 (including last st used in bind (cast) off); rep from * twice more, bind (cast) off 2 sts, k to end.
Buttonhole row 2 K to end, casting on 2 sts over those bound (cast) off in previous row.
Knit 5 rows.
Bind (cast) off.

FINISHING

Block pieces to measurements. Lay buttonhole border over button border and join together at the sides. Join front to backs.

PIPING CORD

Using 2 size 6 (4mm/UK8) double-pointed needles and F, cast on 4 sts.
Work a tubular cord to fit around outside of cushion. Sew it over the seam.

COVERED BUTTONS

Cover four buttons using colours A, B, C and D. Sew into place on button border. Insert cushion pad.

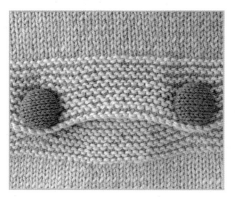

MOTIFS

Intarsia Cushion (page 154)

KEY

☐	MC	▩	B	▨	D	▤	F
▨	A	■	C	▥	E	▦	G

motifs

Flower Top (page 130)

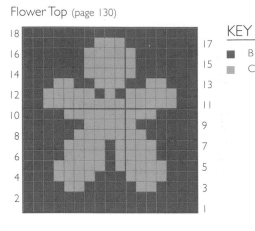

KEY

- ■ B
- ■ C

Fulled Envelope Sachet (page 142)
Valentine Card (page 151)

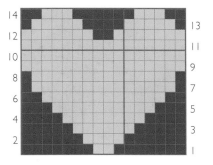

KEY

- ■ C
- ■ B

Gingham Check Bag (page 149)

diamonds

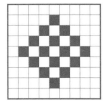

flower

House Sampler (page 153)

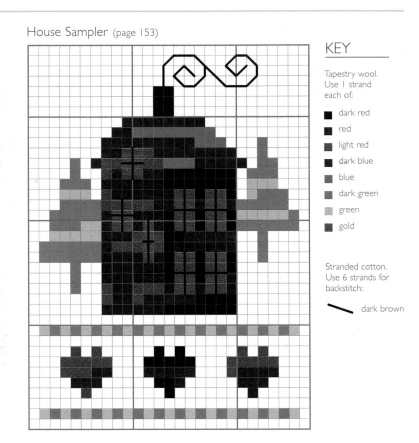

KEY

Tapestry wool. Use 1 strand each of:

- ■ dark red
- ■ red
- ■ light red
- ■ dark blue
- ■ blue
- ■ dark green
- ■ green
- ■ gold

Stranded cotton. Use 6 strands for backstitch:

— dark brown

Christmas Tree Card (page 151)

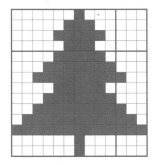

Fair Isle Baby Blanket — alphabet (page 141)

Fair Isle Baby Blanket — pattern rows (page 141)

Chart A

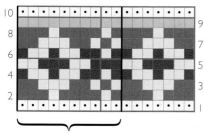

Repeat these 10 sts 9 times

Chart B

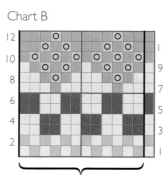

Repeat these 12 sts 8 times

Chart C

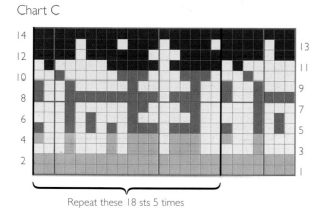

Repeat these 18 sts 5 times

Chart D

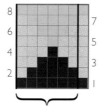

Repeat these 6 sts 16 times

Chart E

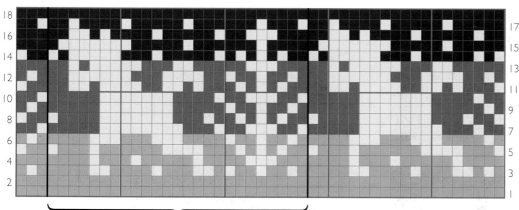

Repeat these 25 sts 3 times

Chart F

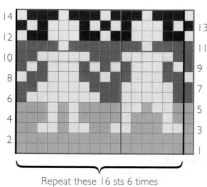

Repeat these 16 sts 6 times

k on RS rows, p on WS rows

- MC
- A
- B
- C
- D
- E
- F
- G

p on RS rows, k on WS rows

- ○ A
- · D

YARN DETAILS

The actual yarns and colours used to knit the projects on pages 129–54 are given below. If you have difficulty in locating yarns see the suppliers list opposite.

page 129
Striped Scarf Jaeger Matchmaker Merino Aran (100% merino wool – 90yd/ 82m per ball) 1 × 1¾oz/50g ball each in colours: **A** 775 Gloxinia; **B** 772 Clover; **C** 663 Light Natural; **D** 662 Cream
Plain Scarf Rowan Polar (60% wool/ 30% alpaca/10% acrylic – 109yd/100m per ball): 2 × 3½oz/ 100g balls in colour 650 Smirk

page 130
Flower Top Rowan Wool Cotton (123yd/113m per ball): 1 × 2oz (50g) each in colour: **A** 946 Elf; **B** 949 Aqua; **C** 952 Hiss

page 131
Striped Bag Rowan Wool Cotton (125yd/115m per ball): 1 × 2oz (50g) each in colour: **A** 805 Wine; **B** 799 Glee; **C** 724 Bubbles; **D** 726 Bleached; **E** 800 Bud

page 132
Cable Throw Rowan Rowanspun Chunky (100% pure new wool – 142yd/130m per ball); 3 × 3½oz/ 100g hanks each in colours: **A** 981 Pebble; **B** 982 Green Water; **C** 983 Cardamom; 2 × 3½oz/100g hanks in colour: **D** 984 Silver

page 133
Place Mat and Coaster Debbie Bliss Cotton DK (100% cotton – 92yd/84m per ball) as follows: 3 × 1¾oz/50g balls in colour 13020 Bright Green

page 134
Mittens Jaeger Matchmaker DK (100% wool – 131yd/120m per ball): 1 × 1¾oz/50g ball each in colours: *Tiger* **MC** 898 Orange; **A** 681 Black; **B** 662 Cream; oddment of pink for nose
Bear **MC** 702 Dark Brown; **A** 874 Light Brown; oddment of black for face
Dog **MC** 874 Light Brown; **A** 663 Beige; oddment of black for face
Cat **MC** 787 Ginger **A** 662 Cream; oddments of pink for nose and black for face

page 135
Rib Stitch Scarf Rowan Rowanspun Chunky (100% pure new wool –

142yd/130m per ball): 2 × 3½oz/100g hanks in colour 992 Hearty

page 136
Short Row Cushion 21st Century Yarns (100% silk): 2 × 1¾oz/50g skeins in colour Azure

page 137
Striped Beret Jaeger Matchmaker DK (100% merino wool – 131yd/120m per ball): 1 × 1¾oz/ 50g balls each in colour: **A** 883 Petal; **B** 894 Geranium
Plain Beret Rowan Yorkshire Tweed (100% pure new wool – 123yd/113m per ball); 1[2:2] × 1¾oz/50g balls in colour 349 Frog

page 138
Garden Plot Squares Throw Rowan Handknit DK Cotton (100% cotton – 93yd/85m per ball): 34 × 1¾oz/50g balls in colour 204 Chime

page 139
Beaded Bag Rowan Lurex Shimmer (80% viscose/ 20% polyester – 104yd/95m); 2 × 1¾oz/50g balls in colour 332 Gold
1 pack of Jaeger beads colour J3001009 Bronze

page 140
Sheep Toy Jaeger Matchmaker DK (100% pure new wool – 131yd/ 120m); 1 × 1¾oz/50g ball each in colours: **A** 661 White; **B** 681 Black

page 141
Fair Isle Baby Blanket Rowan Wool Cotton DK (50% merino wool/50% cotton – 123yd/113m per ball): 1 × 1¾oz/50g ball each in colours: **MC** 900 Antique; **A** 933 Violet; **B** 953 August; **C** 909 French Navy; **D** 952 Hiss; **E** 954 Grand; **F** 910 Gypsy; **G** 951 Tender

page 142
Scented Sachets and Cover Jamieson and Smith 2ply jumper weight Shetland Wool (100% shetland wool – 129yd/118m per ball); 1 × 1oz/25g ball each in colours: **A** 1A cream; **B** 49 lilac; **C** 20 purple

page 143
Lace Bags Jaeger Siena 4ply (100% mercerized cotton –

153yd/140m per ball)
Light pink bag 1 × 1¾oz/50g ball in colour **A** 404 Light Pink
Dark pink bag 1 × 1¾oz/50g ball in colour **B** 423 Dark Pink
Dark purple bag 1 × 1¾oz/50g ball in colour **C** 421 Dark Purple

page 144
Adult's Funnel Neck Sweater Debbie Bliss Merino Aran (100% merino wool – 85yd/ 78m per ball): 15[16:17:18] × 1¾oz/50g balls in colour 325205 Blue Green

page 145
Child's Funnel Neck Sweater Debbie Bliss Merino Aran (100% merino wool – 85yd/78m per ball): 12[12:13:13] × 1¾oz/50g balls in colour 325205 Blue Green

page 146
Lace Cardigan Debbie Bliss Merino DK (100% merino wool – 109yd/100m per ball): 8[9:10] × 1¾oz/50g balls in colour 606 Lilac

page 147
Baby Bootees Jaeger Baby Merino DK (100% merino wool – 131yd/120m); 1 × 1¾oz/50g ball in colour 224 Dawn

page 148
Rose Brooch Jamieson and Smith 2ply jumper weight Shetland Wool (100% shetland wool – 129yd/118m per ball): 1 × 1oz/25g ball each in colours: **A** 43 Maroon; **B** 92 Green
Rose Button Fastening Jaeger Siena 4ply (100% mercerized cotton – 153yd/140m per ball): 1 × 1¾oz/50g ball in colour 421 Dark Purple.
DMC Stranded Cotton embroidery thread: 1 hank in each of the colours: 718 Dark Rose; 605 Light Pink; 472 Green
Leaf Edged Sachet Jaeger Siena 4ply (100% mercerized cotton – 153yd/140m per ball): 1 × 1¾oz/ 50g ball in colour 404 Light Pink

page 149
Gingham Check Bag Debbie Bliss Cotton DK (100% cotton – 92yd/82m per ball): 2 × 1¾oz/50g balls in colour 13002 White.
Rose Brocade Bag Debbie Bliss Cotton DK (100% cotton –

92yd/82m per ball): 2 × 1¾oz/50g balls in colour 13012 Mauve

page 150
Patchwork Cushion Rowan Handknit Cotton DK (100% cotton – 93yd/85m per ball): 1 × 1¾oz/50g ball in colour **A** 204 Chime
Rowan Wool Cotton DK (50% merino wool/50% cotton – 123yd/113m per ball): 1 × 1¾oz/50g ball each in colours: **B** 933 Violet; **C** 952 Hiss; **D** 951 Tender
Debbie Bliss Cotton DK (100% cotton – 92yd/84m per ball) 2 × 1¾oz/50g balls in colour: **E** 13020 Bright Green

page 151
Valentine Card Jaeger Siena 4ply (100% mercerized cotton – 153yd/140m per ball): 1 × 1¾oz/50g ball in colour 421 Dark Purple
1 skein of Caron Waterlilies 12ply silk embroidery thread in colour 084 African Sunset
Christmas Tree Card Jaeger Siena 4ply (100% mercerized cotton – 153yd/140m per ball): 1 × 1¾oz/50g ball in colour 404 Light Pink
1 skein of Caron Waterlilies 12ply silk embroidery thread in colour 066 Jade

page 152
Gift Bags see pages 12–13 for details

page 153
House Sampler Rowan Yorkshire Tweed 4ply (100% wool – 120yd/110m per ball): 2 × 25g balls of colour 264.
DMC Tapestry Wool (100% wool – 8.7yd/8m per skein): 1 skein each of 7110 dark red; 7758 red; 7759 light red; 7306 dark blue; 7304 blue; 7505 gold; 7370 dark green; 7369 green
DMC Stranded Cotton 1 × 838 dark brown

page 154
Intarsia Cushion Jaeger Matchmaker DK (100% pure wool – 131yd/120m): 3 × 1¾oz/ 50g balls in colour **MC** 663 Light Natural: 1 × 1¾oz/50g ball each in colours: **A** 857 Sage; **B** 886 Asparagus; **C** 876 Clarice; **D** 870 Rosy; **E** 894 Geranium; **F** 887 Fuchsia; **G** 896 Rock Rose

SUPPLIERS

Contact the manufacturers for your local stockist or find stockists and mail order information on their website.

Yarns

DEBBIE BLISS
www. debbiebliss.freeserve.co.uk

(USA) **Knitting Fever Inc**
35 Debevoise Avenue, Roosevelt,
New York 11575
www.knittingfever.com

(UK) **Designer Yarns Ltd**
Units 8–10 Newbridge Industrial Estate, Pitt Street, Keighley, West Yorkshire, BD21 4PQ
tel: 01535 664222
www.designeryarns.uk.com

(AUS) **Jo Sharp Pty Ltd**, ACN 056 596 439,
PO Box 1018, Freemantle, WA 6959
tel: 08 9430 9699
www.josharp.com.au

ROWAN YARNS
(USA) **Royal Yarns**
404 Barnside Place, Rockville, MD 20850
online ordering: www.royalyarns.com

(USA) **The Handworks Gallery**
2911 Kavanagh Blvd, Little Rock, AR 72205
www.handworksgallery.com

(UK) **Green Lane Mill**
Holmfirth, West Yorkshire, HD9 2DX
tel: 01484 681881
www. knitrowan.com

(UK) **Shoreham Knitting**
19 East, Street, Shoreham by Sea, West Sussex, BN43 5ZE   tel: 01273 461029
UK online ordering: www.englishyarns.co.uk

(AUS) **The Wool Shack**
PO Box 228, Innaloo City, Perth, WA 6918
tel: 08 9446 6344
online ordering: www.woolshack.com

(AUS) **Sunspun**,
185 Canterbury Road, Canterbury, Vic 3126
tel: 03 0830 1609
online ordering: www.sunspun.com.au

CARON WATERLILIES
(USA) **The Caron Collection**
Thistle Needleworks, Inc, (The Shops at Somerset Square), 140 Glastonbury Blvd, Glastonbury, CT 060633
www.caron-net.com

(UK) **Macleod Craft**
West Yonderton, Warlock Road,
Bridge of Weir, Renfrewshire, PA11 3SR
tel: 01505 612618

(AUS) **Ireland Needlecraft**,
4/2–4 Keppel Ave, Hallam, Vic 3803
tel: 03 702 3222

JAEGER
(USA) **Jaeger Handknits**
4 Townsend West, Unit 8, Nashua, NH 03063

(UK) **Green Lane Mill**
Holmfirth, West Yorkshire, HD7 1RW
tel: 01484 680050

(UK) **Kangaroo**
PO Box 43, Lewes, UK, BN8 5Y.
tel: 01273 814900
Worldwide online ordering:
www.kangaroo.uk.com

(AUS) **The Wool Shack** see Rowan Yarns

JAMIESON AND SMITH
(UK) **Shetland Wool Brokers Ltd**,
90 North Road, Lerwick,
Shetland Islands, ZE1 0PQ
tel: 01595 693579
Worldwide mail order:
www. shetland-wool-brokers.zetnet.co.uk

TAPESTRY WOOLS
(USA) **The DMC Corporation**,
10 Port Kearney, South Kearney, NJ, 070732
tel: 973-589 0606
www.dmc-usa.com

(UK) **DMC Creative World Ltd**
Pullman Road, Wigston, Leicester, LE18 2DY
tel: 0116 2811040
www.dmc.com

21ST CENTURY YARNS
(UK) Unit 18, Langston Priory, Kingham,
Oxfordshire, OX7 6UP
tel: 07850 616537
Worldwide online ordering:
www. 21stcenturyyarns.com

Needles and equipment
Available from your local yarn shop and at the online retailers above.

ACKNOWLEDGMENTS

I would like to thank Designer Yarns for their generosity in supplying all Debbie Bliss yarns. I would also like to thank DMC Creative World for supplying tapestry wools and embroidery threads.

INDEX

Stitch library entries in *italic*

abbreviations, 33
adapting a pattern, 72–3
anchor stitch, 98
aran rib 1 and 2, 107
armhole shaping, 65

backstitch, 84
basketweave stitch, 90
beaded knitting, 54
beech leaf lace, 123
bells, 42
binding off, 20, 25
blanket stitch, 84
blind buttonhole stitch, 105
block quilting, 96
blocking, 66; blocking lace, 36
bobbins, 15, 47, 48
bobble buttons, 81
bobble circle pattern, 104
bobbles, 42
bound off edges, joining, 71
boxed bobble, 103
braid cable, 112
bramble stitch, 102
brioche stitch, 107
bubble pattern, 101
button band, 69
buttons, 80–1
buttonholes, 69

cable cast on, 24
cable edging, 79
  needles, 15, 41
  panel, adding, 73
cables, 40
carrying yarns, 37, 48
cast off edges, joining, 71
casting on, 17
  advanced, 24
  cable, 24
  thumb method, 17
casting off, 20, 25
celtic cable, 110
central decreasing, 29
chain stitch, 83
charts, fair isle, 37
  intarsia, 48
  motif, 155–7
charting a garment, 72
charting a pattern, 74–5
circle cable, 112
circle, knitted, 52, 53
circular knitting, 50–1
  needles, 14, 15, 51
  in fair isle, 37
cobweb frill, 127
cocoon stitch, 105
Continental method, 16
  fair isle, 16, 38
  knit stitch, 19
  purl stitch, 22
cords, 77
covered buttons, 80
crest of the wave, 118
cross stitch, 83
crossed stitches, 40–1, 46

dainty chevron, 120
darts, horizontal, 45
decreasing stitches, 28–9
  central, 29
  decorative, 28–9
  in lace patterns, 74–5
diamond, knitted, 53
diamond lace with rosettes, 124
diamonds stitch, 122
dimple stitch, 104
Dorset thread buttons, 81
double basketweave, 91
double moss stitch, 89
double moss stitch diamond, 100
double moss stitch and rib check, 89
double-pointed needles, 14
  for cords, 77
  in circular knitting, 50
  in medallion knitting, 52
dropped shoulders, 71
dropped stitches, 86–7
duplicate stitch, 85
dye lots, 11

edgings, 78–9
embossed knitting, 42–3
embroidery, 83–5
embroidery threads, 11, 13
English method, 16
  fair isle, 16, 38
  knit stitch, 18
  purl stitch, 21
entrelac, 56–7
ensign braid, 109
eyelets, 34

faggoting, 34
fair isle knitting, 15, 37–9
  correcting, 87
fern lace, 123
five rib braid, 110
flags, 98
flowers, knitted, 82
four stitch cable, 108
four stitch check, 90
four stitch wave cable, 108
french knot, 84
frilled edgings, 79
fringe edging, 127
fringes, 76
full diamonds, 99
full fashioning, increases, 26
  decreases, 29
fulling, 60–1

garden plot squares, 52
garter stitch, 19
garter stitch diamond, 125
gauge, 31, 64
  fair isle, 38
  matching, 45
gingham check, 94
gooseberry stitch, 103
gothic window, 118
grafting, 87
grapes on the vine, 114

heart cable, 115
heart squares, 94
hollow oak, 111
horseshoe lace, 121
humber star, 100

increasing, 26–7
  in cable patterns, 75
  in lace patterns, 74–5
  invisibly, 27
intarsia, 47–9
inverness diamonds, 100

joining, new ball, 32
  new colour, 47
  pieces of knitting, 70–1

King Charles brocade, 92
knit stitch, 18–19
knitting, a garment, 64–7
  a patterned garment, 74–5
knitting on, 24
knitting patterns, reading, 63–7
  sizes, 63

lace knitting, 34–6
  blocking, 36
  pattern, simple 36
  shaping, 36, 74–5
lace mesh, 117
lace rib, 119
ladder lace, 122
ladder stitch, 97
lazy daisy stitch, 84
leaf edging, 126
leaf patterned lace, 122
leaves, 43, 82
lengthening a garment, 72
lightning, 98
loop edging, 125
looped knitting, 55

make one (M1), 27
  spacing, 73
making up, 66
markers, using, 35, 75
marriage lines, 99
mattress stitch, 70
medallion bobble cable, 109
medallion knitting, 52–3
metallic thread, 11
mini horseshoe lace, 121
mistake rib, 106
mistakes, correcting, 86–7
mitred squares, 58–9
mock cable, 93
moss stitch, 89
  double, 89
moss stitch chevron, 93
moss stitch diamonds, 92
moss stitch ladder, 97
moss stitch rib, 92
motif charts, 155–7
motifs, adding, 72

neck shaping, 65
neckband, 66, 69

needle gauge, 15
needles, 14–15
  holding, 16
  sizes, 15
  tapestry, 15, 84
Norwegian fir lace, 43, 120
nosegay pattern, 115

openwork edging, 125
openwork garter stitch, 125
openwork rib, 106
oxo cable, 109

patterns, adapting, 72
  reading, 63–7
  transferring embroidery, 84
pennant stitch, 91
picot bind (cast) off, 25
picot point edging, 79
picking up stitches, 68–9
ply, 8
popcorn, 42
popcorn pattern, 102
pressing, steam and wet, 66
purl stitch, 21–2
pyramid stitch, 91

quatrefoil eyelets, 119
quatrefoil eyelets in diamonds, 119

reverse stockinette (stocking) stitch, 23
  joining, 70
ribs, 30
  double, 30
  for smocking, 62
  joining, 70
  single, 30
rick rack rib, 106
ridged feather stitch, 120
ripple and rock, 112
rose stitch, 85
row counter, 15
rows, counting, 23, 41
ruching, 101
ruffled edgings, 78

scallop border, 125
seam bind (cast) off, 25
set-in sleeves, 71
sewing up, 70–1
short rows, 44–5
shortening a garment, 72
shoulder shaping, 45, 65
side shaping, 65
six stitch cable, 108
size diagrams, 63, 67
sizes, pattern, 63–4
sleeves, 66
  lengthening, 72
  sewing in, 71
  shortening, 72
slip knot, 17
slipping stitches, 32
small gingham stitch, 94
smocked honeycomb, 103

smocking, 62
smocking stitch, 102
snowflake eyelets, 121
socks, shaping, 44
square, knitted, 53
  mitred, 58–9
star in a square, 95
star in a diamond, 96
stepped diamonds, 93
stitch charts, 63
  holders, 15
stitch, mattress, 70
stitches, dropped, 86
stockinette (stocking) stitch, 23
  joining two pieces, 70
stranding, fair isle, 37, 38
substituting yarns, 128–9
swiss darning, 85

tape measure, 15
tapestry needles, 15, 84
tapestry wool, 12, 84
tassel border, 126
tassels, 76
tension, 31, 64
  fair isle, 38
  matching, 45
textured picot stripe, 101
tree, 99
trellis diamond, 113
triple twist cable, 111
tumbling blocks, 95
turret edging, 125
two stitch check, 90
two stitch ladder, 97
twin leaf lace, 123
twisted vine, 116
twisted stitches, 46
twisting yarns together, 48

unravelling knitting, 32, 86–7

vine lace zig zag, 117

weaving in, fair isle, 37, 39
  intarsia, 49
welted ruffle, 127
wrapping a stitch, 44

yarns, 8–13
  carrying, 48
  dye lots, 11
  joining in, 32
  stranding, 37, 38
  split, 87
  substituting, 128–9
  suppliers, 159
  twisting together, 48
  weaving in ends, 32, 49
yarn over, 35
  at edge of work, 36
  multiple, 36

zig zag edging, 126
zig zag lace, 117